I'll Fly Away

I'll Fly Away

Further Testimonies from
the Women of York Prison

EDITED AND INTRODUCED BY

Wally Lamb

HARPER PERENNIAL

NEW YORK • LONDON • TORONTO • SYDNEY • NEW DELHI • AUCKLAND

Disclaimer: The Connecticut Department of Correction neither approves of nor condones the use of vulgar language but recognizes its use as artistic expression in some of the works that follow.

HARPER ⬤ PERENNIAL

Excerpts from or slightly different versions of the following works included in this book were originally published in the *Hartford Courant*: "Revisions and Corrections," "A Gift," "Broken Doll," "'No' Is Not Just a Word," "My Hairstory," "The Lights Are Flickering Again."

Pages 257–258 constitute an extension of this copyright page.

A hardcover edition of this book was published in 2007 by HarperCollins Publishers.

P.S.™ is a trademark of HarperCollins Publishers.

FIRST HARPER PERENNIAL EDITION PUBLISHED 2008.

Library of Congress Cataloging-in-Publication Data is available upon request.

ISBN 978-0-06-162639-5

08 09 10 11 12 ID/RRD 10 9 8 7 6 5 4 3 2 1

This book is for those who live in prisons
of their own or others' making.

In Remembrance

Diane Bartholomew, one of the York writing group's original members, led by the example of her dedication to her own work and that of her peers. She died of cancer in 2002, a few months after her release from prison.

Corrections Officer Jack Mineo balanced professionalism with compassion, never forgetting that the women he supervised were human beings first, inmates second. Officer Mineo died of cancer in 2004 at the age of forty-four.

Barbara Mahon, a member of the writing group for a brief time, succumbed to the feelings of hopelessness and despair against which many inmates battle. She ended her life in 2005.

The State Farm for Women at Niantic, Connecticut, was the precursor of Janet York Correctional Institution. The Angel Memorial remembers and names 116 deceased infants born to State Farm inmates between 1919 and 1967 and buried at the nearby Union Cemetery. Their small, long-forgotten grave markers were unearthed by volunteers and York staff and inmates between 2004 and 2006. A granite monument at the site reads: "Brief sparks of life, on earth for too short a time, now cradled in the arms of God forever."

We hope that *I'll Fly Away* honors the memories of all the above.

Some of the advance received from this book has been donated by the contributors to Connecticut's Office of the Victim Advocate and to the Barbara Fund, a college-in-prison program which seeks to counteract the hopelessness of life in prison with the rehabilitative power of higher education. Established by John and Bette Mahon in memory of their daughter, Barbara, the Barbara Fund is administered through A Sacred Place, PO Box 422, East Lyme, CT 06333. College-level courses are provided through Three Rivers Community College of Norwich, Connecticut.

Acknowledgments

The editor and contributors wish to thank the following individuals for their time, talents, and assistance in the birthing of this book: Eileen Albrizio, Reggie Allen, Ginny Anderson, Martin Anderson, Carolyn Battista, Nancy Birkla, Richard Blumenthal, Aaron Bremyer, Martha Cameron, Susan Campbell, Bell Chevigny, Robin Cullen, Steven Dauer, Judy Dworin, Steven Ecker, Kassie Evashevski, Leigh Feldman, Julia Felsenthal, Jenifer Frank, Sianne Garlick, Kathy Borteck Gersten, Shari Goodstein, Dale Griffith, A. E. Hotchner, Michele Jacklin, Mark Jackson, Terese Karmel, Jeri Keltonic, Steve Kroft, Linda Lamothe, Theresa Lantz, Michael Lawlor, Joseph Lea, Richard Ljoenes, Mary Marcial, Colin McEnroe, Denise Merrill, Graham Messick, Faith Middleton, Calvert Morgan, Ronald Napper, Paul Newman, Diana Pacetta-Ullmann, Jonathan Pelto, Eddie Pettini, Pam Pfeifer, Judith Regan, Lori Ricks, Tabatha Rowley, Robert Shea, Larry Siems, Judith Tannenbaum, Andy Thibault, Nancy Whiteley, and Gale Zucker.

Special thanks to editor Terry Karten and to York Correctional Institution liaisons Monica Lord, Leslie Ridgway, and Karen Oien.

Contents

III. Broken Dolls and Marionettes

IV. Crime and Punishment

V. I'll Fly Away

Revisions and Corrections

BY WALLY LAMB

Oh how glad and happy when we meet
I'll fly away
No more cold iron shackles on my feet
I'll fly away . . .

—ALBERT E. BRUMLEY

I knew from the time I was eight that I wanted to be a teacher but not that I wanted to be a writer. In third grade, my lowest marks were in reading ("Walter needs to check out more library books") and writing ("Walter needs to practice his penmanship and be less sloppy"). If you had suggested to my teacher, prim Miss Comstock, that I'd grow up to be a novelist, she might have slapped her knees and guffawed.

My eighth-grade English teacher, Mrs. Cramer, took us outside to write about nature (which I liked) and made us memorize her favorite poems (which I didn't). Longfellow's "Evangeline," Joyce Kilmer's "Trees," Vachel Lindsay's "The Potatoes' Dance": none of these works spoke to me, and anyway, what kind of men had first names like Vachel and Joyce? At a schoolwide assembly, our class was made to mount the gymnasium stage and recite, in unison, "The Potatoes' Dance." I'd been tapped for a solo quatrain that required me to step to the front and speak the following lines, which, at age fifty-six, I still remember, possibly because of post-traumatic stress syndrome:

There was just one sweet potato
He was golden brown and slim

The lady loved his dancing
She danced all night with him

As I spoke, I could see the science teachers snickering at the rear of the gym. I forgave them immediately. I thought literature was kind of stupid, too.

Later that school year, President Kennedy got killed. Then Beatlemania happened. Then it was eighth-grade graduation. I was only half paying attention when Miss Higgins, the scary teacher at the microphone, called my name. I got off my folding chair and took the perp walk to the front of the auditorium. Miss Higgins handed me an envelope. On the outside, it said "Julia Pease Award for Writing." Inside was a crisp ten-dollar bill. A writing award? For me? As I returned to my seat, Mrs. Cramer's wink implied that there had *not* been a mistake. But later that day at Ocean Beach Park, I spent all my prize money on ski ball and mini golf, just in case.

In high school, I read and wrote because I had to, not because I wanted to. In English, a book report was coming due. I was a pokey reader who favored short books for these assignments, but I'd already reported on Orwell's *Animal Farm* and Steinbeck's *The Red Pony*. From my sister's nightstand, I grabbed the paperback she'd been yapping about, *To Kill a Mockingbird*. The cover had a Technicolor picture of Gregory Peck and some little girl in overalls. I opened the book and read the first sentence: "When he was nearly thirteen years old, my brother Jem got his arm badly broken at the elbow." Three days later, I finished Harper Lee's tale of innocence lost, conscience tested, and hypocrisy skewered. A novel had never kidnapped me before. Until *Mockingbird*, I'd had no idea that literature could exert so strong a power.

I taught high school English from 1972 to 1997, and most of my students read *To Kill a Mockingbird* with me. I still have my coverless teaching copy of the novel, its pages lousy with underlinings and margin notes and held together with a rubber band. Nine years into my teaching life, I, too, became a fiction writer. I hadn't planned it. It was Memorial Day 1981. My wife, Christine, and I had just pulled an all-nighter in the delivery room and the outcome was our first child, Jared. After the new mom went to sleep and the squawking newborn went off to the nursery, I hurried home to call the relatives and grab a shower. Fatigue, exhilaration, and shower water: those were the ingredients that led me to hear my first fictional voice, a wiseass adolescent crabbing about his summer job as an ice-cream truck driver. Unsure of what was rattling around in my head—I certainly didn't imagine it was fiction—I padded naked and dripping down the hallway and scrawled onto a piece of paper what the voice had said.

Two years and umpteen drafts later, Jared was being potty-trained and my first short story was being published in *Northeast Magazine*. "Mister Softee" is a fiction about a smug teenager who has his conscience pricked and his hypocrisy skewered. The day it came out, I drove to the store, bought several copies of *Northeast*, and returned to my car. Staring at my printed work on the page, I began to cry like a newborn. For me, fatherhood and fiction writing are as intertwined as tree roots.

Quickly enough, I hit the wall of all I didn't know about how to write fiction. I enrolled in a master of fine arts program at Vermont College, where my teacher, Gladys Swan, asked me what I hoped to accomplish by writing stories. Because I'd never asked myself that question, I had to wing it. "Well, *To Kill a Mockingbird* never misses with my high school students," I said. "I guess I'd like to write stories that kids would read because they wanted to, not because they had to."

Gladys frowned. "Don't write stories for teenagers or any other group," she advised. "Write them for yourself and let the audience that needs them find them." Nine years after that conversation, I finished my first novel, *She's Come Undone*, a first-person narrative in which a young girl's innocence is stolen by a rapist. Along the way to writing *Undone*, I'd begun to teach writing differently. I sat and talked with kids now while they were drafting their work, instead of writing copious comments about what they *might* have done after they'd already finished the job. I championed the necessity of revision and taught my students how to give feedback to one another. "But two of my girlfriends read it, and they thought it was perfect just the way it is," a big-haired sophomore named Paige told me. Her jaw was set. Her body was clenched with attitude.

"Your girlfriends are loyal to you," I said. "I'm loyal to your work."

A silent staring contest followed, as if Paige and I were two gunslingers facing off at the O.K. Corral. Then she blinked, stood, and walked away. The next day she produced a second draft that hit the moon.

I taught high school kids for twenty-five years, then university students. These days I teach writing to inmates at the Janet York Correctional Institution, Connecticut's maximum-security women's prison. It's one thing to read the statistics about the injustice of the American justice system; it's another to walk the grounds of an American prison. The first thing I noticed was the predominance of black, brown, and cinnamon-colored skin. I'm pretty sure the inmates took note of *my* skin color, too, and my gender. Their body language—suspicious gazes, arms locked defensively against their chests—spoke loudly. What's this guy doing here? What's his game? What does he want from us?

What I wanted from them was whatever they needed to write. Two pages minimum. No bullshitting themselves, or one another, or me. Okay? They nodded in agreement, but just barely.

At the time I began volunteering at York, the governor of Connecticut was John G. Rowland. He'd been elected three years earlier, partly on the campaign promise that convicted felons in *his* state would know they were serving time in prison, not vacationing at Club Med. Governor Rowland had appointed John J. Armstrong as his Corrections commissioner, and Armstrong carried out his boss's vision with a vengeance. Inmates were now "corrected" with changes in policy that degraded and dehumanized them. Several suicide attempts had triggered an epidemic of hopelessness at the prison.

It was suicide that brought me to York CI. Two of the inmates had ended their lives; others had tried. The teachers at the prison school were desperate to equip their students with ways of coping with the despair that had infected the institution. They thought writing might help.

The statistics are alarming: 70 percent of incarcerated women have been the victims of incest and sexual violence. Over time that percentage was borne out in my students' personal essays. Some had landed in prison for single acts of violence committed after years—lifetimes, in many cases—of horrific and predatory abuse. Others were incarcerated for having numbed the pain and become addicted in the process. Some of the writers lost their nerve and left the program rather than reflect honestly about their lives, but the majority hunkered down, struggled their truths onto the page, and read them aloud, often in tears. Doing so was hard, but it made them feel better—less weighted down by the gravity of their histories. Within the confines of the prison, their writing began to give them wings with which to hover above the confounding maze of their lives, and from that perspective they began to see the patterns and dead ends of their pasts, and a way out. That's the funny thing about a labyrinth: what's baffling and illogical on the ground makes perfect sense when you rise above it, the better to understand your history and renovate yourself.

The women's first drafts were almost as bad as my first drafts. Their second drafts were serviceable. I assigned them books on craft and readings from literary magazines. They began giving each other feedback—reluctantly at first, then willingly, then generously. Over time, their writing evolved into prose of publishable quality. Publisher Judith Regan agreed. *Couldn't Keep It to Myself* was scheduled for release in January of 2003. But the week before the book's publication, Connecticut's attorney general Richard Blumenthal, at the behest of the Department of Correction, sued the inmate writers—not for the modest earnings they would receive after they left prison, but for the entire cost of their imprisonment. They charged them $117 per day, as if they were staying at the Sheraton instead of the slammer. One writer, sentenced to forty-five years after a trial that was rife with racism, had $3 in her commissary account with which to buy overpriced toilet paper and shampoo from the prison commissary. She now owed the state of Connecticut $917,000. The lawsuit demoralized and frightened the writers, but it didn't surprise them. Several likened the state's treatment to the treatment they'd received at the hands of abusive men. Connecticut was just the latest in a long line of batterers.

I had neither the time nor the stomach to take on the state of Connecticut in a fight I was pretty sure the women and I couldn't win. But if I had taught the inmates a thing or two about writing, their writing had taught me some things about how and why women land in prison and what happens once they get there. *Couldn't Keep It to Myself* had the power to open minds and challenge stereotypes. The lawsuit had the power to silence writers who had just discovered their voices—women who were in no position to fight back against bureaucratic bullying. So, like it or not, I took up the fight—not alone, but with the help of lawyers, legislators, teachers, and some fair-minded journalists who love the First Amendment and hate the abuse of power.

I got slimed during that fight. Having attempted to communicate with the Department of Correction about the women's book for two years, I now read in the *Hartford Courant* that the department had learned of the project only when book contracts were confiscated in the inmates' mail. And because the DOC didn't like "surprises," my status as a volunteer was being investigated. Until this Kafkaesque turn of events, I'd assumed *I* was the fiction writer.

After the lawsuit had languished for a year, I nominated one of the incarcerated writers, Barbara Parsons, for the PEN/Newman's Own First Amendment Award, a prize that recognizes writers whose freedom of speech is under attack. When Parsons won the award and a $25,000 prize that went with it, things got really ugly. The DOC suspended the writing program, told me to stay away from the prison, and reassigned the teacher with whom I'd run the workshop for six years. A memo was circulated to the school staff: no teacher was to allow workshop members to use class time to write. Worst of all, the women's computer disks were confiscated and their work was erased from the hard drives of the school's computers. Five years' worth of hard-won insights in some cases—eliminated just like that.

The DOC's chief spokesman denied that these things were happening, but CBS's *Sixty Minutes* had evidence to the contrary. And when they aimed their cameras at Attorney General Blumenthal, he suddenly, if belatedly, understood the rehabilitative value of the women's writing and announced the reinstatement of the program and the settlement of the lawsuit.

In the months that followed, ironies abounded. The settlement terms required the inmate writers to donate a portion of their earnings to the very writing program corrections officials had sought to eliminate. With his department facing a wrongful death suit from the family of a mentally ill inmate who had died while being restrained by guards, as well as lawsuits that alleged he had tolerated the sexual harassment of female employees under his command, Armstrong retired as commissioner and headed for Iraq, where he took a position as the deputy director of operations for the Iraqi prison system.

Armstrong's successor, Commissioner Theresa Lantz, directed computer techs to resurrect from those hard drives the inmates' erased work; about 90 percent of it was eventually restored. In 2005, Barbara Parsons was released from prison and Governor Rowland became an inmate. He served a ten-month sentence for felonious "conspiracy to steal honest service"* at a federal prison in Pennsylvania that seems far more like

---

* According to the Associated Press, prosecutors told the judge in Rowland's case that, as governor, he had admitted to having accepted $107,000 worth of vacations, work on his cottage, and free airplane flights from state contractors and employees, and lying about it. Rowland's attorneys bargained with prosecutors and the governor pled guilty to a single count of "conspiracy to steal honest service."

a Club Med resort than the high-tech (and leaky-roofed) gulags built in Connecticut at his behest.

The writing of *Couldn't Keep It to Myself* was wrenching for the women who bared their souls and its publication was hard-won, but the unpredicted ripple effect caused by its existence has proven worth the pain. Without ever having met my teacher Gladys Swan, the inmates had followed her advice by writing what they needed to write and letting the audience that needed to find it, find it. The book has gone into foreign translation, and here in the United States has become required reading for middle school and high school students, sociology and psychology majors, and law enforcement officers. Just last week I received word from the Netherlands that a Rotterdam-based theater group, De Theaterstraat, has made a play based on the women's words. Just last night I attended *Time In,* the Judy Dworin Performance Ensemble's heart-wrenching, spirit-lifting interpretation of the inmates' writing in dance, song, and spoken word. Also seated in the audience was eighty-year-old Janet York, the former warden and namesake of the prison. York's progressive policies, her emphasis on inmate education, and the institution's low recidivism rates while she was warden earned the institution the nickname "the prison that cures with kindness." At the end of the performance, Janet York approached me, took my hands in hers, and squeezed. I've never received a more eloquent thank-you.

And there's more. When SeniorNet, an online website service for people over fifty, featured *Couldn't Keep It to Myself* in its monthly book discussion, the women's essays triggered an initiative. To date, Senior-Net members, under the leadership of Ginny Anderson, have collected and shipped thousands of books to American prison libraries. And back home, the book begat a change in the law. At the urging of Attorney General Blumenthal and several key legislators, the state of Connecticut no longer is permitted to sue its inmates for the cost of their incarceration in response to the rehabilitative work they do. For me, there was a final, personal sweetness: after the dust had settled, I received an unexpected package in the mail from *Couldn't Keep It to Myself*'s publisher, Judith Regan. When I opened it, out slipped a thirty-fifth anniversary edition copy of *To Kill a Mockingbird*. It was signed by Harper Lee.

A fiction writer weaves a fabric of lies in hopes of revealing deeper human truths. I aim for truth in my novels, and in my teaching and parenting. Jared, that infant who helped birth my writing life, is now twenty-five. A Teach for America–trained educator, he's had his heart captured by the inner-city schoolchildren of storm-tossed New Orleans.* Jared infuses his kids with learning and hope, and his dad tries to do the same for *his* students. The blessings we receive in return far outweigh what we give.

My former students—the *Couldn't Keep It to Myself* contributors who have served their time and been freed—are thriving. One, a recovering alcoholic who entered prison after a DUI fatality, now speaks to high school groups alongside members of Mothers Against Drunk Driving. She is in the tenth year of her sobriety. Another has become an advocate for the homeless at Fellowship Place, a New Haven–based organization that services the mentally ill. A third is a hotel chef. A fourth is a property manager for Goodwill of Austin, Texas. Barbara Parsons works at a plant nursery and cares for the elderly. In her spare time, she writes to change things for the better. Shy by nature, Parsons has become an articulate public speaker and an advocate for the victims of domestic violence and the rights of incarcerated women.

Meanwhile, back at York Prison, the writing program has expanded and is going strong. "I know sometimes it's hard to understand those of us in the corrections field," Commissioner Lantz once told me. "Admittedly, we're a different breed." Fair enough. I try to walk around for a while in the spit-shined shoes of those uniformed officers in charge of safety and security so that I might feel what life feels like from a per-

---

*Jared's younger brother Justin, a Teach for America recruit, has also been posted to New Orleans and will begin teaching in the fall of 2007.

spective not my own. Sometimes it helps me understand their actions. Sometimes it doesn't. On my visits to York Prison, I teach, watch, and listen. I speak up when I need to. And to the credit of the current warden, his superiors, and his staff, institutional silence has been replaced with honest dialogue. There are signs, small ones at this point, that the DOC pendulum has begun to swing away from the counterproductive "punishment" model and move instead toward a model that supports rehabilitation, reintegration, and alternatives to incarceration for juvenile offenders, the mentally ill, and others inappropriately imprisoned. I believe it is incumbent on all of us—legislators and justices, policymakers and private citizens—to encourage this more enlightened course.

So call me both the accidental novelist and the accidental activist. I have come to believe firmly that the more transparent the prison walls, the better and more humane the prison—and the world at large. My students believe that, too. They choose as subject matter their past lives, their past mistakes, and their day-to-day existence as prisoners. They have been writing up a storm and *I'll Fly Away* is the result. They are grateful to you for reading their work. I am, too.

I.
When I Was a Child . . .

There is always one moment in childhood when
the door opens and lets the future in.

—DEEPAK CHOPRA

A memory is what is left when something
happens and does not completely unhappen.

—EDWARD DE BONO

And even if you were in some prison,
the walls of which let none of the sounds of
the world come to your senses—would you not then
still have your childhood . . . that treasure-house
of memories?

—RAINER MARIA RILKE

Florida Memories

BY BONNIE JEAN FORESHAW

It's Thursday morning at 6:00 A.M., and we two have just arrived at the open-air flea market, the largest in south Florida. I'm an apprentice shopper and my teacher is my Aunt Mandy. Later this morning, the market will be hot and crowded—alive with music, laughter, gossip, and bartering about the price of everything from necklaces to nectarines. But at the moment, it's cool and quiet. Our focus is fish.

"Pay close attention to the *eyes* of the fish," Aunt Mandy instructs as we walk from stall to stall. "If the eyes are clear, not cloudy, and the color of the skin's not fading, then the fish is fresh." Auntie's dressed for shopping in a pink sleeveless blouse, burgundy pedal pushers, Italian sandals, and a white sun visor. I'm wearing shorts, a T-shirt, and rubber flip-flops. I am tall for my age, and starting to get the kind of shape men take a second look at. My glasses take up half my face. "But you have to shop with your finger and your nose, too, not just your eyes," Auntie instructs. "Poke the fish gently near its fin. If it leaves a dent, then you don't want it. If it doesn't, it's probably part of the morning's catch. And listen to me, Jeannie. Fresh fish never smells foul."

We stop at one of the stalls where the fish are lined up, one against the other, on a bed of ice. The fish man approaches us. He's hand-some—black hair, hazel eyes, tank top and cut-off jeans. "May I help you, ma'am?" I watch him take in Aunt Mandy's curves, her green eyes and honey-colored complexion. I might as well be invisible.

"Well, maybe you can," Auntie says. "Oh, by the way, I'm Mandy and this is my niece, Jeannie. Now what's your name?"

"I'm Ricardo," the fish man says. He's sucking in his stomach, and his feet are moving up and down like he's trying to stretch his height. "It's nice to meet you, Mandy."

"Nice to meet you, too. Now tell me, Ricardo, how much you want for these five yellowtails?"

"Well, let's see. They're seventy-five cents apiece, so that's a total of . . ." He stops to watch Auntie pass her fingers through her shoulder-length hair. It's salt-and-pepper-colored, but Mandy's still got it. "Uh, three seventy-five."

"Oh," Auntie says, half-shocked and half-disappointed. "That fellow three stalls down says he's selling his yellowtails for *fifty* cents each. So unless we can work out a deal . . ."

The smile drops off of Mr. Ricardo's face, but Auntie's smile returns. Her gold tooth is glimmering. She shifts her weight, puts her hand on her hip.

"Mandy, it's a deal," Ricardo says. "Five yellowtails for two-fifty. That's a dollar twenty-five cut I'm giving you."

"Which I appreciate," Auntie says. "And look at it this way: you've just gained yourself a faithful customer. Now, tell me. How much you selling those red snappers for? If I can get them for the same price as the yellowtails, I'll buy some of them, too. And conch."

I stand there looking from one to the other. Auntie touches the small gold cross at her throat. She fingers her earring. I can tell Mr. Ricardo is only pretending to do the math in his head. "Okay," he finally says. "Sold."

WHEN I WAS A CHILD . . .

Auntie pays for the fish and conch, thanks him, and we walk away. A few stalls down from Mr. Ricardo's, she turns to me. "Okay, now," she says. "Show me a fresh fish."

I go up and down the row, looking each fish in the eye, then pick one up by its tail. I turn it, look at its other eye, study its coloration. When I press my finger against its head, near the fin, there's no indentation. "This one."

Her look is serious. "You think this fish is fresh?"

I hesitate. "Yes."

Aunt Mandy flashes me her gold-toothed smile. "Well, Jeannie, now you know how to pick fresh fish."

I'm excited to have passed the test, but I've been wondering something. "Auntie?" I say. "I don't remember going to any other fish stalls before we went to Mr. Ricardo's."

She laughs. "You and I knew that, but Ricardo didn't. It's one of the tricks of the trade when you shop at the flea market. But bear in mind, Ricardo would rather make a sale than not sell. If he has fish left at the end of the day, that's a loss and a waste for him. So we were doing him a favor. Now, come on. Let's cross the street and I'll teach you how to pick out vegetables and fruit."

We meander among the tomatoes and squashes, the potatoes and mangoes and plums. Shopping for fresh produce is a matter of looking and smelling, but mostly of *feeling,* Auntie says. "Fruits and vegetables can get damaged by cold weather, the way they're packed, or how far they've traveled to get to the market. If the skin is firm, that means it's fresh. If it's loose, then it isn't. And always check for bruises."

Although I'm listening to my aunt, it's the peaches in the stall to my right that have my attention. They're big and beautiful, golden yellow with blushes of pink, and their aroma makes my mouth juice up. I'm thinking about how I might get myself one of those peaches.

"Pick us out some bananas," Auntie says. It's test number two.

My eyes pass over several bunches before I pick one up. I check each banana, one by one, then walk over to Auntie, who is examining pears. "These are nice, firm, and yellow," I say, handing her the bunch I've chosen. "Tight skin, no bruises."

She twists the bunch back and forth, then nods her approval. "Good job," she says. Smiling all over myself, I decide to seize the moment. "Auntie, may I get a few peaches?"

"Sure," she says. "Get about six."

I examine the peaches as carefully as I did the bananas, and Aunt Mandy is satisfied with the ones I've chosen. "You've done an excellent job," she says.

We pay up and gather our bags. "I am sooo hungry, Auntie," I say. "May I have a peach?"

"Uh-huh. I'll have one, too," she says.

I hold mine before me and, salivating, take my first bite. Ahhh. My taste buds jump alive; the juice runs down my chin. I eat hungrily, devouring my peach in record time. "Mmm, this peach is *good*," Auntie says. I look at her, enviously. Half of hers is left, but I've eaten mine down to the seed. I suck on it for a while before I pull it from my mouth and toss it away.

Time passes, the sun beats down, and the aisles clog with customers. There's music now. On someone's radio, Bob Marley's singing, *Buffalo Soldier, dreadlock Rasta, stolen from Africa* . . . I can feel the bass vibrate. Although I'm young, I already understand that reggae is the music of history and truth, and that it invites your body to dance and sway to the message. Around the corner, there's Latin music, with its horns and powerful drumbeats. No need to understand Spanish; it's the rhythm that matters. One couple's dancing the salsa, another the cha-cha-cha. Fingers snapping, they move forward, backward, the woman's hips swaying. At the end of the stalls, someone's blasting R & B—Aretha! *R-E-S-P-E-C-T, Find out what it means to me.* Everyone knows the words to this one. People are doing their own little jiggy dances, singing along with attitude.

Auntie's all into it. "Yeah, that's what I'm talking about!" she laughs. "My girl Aretha can sing it for me any time!"

By noon, the flea market's alive and up-tempo—part shopping, part festival. People are smiling, laughing, price-arguing, swaying to the beat. Even the old folks and the little kids are moving to the music. But the noonday heat has no mercy. "Now you know why we come so early," Aunt Mandy says. "We've bought everything we need, and at good prices. Time to go."

And so we do. Walking home, I feel happy and successful. I've learned how to shop. I've eaten the tastiest peach of my whole life. And I can almost taste those pan-fried yellowtails, those conch fritters, deep-fried and golden brown.

"Hey, what happened to you last week? I didn't see you."

"Oh, I was on vacation. Took the family to Virginia Beach."

At the south Florida flea market, the relationships formed between buyers and sellers were lasting ones. Over the years, our family and Ricardo's—his brother Carlos, Carlos's wife Maria, their children Miguel, Ramon, and Sonia, their cousins Ruben and Pedro—came to know each other well. They gave us good deals on the fish they sold, and we, as my aunt had promised, became their loyal customers and friends. I moved away from south Florida in my twenties, but whenever I returned home, I made it a point to go to the flea market to shop for bargains, visit my friends, and savor the sweet sights, smells, sounds, and tastes of life.

And although I listened to these words many, many years ago, I can still hear my Aunt Mandy speak them: "Always remember that the vendors want to sell perishable food rather than carry it home, Jeannie, so you can get a reasonable price if you work at it." I have practiced Auntie's advice all my life, and have taught my children as she taught me.

Here's a recipe for how to live a good life.

When you shop, use your eyes, your nose, your fingers, and your brain. Look both the dead and the living in the eye. Don't just listen to the music—*feel* it—and when you sing along with Aretha, do it with attitude. Dance if you want to, or if you have to. Smile when you're bartering. Laugh any time. Dress up, not down. Buy fresh. Don't pay too much.

Kidnapped!

BY ROBIN LEDBETTER

You're suspended!"

"Suspended? She started it!" I was outraged.

"I don't care, Robin," the vice principal said. "You're *always* being sent to this office. For God's sake, you just got back from suspension two weeks ago."

I was still feeling the effects of the fight I'd just had: the sound of blood thundering in my ears, the bitter taste in my mouth. But I was coming down from my adrenaline high and the reality of my situation was hitting me. I looked the vice principal in the eye. "You can't suspend me, Mr. G. All I did was defend myself."

"Not only can I suspend you, Robin, but I can move to have you expelled if you and Tasha get into one more fight." When he reached for his Rolodex, I sprang from my chair and grabbed him by the lapels of his jacket.

"Don't call her!" I begged. "Don't do this to me!"

He swatted my hands away. "What the . . . Have you lost your mind, child?"

Fighting tears, I sank back into my seat. I hated Mr. G: his push-broom mustache, his stupid baseball trophies, the framed photos of his children on his desk. His cozy, carpeted office with its potted plants was out of place in our rundown school. I looked at a picture of him shaking hands with some guy. He thinks he's such a big shot, I thought; well, maybe he is, but he's not to me.

"Robin? . . . *Robin!*" Mr. G was snapping his fingers in front of my face.

"What?"

"Don't 'what' me, young lady. You'll stay after school for detention tonight, and beginning tomorrow, you're suspended for two weeks. Here's your letter home." He scrawled a few sentences on a suspension slip and handed it to me. "I'll call your grandmother later. . . . I hate to call her again. Lord, I feel so sorry for that lady."

"Sorry for *her*?" I mumbled. "You should feel sorry for *me*."

I walked out of the office and into the girls' bathroom with its stale urine smell, its gray stalls that had no doors or toilet paper, no mirror above the one small sink. I leaned against the wall and started to cry. Damn that "Skanky Tasha" (as we called her). Thought she was better than everyone, but she was fresh—had been sleeping around since before her first period. When we'd fought in first grade, she had won. But I'd won all three of the next ones. I chuckled to myself thinking about our fight that day. Boy, had I ever put a hurting on her. Plus, I'd stripped her shirt off of her and all the fourth, fifth, and sixth graders had seen her topless—every kid in the cafeteria laughing as the teacher tried to shield her C-cup breasts. People thought they could bully me then, and I'd spent most of the school year fighting for the respect that the kids wearing Nikes and new clothes got automatically. Well, I'd beaten Tasha again and people were going to be talking about it for a while. A surge of pride welled up in me. I wiped my nose and my eyes on my shirt and left the bathroom.

As I walked down the hallway toward my class, I caught my reflection in the window. I smoothed my ponytails. The sun shining through the window caught my glasses and created a glare. I took them off and wiped my eyes again. I smiled to inspect my braces. I hated them. They'd brought me many fights. I put my glasses back on and went to class.

"You didn't get sent home?" Miss Sanders, my red-headed, freckle-faced fourth-grade teacher asked, sounding half-angry and half-disappointed. "What do you have?"

"Two weeks' suspension starting tomorrow. Detention tonight."

"Well, you'll spend the remainder of the day in the corner."

"But—"

"No 'buts,' Robin. Get! Right now!" When she turned her back, I gave her the finger. She was always hard on me, yelling in my face with her stale coffee breath and pieces of rice cake flying out of her mouth.

I went to the corner and sat. When classes changed, the kids coming in all gave me "props" about what I'd done to Tasha until I got yelled at by Miss Sanders. Finally, I took out my book, *Indian in the Cupboard*, and started reading. I couldn't really focus, though. It was getting closer to three o'clock and I was scared about what was going to happen then. During my last suspension, my aunt had beaten me every day I had to stay home. *Strip and bend over the toilet.* CRACK! CRACK! CRACK!

I shuddered. I got a beating most days anyway, but when I was good, I'd at least have the hope that I'd be spared. I knew I had a bad one coming, and that's when I made up my mind: I wasn't going home.

After detention, I left the school and sat on the broken-down fence in front of a house I passed every day. What could I do? What could I do? Not go home—that was for sure. I thought back to the first time I'd run away from my grandmother's house. I'd just started living there and it was my first day of school. I was six years old. I'd walked to Kenny Park straight after school, and then at around midnight, I'd sat on the curb in front of the Thomas Cadillac car dealership, waiting for someone to notice me. Eventually, a woman had, and brought me home. My grams and aunt were so glad to see me. I lied and told them I'd gotten lost on the way home. Well, I couldn't say I got lost again. I'd have to make up something else. I'd figure that out later. For now, I'd just head over to the park.

There were lots of kids there. I joined some girls jumping rope and played on the swings and the slide. I was there for hours. The other kids slowly dwindled off, until only me, a little girl, and her mother remained. The sky was orange and the wind was picking up. "Come on, baby," the woman said to her daughter. To me she said, "Little girl, you should go home now. You shouldn't be in this park at night."

"Okay," I said. She smiled and grabbed her daughter by the hand and I watched the two of them leave. I sat alone on the swings for a while. It was cold, dusk settling into nighttime, and I got up and started walking. I had heard lots of stories about dead bodies in Kenny Park, so I hurried past the trees that bordered it. As I was speeding through a wooded area, I tripped on a long stick reaching out of the ground. I picked it up and swung it a few times. This would be good in case someone came after me, I thought. But as I emerged from the trees, it wasn't a rapist or a crazy person I spotted; it was a cop car. As it slowed, I saw the officer in the passenger seat staring at me. My heart stopped. I figured my grams had called the cops by now, and I was scared they'd pick me up and drive me home. Please, God, let them keep going, I said in my head. A few seconds later, the officer said something I couldn't hear to the one behind the wheel and they sped away. I watched the cruiser reach the end of the block and turn onto the intersecting street. Close call, I thought, letting out a breath of relief, which was accompanied by a growl from my stomach. I'm hungry, I thought. Dummy-me had fought during lunch. I had no money to buy food now. Oh, well, I'd survive.

It had grown dark by this time. I started walking but had no destination beyond going in the opposite direction of my house. On Blue Hills Avenue, there were people out on porches and cars whizzing by. Loud music came from both the cars and the apartment buildings I passed. The farther I walked, the quieter it got, and after a while there was just me and my thoughts. I thought about everything except the situation I was currently in. I thought of my mom, my dad, and my sister. I thought about what TV show was on and what dinner I might be eating if I wasn't out here walking. My stomach growled again as I passed the "Welcome to Bloomfield" sign. "God, I could go for some KFC right now," I said out loud. "I'm starving!"

A few steps later, I cried out in pain. Something had slipped under my foot and I'd twisted my ankle. I hit the ground hard. Whatever I'd fallen on was hard but had some give. It felt damp, too. I pulled the object from under my butt: a rotten little crab apple. I looked around— the ground was covered with them. Then I looked up at the branches hovering over me and saw that there were some apples still hanging on up there. Making sure not to step too heavily on my ankle, I struggled to my feet. I used my stick—the one that would help me fight off attackers—as a cane. I picked one of the tiny apples from a low branch. I'd heard these apples were poisonous. Maybe this is what they used in *Snow White*, I thought. Maybe I should eat it and lie down like her. A great tragedy.... Only, with my luck, nobody would see it as that. The paper would end up printing something like, "Runaway Kills Hunger and Self." I dropped the apple and limped on.

It was pitch dark in the boondocks. The streetlights must have been a mile apart. I was starting to get scared and tired, and my ankle was hurting like crazy. Weren't serial killers usually the ones with money and nice houses? Weren't rich people the ones who committed the sickest crimes? How many Jeffrey Dahmers lived out here, I wondered. I could be kidnapped and sent to China to be a sex slave or a worker at a Nike factory. (I'd just seen a show on *48 Hours* about sweatshops.) I'd twisted my ankle, but I could still fight off an attacker if I tried. Any sicko wanted to start something, he'd have a fight on his hand—just ask Skanky Tasha. But as I continued walking, different scenarios of my horrible fate at the hands of maniacs played in my head.

I walked past a church, then stopped and walked back to the front steps. "Church of the Divine Redeemer," the sign said—a big name for a brick building as small as a house. "Well, Jesus," I said aloud, "I'm putting myself in your hands. If a killer attacks me here, then I guess I'll be going to heaven." I threw down my stick, curled up on the steps, and started to drift into sleep. A few minutes later, a white lady appeared out of nowhere.

"Did you miss the van?" she said.

I raised my head from the concrete steps. "Huh?"

"Oh, you're not a member of the church? Where did you come from?"

I blurted it out without thinking. "He kidnapped me!"

"Oh, my God! Come in, come in." She wrapped her arm around me and led me to the side entrance of the building. "Sit down, sweetheart," she said. "I'll call the police. I'll call your home, too. They must be worried sick. What's your phone number?"

I couldn't think of anything else to do, so I gave it to her.

The Bloomfield police came and picked me up. During the ride back to Hartford, they took my statement: "I was leaving school late and he tricked me to come up to the window. Then he opened the door and snatched me."

"Did he touch you?" the officer asked.

"No!" I said, more loudly than I'd intended.

"Okay. Now tell me what else happened."

"He drove me around telling me how he was gonna kill me, and when he stopped at the stop sign, I jumped out. He didn't chase me."

At the town line, I was transferred from a Bloomfield cop car to a Hartford cop car. When I arrived home, my grandmother threw the door open and snatched me in her arms. I started crying. The house was swarming with police.

"Hi, Pumpkin," my aunt said. "Are you okay?"

"Yeah," I bawled.

"Robin, come with me, please," an officer said, taking my hand. "I have to take your statement again." He led me into the kitchen. After I'd retold my story, he said, "Robin, you know that I know you were suspended today, right?"

"Yeah? Well, so what. I could've been killed tonight. I could be half-way to China by now." He gave me a puzzled look.

"Robin," he said. "If you're honest, you'll be fine. But if you're lying, you could get yourself in a whole lot of trouble."

"I'm not lying!" I yelled. "I hate you! Grandma!"

When my grandmother rushed into the kitchen, I told her I was tired and hungry. "Can I go to my room now?"

"Are you finished with her?" Grams asked the officer.

"Yeah, I guess so. We'll put out an APB based on the description she gave us. If we get anything, we'll be in touch. Good-bye, Robin."

I glared at him without returning his good-bye. The nerve of that man, calling me a liar! Everything I said *could* have happened for all he knew. Once the house cleared out, I took a bath, ate my dinner, and went to bed.

My "kidnapping" was never mentioned again. In fact, I was treated very well during my suspension: snacks, TV, no beatings. It kind of made me wish I could get kidnapped all over again.

Shhh, Don't Tell

BY DEBORAH RANGER

My life was falling apart, my arrest was imminent, and I'd been on the road for days, driving everywhere but nowhere. As midnight approached, I headed north on I-95 through Florida with the radio on for company, the volume turned up high. The passing highway lights kept time to Dolly Parton's twangy, upbeat vocal. No matter where in America you drove, no matter what your life had become, you could always depend on those love'em and leave 'em country songs rising up from the dashboard.

I'd grown up listening to Waylon Jennings, Patsy Cline, and Hank Williams; their music was embedded in my bones. My father, his brothers, and their parents had formed a band to pay homage to the country and western greats, and one of my earliest memories is of the time my brother Wayne and I, accompanied by our family band, made our debut singing "Rocky Top" on amateur night at the Grand Ole Opry. I was four years old at the time, still innocent of the ugliness in the world.

Dolly faded away and the car filled with the deep, ominous voice of Johnny Cash. *I keep a close watch on this heart of mine* . . . I reached over to change the station, as I did whenever I heard that voice, but when my fingers touched the knob, I pulled back as if it was white-hot. *I keep my eyes wide open all the time* . . . A bright flash crossed my field of vision. I took several deep breaths, hoping to stop the rising nausea. "For Christ's sake, it's only a damn song!" I shouted. But the voice was carrying me back. As if watching tiny clips from some disjointed movie, I was returning against my will to a memory I had buried for nearly thirty years.

LARGO, FLORIDA
Summer, 1973

Largo was a tiny town just off the coast of the Gulf of Mexico. We lived with our parents in a small two-bedroom house where my brothers, Wayne and Kenny, shared one room and my baby sister Christine and I shared the other. We had moved here from our old house the year I was six.

Because my father was a carpenter, our house in Largo was in a perpetual state of renovation. Mom often complained about how Dad never completed one project before he began a new one. Shortly after we'd moved in, Dad had begun turning our garage into a living room so that the original living room could become a bedroom for Mom and him. Now, a few months shy of my eighth birthday, Dad declared the project completed.

The following day, he drove up to the house with the Silver Bullet.

"Wow!"

"Holy cow!"

"Yessssss!" Kenny yelled, punching the air with his fist.

But our dreams were shot down like birds when I asked if we were going camping. Dad shook his head. "You kids stay away from the camper," he said sternly.

"But Dad, why'd ya buy it for if we ain't going camping?" Kenny inquired.

"Bought it for my trains."

Dad had a fixation about electric trains. I wasn't sure how many crates of miniature locomotives, towns, and track he had at our house, but I knew the shed at Grammy's was filled to the top with them. The day the Silver Bullet arrived, we watched Dad park it under the big tree in the backyard. Then he cut down our tree swing. "I don't want you kids playing on the swing and hitting the side of the camper," he explained.

The next day, after Dad drove off to work, Wayne, Kenny, and I sat outside and stared at the Silver Bullet, each of us dreaming about what fun we would have had camping in it. "It won't be so bad," Wayne said. "We can help Dad build his train town."

"Someday I'm gonna be a conducterer," Kenny stated.

"It's conductor, stupid." Wayne had just turned ten and, being the oldest, thought he knew everything. Although Kenny was only eighteen months younger than me, I often acted as his protector.

"Kenny's not stupid," I said. "You are. At least he knows what he wants to be when he grows up. You're gonna die *before* you grow up, 'cause you smoke cigarettes." That comment earned me a good, hard shove to the ground.

That summer, before Dad could start construction on the camper, his younger brother Lonny arrived, carting his new family with him.

It had been a few years since Lonny's last visit to Florida. As they climbed out of the beat-up station wagon, I struggled to recall that summer when I was five. We'd been living at our other house then, and I'd been playing outside with my brother, hiding under the old oil tank, when Uncle Lonny found me and hurt me. Mom had brought me to the hospital, and after we'd gotten home, I'd heard Mom yelling at Dad that she would kill Uncle Lonny if he ever showed his face again.

I looked at Mom now, wondering if she would keep her promise and kill Dad's brother or at least make him go away, but all she did was turn to my father and say, "Look, Harry. Lonny brought his trailer trash with him." She walked back into the house, slamming the door behind her, and when I followed her inside, she warned me not to go anywhere near my uncle unless she was around.

Dad was the older brother, but Uncle Lonny was taller by several inches. His hair was brown, longer than Dad's, and dirty. Grammy said he was made of "nothin' but skin and bones," and his teeth were yellow from too much smoking.

Aunt Dora Lee, I was sure, weighed at least a thousand pounds. Her long blond hair had been pulled back into a tangled ponytail that hung down her back. Her hair needed a good washing, too. The only good thing about their visit was the babies.

Linda was eighteen months, and she had a full head of blond hair. Her big eyes were as blue as the sky, and when she smiled, her tiny baby teeth gleamed. LeAnne was just two months old. She had a small tuft of fine hair that was soft to the touch. Her eyes were blue, too, but Mom said that could change since she was still very young. She was a quiet baby—nothing at all like my squawking sister Christine when she was that size.

After dinner that night, Dad and Uncle Lonny sat outside, playing their guitars while Uncle Lonny sang Johnny Cash songs: "Hey Porter," "Folsom Prison Blues," "I Walk the Line." Listening through the kitchen window as I did the dishes, I began to feel sick to my stomach. I turned my attention to Mom and Dora Lee's conversation.

"When my pa found me knocked up, he said Lonny and I was getting hitched. Now I got me these here two youngins to haul aroun'," Dora Lee said. A cloud of smoke floated around her while she bounced the older baby on her hip. They'd been sitting at the kitchen table, smoking and talking since dinner ended. In fact, Dora Lee had smoked nonstop since they arrived, even while we ate dinner. I wasn't sure which she did more, smoke or talk, and I wondered if Mom was going to wash her mouth out with soap because of all the bad words she used.

During dinner, Dad had offered to let them stay in the Silver Bullet until they got on their feet, and Aunt Dora Lee told me I could come and help her with the babies any time I wanted. Since Uncle Lonny would be driving away to work with Dad, I would wait until they left and then go over to the camper.

About a month later, in the middle of the night, Uncle Lonny and his family moved on. When we woke the next morning, Dad told us they were gone. "I don't want you kids playing anywhere near that camper," he reminded us. "I'm going to start working on it this weekend."

Nearly a week had passed since Uncle Lonny left. The August day was already hot and muggy by early morning. The Silver Bullet's back half was shaded by the tree and the sun beat down on its front half, causing a glare that made me squint. Wayne, Kenny, and I were playing circus. We were going to join the Big Top one day, we figured, so we were practicing our balancing tricks, me standing atop Wayne's shoulders with my arms outstretched while he walked a circle around the backyard and Kenny did somersaults alongside us. We were just about to circle the yard a second time when we heard the funny noise.

At first we ignored it. Mom had reminded us not to play near the camper every time we headed outside. But as the sounds grew louder, a curiosity took hold of us that we couldn't ignore. Kenny glanced over at the house to make sure Mom was nowhere near the back door. "Coast's clear," he whispered, and the three of us became detectives.

The eerie, whining cry sounded weak, as if whatever animal it was, was trapped or wounded. Standing under the shade of the tree, we looked up, thinking maybe a cat had climbed up and gotten stuck. But the tree was empty. Again the strange cry came, and this time we knew it was coming from inside our Silver Bullet. Without hesitation, all warnings forgotten, we stepped closer and the sounds grew louder.

We could see nothing out in the open. Wayne gave a signal, and we dropped to the ground, slithering forward on our bellies until we were underneath the camper. Rolling onto our backs, we peered up at the bottom, thinking maybe the kitten was trapped there. Disappointed at finding nothing, we crawled back out.

"We have to look inside," Wayne said. Following his lead, we stepped up to the shimmering sunny side of the Bullet. The cry came again, catching us off guard, and we jumped back, breathing hard. "It's in there," Wayne whispered. He reached out and tried the door handle. Locked.

"Wayne, crouch down," I said. "If I stand on your shoulders, maybe I can see in the window." Wayne bent his knees and I climbed up his back. Standing, he moved closer and I hooked my fingers on the window's rim, pulling closer to the screen for a look inside.

"What do you see, Debbie?" Kenny asked.

"Nothin'. The curtains are closed."

"This is stupid," Wayne said. "We're gonna get in trouble, and for what?"

"For nothin'," I mumbled. With a sigh, I jumped to the ground.

We often followed Wayne's lead, him being the oldest and all. But Kenny was hard to resist when he cried. "But the kitten can't get out," he said, in tears.

"If the cat got in there, you dummy, it can find its way out," Wayne said.

"Not if it's hurt. We can't just leave him in there. He'll die."

As we stood there debating what to do, the cries grew louder. And the louder they became, the more scared I got. Something was really wrong and I agreed with Kenny—we had to do something to help. "I think we should go get Mom," I said.

"No way!" Wayne said. "She'll just yell at us for playing near the camper. Then we'll all get switched. I'm not doing it. *Nooo way!*" He stood before us, hands on his hips, shaking his head.

"I'll tell her," Kenny volunteered. He began to shake. "I'll tell her the ball rolled under the camper, and I had to go and get it, and that's when I heard the noise."

"Fine. You go," Wayne mumbled, walking away. "But I'm not going to be a part of this. I ain't taking the switch for no damned cat."

"Come on, Kenny," I offered. "I'll go with you. I'm not afraid of getting switched." Turning, I started toward the back door, Kenny following. "Got switched before for no good reason," I mumbled. Mom often found a reason for one of us kids to climb the big tree and break off the switch she'd then use to hit us with. Mom's rule was that if the switch broke after three whacks, we had to climb the tree again to retrieve another one, and the whacks would begin again, at one, and go as high as ten.

Mom was sitting at the kitchen table reading a magazine and smoking a cigarette when Kenny and I came in. "I'm busy. Can't you see that?" she told us. "If that cat found a way into the camper, it can damned sure find a way out."

"But Mom," Kenny pleaded. "Maybe it ran in there the night Uncle Lonny left. It was dark and they might not have seen it go past them."

Mom still wouldn't budge, so Kenny began to cry, tears running down his cheeks. "*Pleeease,* Mom!"

Mom knew Kenny wouldn't give up; he'd just keep crying until she gave in. Kenny couldn't stand to think of any animal hurting. Sighing, Mom glanced at the crib to make sure Christine was still napping. Then she crushed out her cigarette, pushed back her chair, and followed us outside.

Wayne had moved to the other end of the yard. "What's up?" he called, pretending he didn't know what was going on. Kenny and I followed Mom to the camper. She tried the doorknob. No go. Putting her ear against the door, she listened. Kenny and I held our breath, silently begging the animal to cry out. We got our wish. Just as Mom was turning away, the cat let out a pitiful whine.

"Wayne," Mom called. "Run over to the shed and get me a screwdriver."

Wayne returned a minute later, tool in hand, and gave it to Mom. Pushing Kenny and me aside, he nudged in next to her, fist on his hips and legs spread as if to tell us he was now in charge. Mom pried the screwdriver between the door and the jamb and began to jimmy it back and forth. The lock popped and the door swung open, the sudden motion causing Mom to jump back to avoid being hit.

Mom waved away the stench. "You kids stay back. We don't know what kind of animal is inside. From the smell, I'd say it's already dead."

"It can't be, Mom," Kenny said. "We all heard it crying."

Mom turned to me, "Debbie, go get me a dish towel off the clothesline." I did as she asked. Covering her nose and mouth with the towel, Mom stepped up and into the camper and disappeared.

Seconds passed before Mom called out to us. "Wayne! Go call the police. *Now!*" Without asking why, he took off toward the house. "Debbie? Kenny? You two stay right where you are. Don't come any closer, you hear me?" Kenny looked at me, and together we nodded. With the camper door open, flies swarmed above the doorway. A minute later, the stink reached us; it was so sickening that I thought I was going to vomit.

"You think it's some kind of monster, Debbie?" Kenny whispered through the fingers covering his nose and mouth.

"I don't know, Kenny, but I don't think it's a kitten." Why did Mom want the police? I knew Kenny was scared, and so was I. Reaching out, I put my arm around him. And as the minutes passed, I became more and more frightened. "Mom?" I called. "Mom!" There was no reply.

Then Mom reappeared. Jumping down from the camper with the dishtowel held tightly against her face, she ran to the side of the camper and vomited.

"Mom, what is it? What did you find in there?" Kenny asked as I ran toward her. But before I reached her, Wayne came slamming out the back door.

"Mom, the sheriff's on the phone! They want to know what the emergency is! What do I tell them?"

"Tell them ... " Mom stopped as another spasm overtook her. "Tell them to send an ambulance." She turned to face us, tears running down her face.

"*Oh God*," she cried. "The babies are in there."

We watched as two paramedics entered the camper and waited for them to emerge. When they did, several minutes later, each was carrying a small unmoving bundle. They had wrapped the babies in blankets so we couldn't see them, and I wasn't sure if they were dead or alive. After the ambulance left, we all followed Mom and the police officers into the house. "You kids go to your rooms now," Mom told us.

Wayne, Kenny, and I left the kitchen but didn't do as we were told. In tears, we listened from the hallway to the policemen's questions and Mom's replies.

"Lonny Lawson—he's my husband's brother. He and his wife Dora Lee came to stay with us about two months ago. They left about five, six days ago . . . in the middle of the night."

"You didn't realize the children weren't with them?"

"No. Like I said, they left unexpectedly. Harry told me the next morning they had gone. He found the note they had taped to the back door."

"Do you still have that note, ma'am?"

"I never read it. Harry just said they were gone and didn't say where they were headed. I assume they may have gone back to Connecticut, or maybe Tennessee. Dora Lee has family there." Mom paused to light a cigarette. She only smoked when she was real upset, which seemed like most of the time. "I'm telling you, if it hadn't been for the kids playing near the camper, we never would have found those babies alive."

"Ma'am, can you tell me how we can contact your husband?"

"He's on the road, delivering cabinets. There's no way to reach him."

"Well, when he gets home, have him call the sheriff's office right away. And if you hear from either Lonny or Dora Lee, call us immediately."

As Mom walked them to the door, we heard her ask, "Do you think the babies will be all right?"

"Don't know, ma'am, but at least they have a chance, thanks to those kids of yours."

That night at dinner, Mom repeated the story to Dad. "I'm telling you, Harry, if it hadn't been for the kids playing near the camper, those poor babies would've died in there." Dad looked up from his plate and glared at us. He was mad that we'd been playing around the Silver Bullet.

"They were so sickly looking. Starving, bleeding all over. They had open sores all over their bodies. Linda had managed to pull her diaper off so she was in better shape. But LeAnne was too young to do anything but lie there in a bed of her own filth. She was covered in maggots. The camper's filled with flies."

From my place at the other end of the table, I kept watching Dad, staring down at his plate, putting food in his mouth, chewing slowly.

"I could expect this from Dora Lee," Mom said. "She doesn't have the two cents that God gave her. But that brother of yours—what's *wrong* with him?"

My stomach turned at the mention of Uncle Lonny, and I gave up trying to eat. Maybe it was just too much for Dad, and he'd had to stop listening.

"I hope Lonny rots in hell for this, and Dora Lee along with him," Mom said. "They better never show their faces around here again. That's all I'm saying."

Finished with his supper, Dad got up from the table and walked out the back door.

The flashes subsided, the images faded, and I was back in the present, driving along the interstate. I pulled my car into the Georgia Welcome Center and veered toward an empty lot. Hitting the brakes, I brought the car to a sudden stop, threw the door open, and emptied my stomach onto the asphalt.

I don't know how long I sat there, vomiting and crying. My stomach hurt with the pain of being sick, my head with the pain of those ugly memories. Inside the welcome center, I entered the ladies room, rinsed my mouth out, and splashed cold water on my face. Outside again, I fed change into a machine and bought a coffee.

Mom had told us we were never to talk about what had happened that day. It was a family secret. Later, Uncle Lonny was arrested in Connecticut for molesting a young girl and sent to prison for twelve years. We never knew what happened to Dora Lee—if she'd been caught and punished. We never spoke her name again. We never mentioned the babies.

What I now knew, for certain, was that I'd been lied to my whole life. Uncle Lonny hadn't just "hurt" me when I was five years old. He had molested me. And knowing he had, my father had let him come back and stay in the Silver Bullet.

There was a part of me that wanted to go backward—to forget it all over again—but I knew that was no longer possible. The time had come. And for the first time in five days, I had a destination. I pulled my car back onto the highway and drove toward the exit that would take me to North Carolina, to my mother, to rip open family secrets.

In the Mood

BY "SAVANNAH"

While twisting the radio dial, I hear, unexpectedly, one of my grandfather's favorites: Glenn Miller's joyful big band song, "In the Mood." But it's not joy I'm feeling as I recall that old 78 rpm record rotating around and around on my grandparents' cabinet-model record player. Against my will, the music takes me back there, one more time, to that place where I hated to go.

In laying down the guilt trip about visiting her parents, my mother was perpetuating their techniques. Guilt, she had learned, was a great motivator. Mom would begin prepping me for those Sunday evening visits on Friday afternoons. "Do it for *my* sake," she'd say. Or, "Years from now, after they're gone, you'll regret not going." She thought she was doing me a favor, I guess, but what she was really doing was poking at the smoldering embers of my disdain for her abuser.

From the moment I learned the horrible family secret, I felt protective of Mom—but frustrated, too. Didn't her ugly childhood memories return each time she set foot in her parents' home? How could she be so damn passive and compliant? I wanted her to stop pretending everything was hunky-dory—to stand up for herself and stop being a pushover. But how could I fault her submissive nature? I, too, had been raised to be obedient and subservient. To speak only when spoken to. To keep the family secrets.

So I was frightened on those Sunday evenings when we'd round the corner and 157 Maple Avenue would come into view. But it was *myself* I was afraid of, not my grandfather. I was fearful that, while playing checkers or rummy or old maid, I might snap. Run up those railless stairs, smash Glenn Miller into two perfectly symmetrical pieces, and, with the jagged edge of one of them, slice my dear grandfather's throat.

That's what I was "in the mood" for: avenging my mother's horrific childhood. Confronting the man who had squashed her spirit and making him pay, at last, for what he'd done.

Tinker Bell

BY BRENDALIS MEDINA

It was June of 1994. I was going on fifteen months in jail and feeling depressed. Still unsentenced, I was scared of what my future would hold. I was faced with the possibility of spending the rest of my life locked up. That thought was weighing hard on my mind.

"What's wrong, Brenda?" Ebony asked, plopping herself next to me. "I can tell something's bothering you."

"I'm okay—just a little tired." I stood up to escape her look of concern. "I'm going up to my room to lie down," I said.

I left the TV room and headed upstairs. I didn't want to admit it to her, but Ebony was right: something was bothering me, and it scared me to think I was readable.

Since they had moved my roommate to another unit, I was bunking alone. I sat on my bed and looked at the wall I'd covered with my family's pictures. My sister Mimi's face beamed down at me as she held up a present from her baby shower. My father, with his blue jeans and black Nikes, sat on a big rock wearing a wide smile. My nieces, Nicky and Jascelyn, struck their sassiest poses and stuck their tongues out at me. Smiling to myself, I remembered the good times I'd spent with my family—the parties and holidays, the silly arguments my parents used to have about who was a better singer: Julio Iglesias or Jose Luis Rodriguez. Would I ever be among them again? As I pondered that difficult question, the good memories blurred into bad ones and my face turned damp with tears.

The faces on my wall became those who had hurt me and whom I had hurt. Gang members who'd called themselves my brothers and sisters floated in front of me—Albert, Manny. I saw my victim—the way she looked the night she died—and, circling around her, images of her son. I saw the fear in my father's eyes and my mother's sobbing face as the cops took me away. I was crying uncontrollably now, self-loathing pumping through me like blood in my veins.

Exhausted, I no longer had the strength or the energy to fight despair. Without thinking, I yanked at the cords at the back of my TV. I found the sharpest metal wire and, lost in my ugliest memories, began digging into my wrist. . . .

I remember sitting there, watching without emotion as blood gushed and some annoying girl screamed. I don't recall who she was or why she was at my door, but the next thing I knew, my room was crowded with corrections officers. One tied a rag to my wrist to control the bleeding until I got to the medical unit. I was put in a van and driven away.

At the med unit, a nurse cleaned my wounds. In spite of all the blood, the cuts weren't deep. When she finished, I was escorted to the mental health unit. A counselor questioned me, but I can't remember much. I do remember saying, over and over, "I'm tired. I'm just so tired."

The counselor decided I should stay in Mental Health for observation. I was taken to a small, dim room, empty except for an unmade bed. I was allowed only a blanket to put on the dirty mattress and cover myself with. Then I was stripped and left with a thin paper gown. An unfamiliar male CO with salt-and-pepper hair was posted in front of my door because I was on suicide watch. Embarrassed and confused, I sat on the bed and cried. I must have looked pathetic because the officer approached me with a look of pity in his eyes. Without saying a word, he stretched out his hand and offered me a tortilla chip. I didn't want the chip, but I snatched it anyway, quickly looking away. He returned to his place at the door. I held the chip tightly in my hand, and when it crumbled, I cried harder than ever.

Two days later, the doctor declared that I was no longer a danger to myself, but I was to remain in the mental health unit a while longer. The counselor and the doctors thought I could benefit from group therapy. I, of course, thought otherwise, but I went through the motions, faking my way through the groups.

Group was held in the TV area. The counselor, Sherrie, a short, thin woman with bright red hair, wore the outfit she'd probably worn at Woodstock. Seated on a chair in the middle of the room, she coaxed the rest of us to speak. There were about five or six women in the group, but the only one I remember clearly was Trisha, a short white girl with curly black hair and big potholes in her face. Trisha didn't share, but she would jump up and scream, out of the blue, "I forgot to lock my door!" Then she'd make a run for it. Sherrie would remind her that her door was locked, and Trisha would return to her seat and be calm until she repeated the whole scene five minutes later. I sat on the couch, knees pulled up to my stomach, thinking, Trisha, you're doing this all wrong.

I shared with the group, telling them what I knew they wanted to hear but burying my real feelings. I said things like, "I want to help myself," and "I never want to try and end my life again." It worked; I was finally released. For the first time in my life, I felt grateful for the lessons my family had taught me. Going back to never-never land had just gotten me out of the nuthouse.

My family believed strongly in the code of silence. Whenever life dealt them a shitty hand, they'd fly off to never-never land and pretend everything was fine. It was no wonder *Peter Pan* became my favorite childhood story, Tinker Bell my favorite character. I envied her for being able to fly away whenever she felt she needed to escape the crocodiles and Captain Hooks of life.

I was only six when my Captain Hook molested me. My mother

and I were visiting my aunt. I went into the bathroom, but couldn't unbutton my pants. When I returned to the living room, looking for my mother's help, the only person there was my mom's cousin, Albert. Albert was a tall, dark-skinned man who had greasy black hair and always wore the same dirty blue jeans. He was sitting on the couch holding a brown paper bag with a can inside. I turned to leave so I could find my mother.

"I'll help you," he said, grabbing my arm and pulling me close. Albert managed what I couldn't, but after he'd freed my button, he kept his hands on my pants. I felt his warm alcohol breath on my face and his cold, sweaty hands sliding past my stomach. I shut my eyes when I felt the strange pain. He was touching me and pushing his fingers inside me in the one place my mother told me no one had the right to touch. I stood there, frozen, until he finally released me. Then I ran back into the bathroom, locked the door, and waited. It seemed like hours passed before anyone came looking for me.

When we were leaving, I tugged at my mother's shirt. I wanted to say, "Mommy, he touched me there." I wanted her to hug me and tell me that no one would ever hurt me like that again. But when I opened my mouth, no words came out. I was afraid Mommy would get mad at me for speaking about the bad thing. Although I was only six, I instinctively observed the code of silence. Whenever something bad happened in the family, we weren't to speak of it—not in the house and especially not *out* of the house. Yet I was confused and scared about what Albert had done. That night, wrestling in silence with my fears, I turned into Tinker Bell and flew away.

My parents and my older brothers and sisters schooled me well in the code of silence—not by speaking of it, but by their example. As time went on, I became proficient at denying my fears and numbing my emotions, but the pain lived inside me like the sleeping dragon in a fairy tale. I needed to escape from the memories and, for a time, I did. But on July 15, 1988, the dragon awoke with a vengeance.

WHEN I WAS A CHILD . . .

My parents had gone to New Jersey to visit my aunt. At thirteen, I was too old for a babysitter, but since my parents would be away the entire weekend, they wanted someone to stay with me. I didn't mind their decision to leave somebody with me; the truth was, I hated my house at night because that was when my fears and demons came alive. My brother David still lived at home, but he wasn't reliable enough to stay with me because he was always out with his friends. Instead, my twenty-year-old sister Jeannette was recruited for the job.

Jeannette had been staying at our house for a few weeks since she'd broken it off with Luis, the father of her kids. She had agreed to stay with me, but the kids were with Luis. A free agent for the night, Jeannette had no interest in keeping me company. She was going out, she said, but she promised she'd hurry back since she knew how I felt about being in the house alone. And she *did* come back quickly, with a weird look on her face and a bribe from McDonald's. My friend Lisa was standing beside her, duffel bag in hand. I knew what was coming.

"Here. Take this," Jeannette said, handing me the McDonald's bag. "I have to go out again, but I'll be back soon."

"Where you going?" I asked.

"Out."

"But it's late."

"You'll be okay. Besides, you're not alone. Lisa's mother said Lisa could sleep here tonight." Jeannette had planned her escape carefully.

I liked having Lisa over, but I didn't feel comfortable knowing that it was just her and me. As Jeannette headed for the door, I made a desperate attempt to stop her. "You promised you'd stay with me," I said, tugging at her shirt. I could feel my eyes burning from the tears that were about to pour out. For a moment, my sister's face softened. She wiped my tears, sighed, and said, "I'll be back fast. I promise."

"Jeannette!" I cried. But out the door she went.

My sister had shown me many times how good her promises were, so I knew it was just Lisa and me for the night. When I went back into my bedroom, Lisa was sitting on my bed, rummaging through her duffel bag. With a huge smile on her face, she pulled out a bottle of Hennessey. I had never drunk alcohol before, and I knew I shouldn't have started that night, but the longer I looked at the bottle, the more it promised escape. Besides, nobody cared what I did. I was always being left alone.

"Where you get this?" I asked Lisa, grabbing the bottle.

"I have connections."

Her answer was good enough for me. I turned my stereo up loud and began chugging the Hennessey.

About halfway through the bottle, I started to feel weird. A deep sadness came over me. The more I thought about my life, the worse I felt. It was a hot, humid summer night. I was seated on the windowsill of our upstairs apartment with my head out, breathing fresh air. Lisa stood behind me, babbling about some boy who was trying to get with her. Her voice became a stream of noise.

Then, without warning, my demon arrived at the party. Half devil, half Albert, he hovered just outside the window. My body shook, my heart pounded. The screaming in my head grew louder and louder. He had haunted my dreams since I was little, and because he wouldn't leave me alone, I had no choice. I looked at my friend, then looked straight ahead. I grabbed my demon's hand and leapt.

Ironically, that same night that my demon came to visit, God must have been there, too. That's the only explanation for what happened next. As I left the window ledge, Lisa, a scrawny little thing, leapt forward and somehow mustered the strength to grab me in midair and pull me back in. We both fell back, landing on the floor.

I blocked out most of the rest of that night, but I do remember waking up later in a hospital with my arms and legs restrained. Lisa was there, too, asleep, her head resting on my stomach. Later I learned that Lisa's screaming had alerted the neighbors, one of whom had called an ambulance. I felt scared and irritable, and the pounding in my head didn't help my situation any. When I tried to move, Lisa awoke with a start, her eyes puffy and red. "Brenda, you scared me. Are you okay?"

I nodded, unable to speak from the dryness of my throat. Lisa's tears streamed down her face. "They called your parents, Bren. They should be here any minute."

When they came into the room, my mother ran to me and stroked my hair. Sobbing uncontrollably, she asked God why this had to happen to her youngest child. My father just stood over me, looking as if he were trying to figure out who or what I was.

Now that my parents were there, a shrink came to talk to me. "Do you know the date?" he asked, without looking up from his pad.

Judging by the sun coming up, I knew it was early in the morning. I held my head up a little and croaked, "July sixteenth."

"What's the year?"

"1988."

"And do you know who the president of the United States is?"

"George Bush."

After a few more easy questions, he looked me in the eye and asked the hard one: "Brenda, why were you trying to end your life?"

Resting my head against the pillow, I looked from my mother to my father and back again. Mom and Dad didn't say a word, but I knew what they were thinking. In my head I heard a little voice reminding me. *The code. Don't forget the code.* I cleared my throat and gave the doctor the answer I thought my parents wanted him to hear. "I wasn't trying to kill myself. I was drinking even though I'm not supposed to, and, when I was sitting in the window, I felt dizzy and slipped."

I put on my best innocent face, hoping the shrink would buy it. He raised his eyebrows and wrote something down on his pad. Then he took my parents to the doorway and they talked in whispers. Either the doctor believed me or my parents convinced him that I was sane, because when they returned to my bedside, he told me he'd decided to let my mother and father take me home. As they removed my restraints,

I recalled how I'd felt just before I jumped. Then I buried the incident so deeply that to this day I don't remember most of it. Sometimes it seems like nothing more than a bad dream.

My family truly believed that ignoring hard truths was a way of making them go away. That belief had been passed down to me. So on the day I left the hospital, I returned with my mother and father to never-never land. I went on living my life as if I didn't have a care in the world—until I met Manny, my very own Peter Pan. Manny was all about having fun and breaking rules, and I loved every minute of the roller coaster ride he took me on. But following Manny, joining a gang, and avoiding the real world gave me a lifestyle that landed me in prison. It was there, while I waited to hear if I would be sentenced for life, that my old ghost flew past the security gate and through the razor wire fence and returned to me. His visit filled me with the same dread I'd had five years earlier on the windowsill—the same desperation to escape from the pain and from myself.

On my eleventh day in the mental health unit, I was told my madness had been cured and I would be going back to the Fenwicks. When I got to the building, my friends were gathered in the TV area waiting for me. Some ran up and hugged me; others stood at a distance and stared, unsure of what to say. I put on my biggest smile and did what I do best: I pretended everything was okay. "Hey, they decided I'm not crazy after all, but what do they know?" I said, laughing and pulling laughter from them. They filled me in on all the jailhouse gossip I'd missed, as if I'd just returned from a vacation instead of a suicide attempt. We talked about everything except what had happened, and the smile didn't leave my face until I returned to the privacy of my room.

I couldn't help thinking that my family would be proud of the way I was handling my reentry from the mental health unit to the everyday craziness of prison life. Tinker Bell was flying again.

One Saturday Morning

BY CHASITY C. WEST

W ake up, Chas. I made breakfast. Hurry up so you'll have time to eat." My mother poked her head in and out of my bedroom before I had the chance to object. As the aromas of cinnamon and bacon wafted into my room, I heard Mom knock on my older brother Sterling's bedroom door. Another dreaded Saturday morning had arrived.

Sterling and I were to be up and ready to leave within an hour in order to meet the others by 9:00 A.M. Yawning, I dragged my thirteen-year-old self out of bed and headed to my brother's room. He had pulled the blankets over his head. Plopping onto the edge of the mattress, I shook his shoulder. "Sterl, Mom said to get up. You better be ready by the time Dad comes in." Our hardworking father was a no-nonsense man of few words whom my brother and I both feared and loved. The answer to Sterling's and my requests was almost always no unless our easygoing mother served as our diplomatic liaison. Dad had a definite soft spot for his wife of seventeen years.

"If Mom and Dad want to do house calls, *they* should go," I complained to my blanket-covered brother. "Why do they always have to drag us with them? I'm never going to make *my* kids do anything this humiliating."

"You're doing way too much talking so early in the morning," Sterling mumbled. "Go get ready. I'm telling Mom I have a stomachache."

"Sterling, no! Don't make me go with just Mom and Dad." I shook him hard, and when he still didn't respond, I flung my body over his blanket cocoon, hugging him tightly and pleading, *"Pleeease!"* Sterling's arm appeared from beneath the covers and he began to pummel me with his wadded pillow until I released him. When I did, he repositioned himself again, poised for sleep.

"You know Dad's going to make you stay in all weekend if you don't go."

"So what?" he said. "I'll just spend the weekend watching TV." He popped up, suddenly wide awake. "What time is it? Did I miss *Looney Tunes?*"

What I wanted was to go to the movies that night, and I had a better chance of being allowed to go if Sterling went with me. If he was grounded, then I would be, too. Every Saturday night at seven o'clock, the Windsor Cinema featured a ninety-nine-cent movie, so it was always flooded with teenagers from Sage Park Middle School, Loomis Chaffee, and Windsor High. This was the hangout for anybody who was anybody. I was allowed to go occasionally, depending on what type of movie was playing; R-rated films were still off-limits. Although I always looked forward to viewing the show, there were other attractions besides the movie. Each Monday morning, the popular girls would be in the bathroom, puffing on their cigarettes and gossiping about whose fingers and mouths had pleasured whose privates the Saturday before at the ninety-nine-cent show.

I smiled in Sterling's direction, knowing that television was his Achilles' heel. "Aren't you forgetting the new policy? Remember last week, when Dad said if we're too sick to make house calls, then we're too sick to watch TV."

Sterling punched his pillow. "Darn! I forgot about that dumb rule," he groaned.

Bible in hand, I fidgeted in my chair. Before doing house calls, it was customary to meet at our house of worship, where we would pair off with others, working to spread the word to our assigned territories in residential, rural, and industrial areas.

"Jesus Christ has commissioned us to continue this preaching work," an elder member of our congregation, Brother Greene, reminded us as he addressed the small group. "We are delivering the same message of hope he and his apostles did centuries ago: that all the wickedness that plagues the earth today will be done away with, replaced with worldwide peace and security as originally intended by the Creator of the heavens and earth." Brother Greene droned on in his melodic baritone. "Now, brothers and sisters, the topic for this morning's door-to-door discussions can be plucked right from the morning headlines." He spent the next few minutes discussing current events that mirrored biblical prophecy. Seated beside my brother, I snickered at the woman who sat directly in front of us. Sister Pearlette Mackey had worn that same auburn wig for as long as I could remember, but today the manufacturer's tag was sticking out in back. Sterling and I passed a note back and forth, scribbling dares.

I dare you to tuck the tag in, I wrote. He smiled into the palm of his hand, then scribbled a reply and handed it back. *I dare you to rip the tag off and hand it to her.* Our snickering, which had become audible, was silenced by our father's stern gaze. My brother and I straightened up and peered into our Bibles.

We were both dressed for walking in the late autumn weather, me in a corduroy jumper, white tights, and leather mary janes, my hair held in place with a plastic headband. Sterling, two years my senior, wore a tweed blazer, a waffle-textured clip-on tie, and brown oxfords. We both carried thin attaché cases in which we held our magazines, brochures, and other publications necessary for door-to-door preaching. These items were to be offered at the end of a brief but well-rehearsed sermon that I could have said in my sleep. We'd been taught the fundamentals of the Bible at a very young age and had learned how to present a sermon for our Saturday work by the time we were able to complete whole sentences.

"I hope the territory we get isn't in Windsor," I whispered to Sterling as Brother Greene pulled out his map of the surrounding towns. The most horrifying thing that could happen would be for us to be assigned house calls in the vicinity of our neighborhood, the school we attended, or the town where we lived. Any of those factors increased the risk of running into our classmates. And on Saturday mornings, everyone was home. My brother and I had gotten pretty good at dodging the houses where we knew someone from our school lived, but our techniques weren't error-proof. Nor could we prevent an unforeseen spotting or encounter.

"Now for carpool arrangements," Brother Greene began. "Do we have any volunteers to drive?" Hands went up, including my father's. Dad was driving the Buick this morning. It would be a tight squeeze, but we would be able to accommodate one more person, he explained to Brother Greene. Brother Greene began to arrange everyone and their partner into cars. Within minutes everyone had a ride—that is, everyone except ancient Brother Ghedvides, slumped in his chair near the wall. If not for an occasional snore or snort, it would have been hard to tell if Brother Ghedvides was still alive. The most senior member of our congregation, he looked old enough to have been one of the original apostles.

"Brother Ghedvides?" One of the sisters leaned forward and tapped his shoulder, gently awakening him from death.

"Good morning! My name is Sam Ghedvides and this is my lovely wife, Noreen." He licked one of his rickety old fingers and flipped through his large, worn Bible. Sister Ghedvides, his wife of over seventy years, had passed away three months earlier, but Brother Ghedvides sometimes forgot that she was gone. The woman seated behind him leaned forward and rested her hand on his shoulder.

"Sam, Brother Greene is asking if you'd like to ride with the Wests."

"With who?" he asked loudly, annoyed.

"The Wests!" she repeated, directly into his ear. "Aaron and Jennifer! And their children!"

"Yes, yes, whatever." His hand swatted impatiently at nothing and he fell back to sleep. Sterling and I looked at our mother in silent protest. She did not look back.

"Very well, then. Brother Ghedvides will ride with the Wests."

I turned to my brother. "I'm not sitting next to him."

"Yeah, you are."

"No, I'm not. You sit in the middle."

"No way." He gave me a quick shove, and I had to catch myself from being knocked off my chair. I knew I would not win this battle no matter how much I protested. Glancing over at Brother Ghedvides, I wanted to cry.

Brother Ghedvides had stark white hair and a nose that seemed too large for his face. His bottom lip, pink and fleshy, appeared to weigh down his entire head. Whiskerlike hairs grew wildly from his ears and nostrils, begging to be trimmed, and the lobes of his ears dangled at the sides of his head, touching the collar of his shirt. An elastic strap held his metal-rimmed bifocals in place. Accessorizing his mismatched clothes was a large polyester tie so wide and gaudy it probably could have been flown as a kite. He had a sickening odor that seeped from his colostomy bag whenever he moved.

As expected, Brother Ghedvides insisted on a window seat and, as my luck dictated, I got stuck sitting in the middle, wedged between him and Sterling. Every few minutes, Brother Ghedvides let out an incoherent mumble or released some gas. On my opposite side, Sterling kept nudging me with his elbow and chortling softly. I rolled my eyes and tried squeezing closer to my brother, who kept laughing with his eyes and shoving me back toward Sam Ghedvides.

We parked the Buick at the top of Wilson Avenue. It wasn't our neighborhood, but close enough to our school for us to worry. In the past, Sterling and I had been able to avoid embarrassing run-ins by being vigilant about reading the family name on the mailbox before ringing the doorbell. We hoped our luck would hold.

"Osweiki. Could be Jason and Tina Osweiki. I mean, how many people have the last name Osweiki?" I asked my brother. We'd definitely skip that house. But there were many variables to consider. What if the last name of a classmate wasn't on the mailbox? We'd have no way of recognizing some stepparent's name. What if someone happened to be skateboarding down the street or mowing the lawn or carrying groceries into the house from a parked car in the driveway? Then it would be too late. They would've already spotted us in our good clothes, attaché cases in hand. And if that happened, I'd rather die than to have to face them Monday morning.

Brother Ghedvides shuffled from house to house as if at any given moment he might topple over. His grip was strong around the handle of his well-worn, hand-stitched leather briefcase, and I noticed the bulging veins in his hand and his pale knuckles. I looked down at his shoes—artifacts that looked as if they'd walked around the world and back. They'd obviously been worn during decades of faithful service.

I flashed my brother a Cheshire cat grin when Brother Ghedvides grabbed hold of his arm to be guided up a set of concrete stairs.

"Do you want to ring the bell, little lady?" Brother Ghedvides asked me when we reached the top. My eyes jumped to the mailbox that was affixed to the house. The Walters. Not familiar. I looked over at Sterling, who shrugged his shoulders. I reached out and rang the bell. A moment later, a pair of eyes scanned us suspiciously from behind a front-room curtain. To my surprise, the door was unlocked and opened.

"Good morning! My name is Sam Ghedvides and these two little whippersnappers can tell you their own names 'cause for the life of me I can't remember 'em." The woman, wearing hair rollers and carrying a mug of coffee, cracked a smile. I had half-expected that Brother

Ghedvides might fall asleep midsentence and Sterling or I would have to apologize, complete the sermon, shove magazines at the listener, and get away as quickly as possible. But I was mistaken. Brother Sam delivered an eloquent sermon and placed a book and a set of magazines in the nodding woman's hand.

As our party of three teetered from door to door, Brother Ghedvides told us of an earlier time when, as part of his missionary work, he had carried a heavy phonograph with a prerecorded message for miles at a time. He described the persecution he had endured for simply wanting to share with others what he had learned about God. He told us of his imprisonment by the government in his native country during a time when preaching work was forbidden. And when he told us the story of how he had met his wife, Noreen, I couldn't help but notice the way his watery blue eyes lit up with radiance and love at the mention of her name.

"I've been alive nearly a century, and so I've witnessed how the ministry's evolved," he said. "These old eyes have seen a lot." He sighed deeply and I wondered if he was thinking of his own mortality. Then, as if he had read my mind, he said, "I know I won't live much longer, but I have the hope of the resurrection and the everlasting life that the Bible promises." Then his voice took on a strong, commanding tone and he smiled. "You kids nowadays don't know how to have fun, but my Noreen and I could show you a thing or two." My thoughts wandered to ninety-nine-cent movie night, and the girls' room conversations the following Monday, and all the desperate ways we kids struggled to impress one another and dodge each other's harsh judgments.

I survived that memorable Saturday morning without bumping into anyone from school, although in the lunchroom the following Monday, Jonathan Colton asked me if I'd been around Wilson Avenue Saturday morning "selling books." I said no and continued to eat my soup—end of conversation. I didn't get the chance to go to the movies that Saturday night; the featured show was rated R. But the evening wasn't entirely wasted. I had figured out something about my faith. And though I still vowed that I would never force my own children to go door-to-door spreading the word of the Lord, I now understood and accepted why my parents made my brother and me do it. And when Brother Ghedvides died in his sleep nine days later, I thought about him and his Noreen, united again in a deep, peaceful slumber, awaiting the resurrection.

II.
Gifts My Family Gave Me

*You don't choose your family. They are God's gift to you,
as you are to them.*

—DESMOND TUTU

*Making the decision to have a child—it's momentous.
It is to decide forever to have your heart go walking outside
your body.*

—ELIZABETH STONE

*Family faces are magic mirrors. Looking at people who
belong to us, we see the past, present, and future.*

—GAIL LUMET BUCKLEY

When I count my blessings, I count you twice.

—IRISH PROVERB

The Captain

BY KATHLEEN WYATT

When I was a child, I acquired a number of exotic dolls from around the world, each one beautiful and unique. My favorite is a Spanish flamenco dancer, over a foot tall. Her thick black hair tumbles down her back and her long legs peek out of a ruffled red silk dress. Arms extended above her head, she snaps castanets, eyes closed, lost in the dance. This beautiful woman is kept in her own glass case, displayed alongside dolls from Africa, Japan, and around the globe. The dolls were gifts from my father's bachelor brother, Mitchell. As a ship captain for the U.S. Merchant Marines, Uncle Mitchy traveled to the most fascinating spots on earth, returning to port with tales of adventure and bounty from worlds far away.

In my earliest memory of Uncle Mitchy, he emerges, dreamlike, during a Massachusetts nor'easter. My family lived outside New Bedford, Massachusetts, in the seaside village of Padnarum. Heavy snow was coming down and I was out front making a snowman while my parents shoveled. A taxi pulled into the driveway, its headlight beams barely cutting through the falling snow. The passenger door opened with a sharp creak, letting out a massive form that resembled a man. He had bulky duffel bags slung over each shoulder, as he stood looming in our driveway. "Is that my Kathleen?" he roared. Terrified that I was about to be kidnapped, I hid behind my mother. I was sure it was the man who steals children, the villain from *Pinocchio*. But my father seemed happy to see the kidnapper. A tall man, Dad was an imposing figure in his snow gear, but the stranger approached him fearlessly. "Captain!" my father shouted. "What a great surprise! I thought you weren't due back to the States until next month." As the two men embraced, the stranger howled. "For heaven's sake, Mitch, stop!" my mother scolded. "You're scaring Kathy half to death."

Back inside, safe and dry, over a hot chocolate for me and something stronger for Uncle Mitchy, we became fast friends. I have pictures of that visit. I am bundled in a snowsuit, perched atop a six-foot mound of snow. Mitch, in his pea coat, is at the bottom, his arms open for me to jump into.

Whenever Uncle Mitchy came to town, our family life was turned upside down. Neighbors were over until late at night, their laughter and voices keeping slumber at bay. It was Mitch's violin that would finally lull me to sleep. Haunting melodies of "The Wild Irish Rover" or "Danny Boy" drifted upstairs into my room, bringing with them comfort and an enchanting world of dreams.

When my uncle visited, we went out to eat on weeknights. At the restaurant, Mitch would raise his beer glass and proclaim his love and respect for my parents, or for the long-suffering Irish and the sea. The ending of his toast never wavered: "And God bless my precious niece, Kathleen Bridgett." Pleased with my uncle's closing, I would raise my cherry-laden Shirley Temple and clink glasses with the adults. During dinner, I'd listen, mesmerized by Uncle Mitch's tales of trips to the Tropic of Capricorn or the frozen ports of the Bering Sea.

"I won eight out of eight and walked out with a fist full of diamonds," Uncle Mitch boasted. "There isn't a watering hole in Cape Town where I haven't beaten their best man at arm wrestling!" As he flexed his tattooed biceps, I would squeal with delight. But I was not the only female taken with this handsome sea captain. The waitresses would make a fuss over me, lingering at our table, hoping to catch his eye. The pretty ones always did. By the time my parfait arrived, Mitch was usually getting fresh with one. Wide-eyed, I'd watch his every move, savoring each spoonful of vanilla ice-cream and chocolate sauce. The evening would close with my mother announcing it was past my bed-time. My uncle would shoot me a quick wink and, despite my firm dissent, the evening's fun would be over.

Mitch's visits were rarely scheduled, and I never knew when I would see him next, but he always arrived on our doorstep with treasures from faraway ports: rubies and sapphires loose in velvet pouches; busts of tribal chiefs, hand-carved from the finest wood by the natives of Bali; silk kimonos; solid gold tableware. He brought us wooden shoes from Holland, bolts of fine Irish lace. No gift was run-of-the-mill, nor was its giver.

"I love ponies and horses," I told Uncle Mitchy one night during a restaurant outing. "I'll show you my collection when we get home."

"Honey, it may be too late by the time we leave here," my mother said, smiling. "Tomorrow's another day." Mom wore her blond hair short, teased, and styled high according to the 1960s fashion, and she complemented whatever dress she was wearing with a strand of pearls around her neck and simple gold earrings. "Kathy, I'm going to the ladies' room," she continued. "Do you need to go?" When I declined, she directed the next statement to my father and uncle, and to our neighbor, Mr. Barrett. "No more drinks. Okay, fellas? It's getting late." With that, she and Mrs. Barrett left the table.

"You know, Doug," Uncle Mitchy said to my father. "Your yard's big enough for a horse."

"Sure is," Dad said. "Two and a half acres. And a horse would defi-nitely cut down on lawn maintenance." The men laughed, and I pushed over and rested my head on my uncle's forearm, fighting off sleep.

The following morning, I woke to raised voices downstairs. Confused and half-asleep still, I listened intently. "Mitch, if they hadn't called to verify the address, there'd be a horse in our backyard right now!" My mother's voice was shaky.

A horse! I couldn't believe it. I was out of bed like a shot and looking out the window, but all I saw was rolling lawn and weeping willows. I crept into the hallway and to the top of the stairs, the better to eavesdrop.

"A horse? Aw, go on. What are you talking about?"

"Yes, Mitch. A horse," my mother said. "You called sometime last night to the stables out on the Cape and rented a horse for three months." It sounded like Mom was going to cry, and I felt bad, as if I'd done something wrong. I stayed crouched against the banister. "Mitch, your drinking is out of hand. We love you. For heaven's sake, you're Doug's brother! But this can't go on with Kathy here. She adores you."

My mother's weeping frightened me. So did the slamming of the door and the silence that followed. After a while, I crept down the stairs to find my mother sipping tea and staring out the window.

"Mommy? Where's Uncle Mitchy?" I asked.

"And good morning to you, too, young lady." She paused for a second before continuing. "Your uncle walked down to the bay, I think. He said he missed the sea air." My mother's eyes would not meet mine. Somehow I knew she was not telling me everything. "Kathy, why don't you color a picture for Uncle Mitch while I fix your breakfast?" Her smile seemed forced as she handed me some paper and crayons. "Here—go ahead. It'll be a nice surprise."

"Mom, am I getting a pony?" I asked. "I promise I'll take care of her. I'll get up early every day and—"

"Kathy, there was a misunderstanding," Mom said. "Mitch didn't realize horses aren't allowed in neighborhoods like this, with children, houses—and especially cars. Sweetheart, a horse could get hurt living here."

"But Mom!" I whined.

"No 'buts,' Kathy. It's the law." My mother's tone let me know that was the end of our debate, so I picked up a crayon and drew a pony, dreaming about the day when I had my own.

After the pony incident, Mitch's visits became less frequent and more strained. The years slipped by, and Uncle Mitchy retired from the Merchant Marines to a log cabin in Sunnybrook, New York. My parents and I settled in Connecticut. Then, while I was still in grammar school, my father died suddenly one Christmas.

It was a painful time for my mother and me—and for Uncle Mitchy. Unable to accept the premature death of his older brother, my uncle's drinking escalated. Phone calls in the middle of the night to my grieving mother were common. On the other end of the line was Mitch, slurring his words as he reminisced about the good old days when my dad and he were young. As upsetting as these phone calls were, my mother did her best to soothe her late husband's brother and get him off the line without a fuss.

I was a teenager when Uncle Mitchy moved his lady friend, Maggie, in with him. This arrangement caused an uproar among my aunts. Branded as licentious, Maggie was disliked by the female elders of the family. I liked her, however. Maggie loved my uncle; she made him happy, and I thought that was what truly mattered. Maggie proclaimed that she was a self-taught pianist, and she was reasonably good. I always envisioned them nestled in the woods of Sunnybrook, Mitch on his fiddle and Maggie tickling the ivories, the two of them playing songs into the wee hours of the morning. Maggie was a character, with her platinum blond hair piled high on her head, her eyes streaked with turquoise shadow and heavy black liner. I think what appealed to Mitch, besides her buxom figure, was her talent for banging back boilermakers alongside him. Maggie also whipped up a first-rate mutton stew. "Sticks to a man's ribs and keeps him warm on a frigid Arctic night," Mitch would laugh. "If he doesn't have a willing colleen or a bottle of Irish whiskey close by, that is."

As adulthood sneaked up on me, my favorite uncle, anchored permanently in home port, became a recluse. Mitch's eccentricity increased over time, as did his alcoholism. Drink became the source of his delusions, although the aunts preferred to blame Maggie. On a raw February night, in a log cabin tucked in the woods of Sunnybrook, New York, with the woman he loved by his side, the captain passed away peacefully in his sleep at the age of eighty-three.

We celebrated Mitchell James Wyatt's life at a local hall in the true Irish tradition. Glasses raised, we toasted his generosity and repeated the tall tales he had spun on his trips home from the ports of the world. Guests dined on roasts, casseroles, wine, and—of course—Maggie's mutton stew. Irish folk songs triggered cheers and foot stomping, and when "Danny Boy" was sung, there wasn't a dry eye in the hall.

The nieces, nephews, and grandchildren—those family members too young to remember Uncle Mitchy—know him through his stories and the gifts he gave. Mitch's stories are *our* stories now, told with humor and love, but the greatest of my uncle's gifts are my vivid memories of those restaurant nights. . . .

Whenever I want to, or need to, I can close my eyes and again become the wide-eyed little girl whose dimpled, blue-eyed mother is young again and pretty, and whose father, alive once more, sips his drink and laughs along with the brother seated beside him. Uncle Mitchy has returned from his latest voyage, laden with seafaring stories and exotic dolls. Seated across from him, I watch with delight as he holds court, winks at the prettiest of the waitresses, and, raising his glass, asks God to bless Kathleen Bridgett, the niece who is lucky enough to have his attention and his love.

A Brother's Gift

BY JENNIFER RICH

The summer I was ten, we sat together on the back deck. You had Mom's ancient acoustic on your knee. I was transfixed by your fingers as they danced across the frets.

The melody sprang to life with each chord strummed, notes bouncing from leaf to leaf in the huge red maple that shaded us from the sun. The song was the same one I heard each night, muffled by the wall that separated our rooms.

After the last riff, you pushed your hair away from your eyes and broke the trance. You seemed to notice for the first time that I'd been staring at you. Lifting the ornate strap from its resting place at the back of your neck, you ducked your head underneath and raised your eyebrows as if asking, *Well?* You were holding the relic out to me.

I set the guitar on my thigh and wrapped my left hand around its neck. Instantly, I was in love with the feel of its polished body in my lap.

Patiently, you positioned my small, stubborn fingers again and again until the bats and fireflies came out. And on that day, my passion for playing was born.

The Rainbow Ring

BY CARMEN RAMOS

It was May of 1988, and I was living in Trujillo Alto, Puerto Rico, with my two boys and a dog named Cindy. Our little apartment was perfect for us.

Early on the morning of Mother's Day, my eight-year-old son Hector handed me a little box—a gift to celebrate the occasion. I was surprised that he had remembered what day it was because he was only eight years old. My charming, sweet boy looked at me with those beautiful brown eyes that always made me melt with love. Hector was a funny and lovable kid, neither chubby nor skinny. Just right. I loved the caramel and cinnamon tone of his skin. And did I mention that Hector was smart? Yes, he was.

Hector broke away from my hug and pointed to my present. "Open it, Mommy! I know you'll like it." When I unwrapped the paper and opened the box, tears fell down my cheeks. Inside was the most beautiful candy ring I had ever seen. "It's not a real diamond ring, Mommy. It's candy. But don't eat it yet, because I'm going to tell you a little secret I know about this ring. When you move it, it makes different colors like the rainbow!"

I was so happy and amused that I forgot to thank my son. Instead, I asked him where he'd gotten it. "I bought it from the store we went to last week," he said. "You were busy buying other stuff, so I whispered to the lady behind the counter that I wanted a candy ring to give my mom for Mother's Day. I got one for myself, too, and you wouldn't believe what my eyes saw. When I was ready to eat mine, I stopped because the colors were swirling."

"Or maybe that's what you wanted to believe," I said. But Hector's face turned serious, and I thought, well, I'll just listen without interrupting him.

"Mom," he said. "You know how you're always saying you don't have any patience? It's the same with me sometimes, too. But when I looked at my ring, I stared at the color yellow and thought maybe I *can* have patience, even when my work at school is hard. I know I can do it if I believe I can."

"How is it that yellow stands for patience?" I asked my son.

"Because it's like the sun," he said. "It has a warm touch that says, 'Breathe in, breathe out, and everything will be all right.'"

I just stood there, listening; I had never imagined my young son could be so philosophical! Hector said, "Mommy, I saw these two colors come together—orange and green. The orange reminded me of the sunset, peaceful and calm. The green made me think of nature. Look around, Mommy, at the plants, trees, and grass. All this green gives me the freedom to run around. Nature is an invitation!"

I couldn't believe what I was hearing. Hector, my charming son, sounded like a little man. I looked at my candy ring, turning it to see if I could see or feel what he had seen and felt. What I saw was that belief is a powerful thing, *if* you have faith in yourself.

Hector continued. "The color pink in the ring is not for me. It suits you better, Mommy, and let me tell you something. You should wear pink more often. You look pretty when you do, and I think your days will go better if you feel pretty." That made me smile sadly. If my son saw the beauty in me—something I struggled to see in myself—then

I would wear pink more often. Maybe I would look in the mirror and see someone beautiful, too.

As Hector continued, a worried look crossed his brow. He said, "Mommy, you and I are the same. When we get mad, our faces turn purple, as if we might explode. But purple doesn't suit us. We look better when we smile than when we wear our angry purple faces." As Hector spoke, my heart filled with sadness. I thought about all the ways in which anger had interfered with my happiness, and I vowed then and there that I would learn from the wisdom of this wise and special child.

"Keep turning the ring, Mommy," Hector advised. "Do you see the color blue? Blue makes me feel sad. When I'm not around you, I miss you, Mommy. But when I see you again, your hugs say you love me and the blue goes away."

Hector paused before continuing and his eyes widened. "The color red is God for me," he said.

"Yes? Why God?" I asked.

"Because you always tell me that God loves us, and that he gave his life for you and me on the cross. Mommy, you said God created the world in seven days and gave Noah the seven colors of the rainbow as his promise of love for us. So that's why I gave you this candy ring. I know sometimes we get out of control, but I also know that every day you give us the gift of love."

My tears fell again. Wow, I thought. Even though I spend most of my time with Hector, he is a mystery, wise beyond his years. My sweet little boy has such a vivid imagination—such a gift with words. I, on the other hand, was speechless. I just kept hugging my son. And when at last I could speak, I said, "Hector, you've grown up so much. The things you just said? They touch my heart and I will remember them forever." And I have. To this day, I recall my little present—a candy diamond and a Mother's Day I will never forget.

You don't need much money to give the gift of love.

Pictures of a Daughter, Viewed in Prison

BY CHRISTINA MACNAUGHTON

You set the photos down,
spreading time around you panorama-style.
Button-nosed baby, toddler, little girl, bigger girl:
Your eyes roam the chain of living paper dolls,
the side-by-side smiles posed just for you.
Time cannonballs you in the gut.
You think, When the hell did all this happen?
How did I miss so much?
Too late to cry, too late to mourn
the baby smell, the small heft, the music of her giggles.
The middle photos blur, become
the space between your first photo and your latest.
This is the abyss into which time has fallen.
Your reverie broken,
you gather up your painful collection and rise.
The clock reads 2:28.
Time has just stolen another hour.

Under-Where?

BY LYNNE M. FRIEND

My sister Andrea was adamant. "Lynne, I mean it. Please don't get me laughing at some inappropriate moment and make me look like a fool!"

A big family event was coming up: our brother Gary, who'd borne the burden of growing up with four older sisters, miraculously still liked women enough to marry one. Gale was the girl of Gary's dreams and their wedding would be the first time in over nine years that we five siblings and our divorced parents would be in the same state together, let alone the same church. The wedding couple was "opposites attract" in some ways; Gale had grown up with horses and her own credit card and Gary had grown up in a family on a budget. So the stakes were high, and my sisters and I were hoping not to come off like too loud and lively a bunch in front of Gale's staid and proper relatives.

But there's a history between Andrea and me. On many, many occasions, I have gotten her guffawing at the *most* inopportune moments. Here's an example: once when we were kids, Gary accidentally passed gas in church during the minister's sermon. I leaned over to Andrea and whispered, "Gas who?" She tried laughing silently at first, her shoulders rising and falling, but it was no use. She broke out in full-scale chortling.

Mom frowned, heads swiveled, and Reverend Fortin stopped midsentence, all of which made Andrea laugh harder. Well, she was not about to let it happen again. She wanted to be solemn and thoughtful during the upcoming nuptials, and she made me promise not to derail her in that effort. But it was not to be.

My husband, Bob, and I flew from Colorado back to Connecticut a week or so before the wedding. Andrea and I had always been close with Gary, so we were thrilled that Gale had asked us to be in the bridal party. And because our future sister-in-law had a great fashion sense, we were looking forward to wearing the bridesmaid dresses she'd chosen. Until we saw them, that is.

They were pink satin, low-cut, and gathered at the waist, with short sleeves that puffed out like a car's air bags on impact. Andrea and I had given Gale our dress sizes over the phone, so at least the gowns fit us. In the bridal shop dressing room, with Gale waiting outside, my sister and I stood side by side before the mirror. Two look-alikes in matching cotton candy getups looked back at us. The shoulders of our mirror images moved up and down with stifled laughter. "The Shoulder Sisters," our family had nicknamed us, and we were at it again.

"Oh well," I whispered, when I could finally speak. "He's our only brother, right? These dresses aren't *his* fault. And look, we only have to look ridiculous in front of a hundred and fifty people or so. We've seen worse dresses, haven't we?"

Andrea didn't answer me.

"Well, *haven't* we?"

"Maybe *you* have," she said.

But ugly dresses or not, I was determined to be a good sport and a supportive sister-in-law. When I emerged from the dressing room and faced Gale, I gave an Academy Award–winning performance of enthusiasm.

The day before the wedding, I pulled Gary aside for a serious talk. I was having a bit of difficulty letting go of my "baby brother," but he reassured me that we'd remain close. "Married or not, I'll probably still call you from time to time for advice about women," he said.

"From time to time?" I said. "You better call me every chance you get, or I'm going to call you every chance *I* get. Collect!"

Gary rolled his eyes and laughed. "Wouldn't want that," he said.

At the rehearsal dinner that night, Mom turned to me with a look of concern. "Now, Lynne, try to be graceful when you walk down the aisle tomorrow, okay? You don't want to trip like you did at your cousin's wedding."

"But Mom, there was a rip in the carpet," I reminded her.

"Sure there was," Dad chimed in. He turned to his ex-wife. "We should have named her Grace, don't you think?" Mom smiled and nodded.

The big day arrived: Saturday, August 17, the hottest and most humid day of the summer. "Oh my God, it must be a hundred degrees out there," I whined to my husband, Bob. "I'm going to be miserable in that puffy satin dress all day. Where are my dress shields?"

"Chill out," Bob said. "It'll probably be air-conditioned in the church and at the club for the reception."

"Yeah, but we'll be outside before the wedding and in the receiving line afterward. You know how cranky I get when I'm sweltering."

What could I do? Well, I reasoned, I wouldn't be leaping up to catch the bridal bouquet with the single women, or showing my legs for any other reason. Why not just wear knee-high stockings under my gown? Nobody would know and I'd be more comfortable. I'd packed my favorite underwear to wear for the wedding—green satin panties with lace, hand-sewn by a friend in Colorado. I slipped them on, then a half-slip, then the knee-highs, then the dress. I was still hot, but not as hot as I'd have been in pantyhose.

Bob and I drove to the church with Andrea, her husband, Corey, and my nephew Michael. "I wish I'd thought about the knee-high thing," Andrea said. "My legs feel like they're in a toaster oven."

In the bridal room, Gale gave us each a strand of pearls to wear. She was nervous, of course, but she looked beautiful. And now I realized why she'd picked out our dresses. Her off-white satin gown was low-cut with puffy short sleeves. We blended together perfectly. As Bob had predicted, the church was air-conditioned. I would be walking down the aisle with Dan, a good friend of Gary's who was both nice and funny. Okay, smooth sailing, I thought.

We all took our places at the back of the church and the organ music began. Everything went fine as we proceeded down the aisle to meet the minister and the handsome groom. My brother, six feet tall, with dark brown hair and eyes, was wearing a black tuxedo with a cream-colored shirt, and a white rose in his lapel. The guests gazed lovingly at us all, especially the bride and groom.

During the ceremony, I looked from the bridal couple to the gathering of friends and family who had come to witness their union. Swept up in the magic of the day, I was listening intently to the minister's meaningful words about holy matrimony and unconditional love when, without warning, *it* happened. The elastic waist of my elegant hand-sewn underwear had just broken and that fancy underwear was heading south. Oh, no, I thought. This could only happen to me!

Andrea was standing next to me. I leaned toward her and whispered, "You're not going to believe what just happened to me."

"Lynne," she whispered back, "I swear to God, leave me alone right now or there's going to be hell to pay!"

"Yeah, but the elastic on my underwear snapped, and they've fallen down to my knees." I shifted my position a bit. "Whoa, make that *below* my knees!"

Andrea's shoulders started moving up and down. That started me going. The "Shoulder Sisters" were at it again. If only I'd worn panty-hose!

I turned back to look for my mother, but all I could see were Gale's relatives in their conservative suits and tasteful dresses. And when I finally did spot Mom, the scathing look she gave me let me know I was on my own.

I placed my hand just below my knee—along the outside of my dress, of course—and managed to pinch a little of the lace trim. I tried inching the underwear, little by little, back up toward my rear end. I couldn't get a strong enough hold, though, and they kept slipping back down to my knees.

Oh my God, I thought, they'll be saying their vows soon. I had to figure out something quickly, because once the minister invited the groom to kiss the bride, I'd have to take Dan's arm and walk back down that aisle. How the heck was I going to get myself out of *this* one?

Half-composed, Andrea whispered, "Have you pulled them back up yet?"

"I've tried," I said. "But they have a mind of their own!"

More shoulder action from both of us.

At that point, my brother, who'd been trying to concentrate on his wedding vows, turned and glared at us. I felt terrible—I certainly didn't want to ruin his big day. My forehead and upper lip broke out in a sweat. I tried a few more unsuccessful hoists. Then, just as things were wrapping up, I got a good grip on the underwear and formulated a plan. I would carry my flowers in my left hand and hold on to my underwear with my right. I wouldn't be able to link my right arm with Dan's left on our way back up the aisle, but no one would guess what the problem was. I would quietly tell Dan, "I can't hold on to your arm. I'll explain later."

The music played, the bride and groom began their exit, and I stepped forward to meet Dan. I tried to tell him I couldn't hold on to him, but he wouldn't listen. "Aw, come on. Don't be shy," he said and hooked his arm around mine.

One or two steps into it, my underwear dropped back to my knees. I couldn't let them fall to the floor. What if people saw them dragging beneath my dress? What if they tripped me up and sent both Dan

GIFTS MY FAMILY GAVE ME

and me toppling? I clamped my knees together and took a few baby steps forward, my feet turned inward, my knees scrunched against each. Puzzled looks fell over the faces of the wedding guests as they watched our curious progress up the aisle.

Midway there, I spotted my husband, standing at the end of his pew and laughing. He knew something had to have happened to make me walk so awkwardly—he just didn't know what it was. But Bob wasn't about to pass up the opportunity to immortalize the moment of my mortification. He raised his camera and began snapping away.

It took several minutes for me to make it to the vestibule. I was in tears at that point, but Andrea, wearing her stupid pantyhose, was doubled over. As the others in the wedding party gathered for the receiving line, I ducked into the ladies' room and took off my underwear, rolled it in a ball, and crushed it inside my fist. Once I located Bob and got him to pocket the evidence, I'd just have to stand in the receiving line *au naturel*.

The problem was: I couldn't find Bob. As I got in line, I transferred the underwear from my right hand to my left and put it behind my back. My whole body trembled as I shook hands and greeted guests. "Hello. So nice to meet you. Yes, it was a lovely service."

At long last, Bob materialized behind me. "What the hell was going on with you and Andrea in there?" he asked. "Your shoulders were shaking for ten minutes."

"I need you to take these," I said. I placed my underwear in his hand.

Bob's eyes widened. "What the ... what are you wearing under your dress?"

"Nothing," I said. "Just my slip and my knee-highs."

"Ooh, baby," he said.

I rolled my eyes and told him to get a grip. And when he gave my behind a squeeze, I said, "That's not what I meant, but hold that thought for later." He walked away, laughing and shaking his head.

When the last of the guests had made their way through the receiving line, my mother approached me. "Lynne, I want to talk to you," she said. "Would you mind telling me what was going on up there during the service? Whatever it was, everyone noticed. And why were you walking up the aisle like a crippled person?"

By the time I finished telling her the underwear saga, she was laughing so hard, she was holding her stomach. "Oh my God, you poor thing!" she said. "You'd better go tell your brother what happened. He's looking for you and he's not too happy."

I found Gary in the parking lot, pulled him aside, and told him the whole story. Howling with laughter, he repeated it to Gale, whose proper bride behavior collapsed into belly laughs. "My bottomless wedding!" she said.

"Yeah," I said. "Welcome to the family."

By the time I arrived at the reception, the story was all over the place. As I stood there in the air-conditioned room, freezing my butt off, I tried to maintain some sense of dignity. And when that proved hopeless, I gave up and simply maintained my sense of humor. "Butt anyways . . ." I'd say.

The groom made fun of me all afternoon and, by midreception, he was even imitating my perilous walk up the aisle. Little brothers, I thought. Some things never change.

Why I Write

BY CAREEN JENNINGS*

My great-great-great-uncle marched with General Sherman's army through Georgia in 1865. Back home in Indiana after the war, he took up his quill pen and wrote: "*In the city of Savannah a colored school was now established and the children liberated by the sword sat with books in their hands and teachers before them on the same platform where slaves had but a short time before been bought and sold like brutes. Tears filled the eyes of parents as they gazed in wonder and thankfulness to God.*"

My mother wrote of her girlhood in the 1920s: "*I remember waking to the clip-clop, clip-clop of horses' hooves just after daybreak on weekday mornings. Farmers were taking produce to town. The milkman rattled his bottles saying, 'Giddap' and 'Whoa' alternately. During summer vacation the horse brought the ice. We children gathered round saying, 'May I have a piece of ice?' He gave us each a chip.*"

Photos from the past are priceless, but words from the past give meaning to the lives of those who have died.

Why did they write? I think it was to help them remember that they had seen and done something significant, and they wanted to share

* Careen Jennings, a retired high school English teacher, is a writing workshop cofacilitator.

their lives with others, others they would never meet. They knew that their lives meant something, and they wanted to speak to the future.

Why do I write? As was my great-great-great-uncle, I have been a witness to history. I was in the crowd of college students when Martin Luther King Jr. rallied us for the passage of the Civil Rights Act. I was sitting at the makeshift press table (no one cared in those days of innocence) when Robert Kennedy came to a nighttime rally for his brother John, who was trying to win the Democratic nomination for president.

But like my mother, I mostly write of my own life: my childhood, my own children, my losses, my joys, fears, dreams, angers, questions. I write in order to be able to think, to sort out confused emotions, to record my life and the lives of those around me, to find meaning, to *Be*.

As he was dying from brain cancer, my twenty-seven-year-old son said, "Remember me." He'd never read much Shakespeare, but Hamlet's father returned from the dead to speak these same words to his son.

So I remember my great-great-great-uncle who died many decades before I was born. I remember my mother's childhood. And maybe my writing will be read by my unborn great-grandchildren, and they will learn of my world—not as the history books will describe it, but as I lived in it. Maybe they will remember me.

Lavender and Vanilla

BY KIMBERLY WALKER

Mom lies still
in the hospital bed—

lavender and vanilla
radiating from her skin.

Spirit at peace, body at rest,
she is in her father's arms.

Upon her face,
glorious light shines.

The wind blows
I love you kisses.

The rain falls,
tears of I miss you.

The scents of lavender and vanilla
say, I will always be with you.

A Gift

BY ROBIN LEDBETTER

I stared in disbelief at my grandmother's door—the locked entrance to the apartment where I'd spent most of my life. "What do you mean, 'How are you?'" I shouted. "You're not even going to open the god-damned door?"

"I'm glad you're all right," she called out. "Okay, then. Bye."

I pounded the door with my fists and screamed. "Grandma! Grandma! I can't believe you!" But I could. My grandmother had three major flaws: number one was too much pride; number two was her secretive-ness; and number three—her worst flaw—was her ability to completely ignore any situation or conversation that caused her the slightest dis-comfort. And that was exactly what Grandma was doing.

I turned to Barbara, my new foster sister, who had come with me. She was staring strangely at me, her normally pale skin flushed, her big brown eyes large with fear. "Sorry, Barbie. I thought she'd . . ." My words trailed off and I rested my head against the apartment door and began to cry. I was thirteen. I hadn't lived with my grandmother for almost two years, and when I had, I'd always felt like an intruder. But for some reason I didn't really understand, I still considered her place home.

I'd gone to live with my grandmother when I was five years old. My parents were drug addicts and couldn't raise me, so Gram had stepped in, offering me a home inside the red brick building in the projects where she lived. Life with Grandma had been isolating. She was as proud as she was uneducated, and because she lived in fear that her limitations might be exposed, she lived a very private life, with few connections to the outside world. I was, for the most part, a good kid, but by the age of ten I had become restless. I'd found my voice, too—a voice of indignation and ferocious rebellion. Grandma's apartment became a battleground, and each day the war between us escalated. By the time I was eleven, Gram had had enough and kicked me out.

In the two years that followed, I'd bounced from the apartments of other family members to mental hospitals, from shelters to group homes. Now, at thirteen, I'd landed at my current residence, a foster home I loved. Despite the battles I'd waged against my grandmother, despite all the bad blood between us, I wanted to reconnect with her—to show her how well I was doing and introduce her to my new foster sister. What I wanted most of all was Grandma's approval, and in my youthful ignorance, I thought I could show up at her house by surprise and she would toss aside my history of bad behavior, throw open the door, and welcome me in with open arms. So her "How are you?" from behind the locked door was a slap in the face—a stinging wallop back to the reality that she had never fully accepted me. She didn't *want* to see me? Not even through a crack in the door with the safety chain on? A hundred painful emotions churned inside of me, and with them came the involuntary tears I was furious at myself for shedding.

"You won't open the door? It's okay. Fuck you!" I screamed. "Come on!" I ordered Barbara, flying past her and down the hall, out the doors of the apartment building, down the front stairs.

"You okay?" Barbara called after me, her voice thick with concern and heavy with accent.

"I'm fine!" I declared, though I was anything but. Grandma had wounded me and I wanted to wound her back. My face cast downward,

I wiped fiercely at my eyes and rounded the corner of the brick building where I'd been raised. I had no idea what I was going to do until I looked up at the parking lot behind the building. There was my grandmother's beloved car, parked behind the crippled fence. "I got a trick for *her* ass," I muttered to myself and headed toward the back of the building.

"What are you doing?" Barbara asked as she watched me struggle a few bricks loose from under the stairs of the back porch. Without answering her, I headed straight for Grandma's silver Buick Thunderbird. She had bought it with the insurance money she'd gotten after a driver smashed into her other old clunker a few years earlier. A year ago, some kids had busted out one of the Thunderbird's windows by accident and she'd been upset. Well, she'd be *devastated* by the time *I* finished with that car. The bricks I was holding fell to the ground—all but one. As I took aim at the front windshield, I felt strangely calm. With all my might, I hurled the brick. The alarm began wailing as soon as it made contact, but I'd only made a dent, not a smash. I picked up the brick again. I could see a few bystanders peering at me as I took aim the second time and fired.

It took four more hits before that front window was smashed to my satisfaction. I moved on to the passenger's-side window. Again, I took aim—but this time, when the brick hit the glass, the window exploded. I think the mixture of exploding glass, shrieking car alarm, and my own fierce emotions made me high. By the time I'd busted out the last window, I was laughing and crying hysterically. The last thing I remember is my foster sister grabbing me by my arm and dragging me away from the scene of my crime. As she did, I caught a glimpse of my grandmother peering out of my old bedroom window. She was a shadowy figure behind a curtain, and I was a feverish thirteen-year-old in a yellow sundress and white sandals, an outfit I'd put on that morning to show her how well I was doing.

I know this sounds like the memory of a disturbed young girl—and it is. But it's more than that. This is a story of gratitude for the gift of forgiveness—for the gift of abiding love.

A year after the window-smashing incident—the year I was fourteen—I was arrested for murder. Stretched out on my bunk on my first night in a juvenile detention center, I thought about how completely alone I was. Both of my parents were messed up, and as for the rest of my family, I'd let years of anger burn every bridge between them and me. There'd be no one in the world to stand by me while I fought to survive in the face of hopelessness and despair. So I was taken by surprise when, the next morning, I was called for a visit. And what surprised me even more was that the visitor was my reclusive grandmother—a woman who preferred solitude to company, isolation to connection. Yet there she was, in a floral dress and matching headband, walking her proud walk, her hands turned out to show off her ring. I braced myself as she approached me, thinking I was in for a verbal assault that I didn't have the energy to endure. But the biggest surprise I got that morning was the kiss and the hug Grandma gave when she reached me. No judgment, no harsh words, no bitter tone.

We visited for two hours and she promised me she'd be back the next day—that she'd always be there for me as long as she had breath in her body. And you know what? She did come back the next day, and the day after that, and the day after that. Grandma has continued to be there for me until this day ten years later. For that, I'm grateful beyond what these words can express.

My grandmother has never brought up that day I destroyed her car. On the day of her first visit—the first full day of my imprisoned life— she and I had a new beginning. I believe my grandmother has blessed me with many things over the years, but the most precious gift she has ever given me came ten years ago in that visiting room. To this day, I can see her approaching me in her colorful dress, walking across a bridge of love to give me the gift of a second start.

III.
Broken Dolls and Marionettes

*The heart of a hurt child can shrink so that forever
afterward it is hard and pitted as the seed of a peach.
Or, again, the heart of such a child may fester and swell
until it is misery to carry within the body, easily chafed
and hurt by the most ordinary things.*

—CARSON MCCULLERS

*Sexism is the foundation on which all tyranny is built.
Every social form of hierarchy and abuse is modeled on
male-over-female domination.*

—ANDREA DWORKIN

*Those children who are beaten will in turn give beatings,
those who are intimidated will be intimidating, those who
are humiliated will impose humiliation, and those whose
souls are murdered will murder.*

—ALICE MILLER

Broken Doll

BY LYNDA GARDNER

I begged Daddy to stop. I begged him not to.

"Please, Daddy! My skin is burning up. Please stop! I'll be a good girl. I didn't mean to make you so mad. I didn't mean to be a bad girl, Daddy! Okay, I'll stand in the closet with my arms out. But Daddy, it's so hard to keep them up for such a long time—I'm only little, Daddy! Please don't get mad at me again. My arm's burning and it smells like bacon. Could you please put some of Mommy's medicine on it to make it feel better because it hurts so much. It hurts bad, Daddy! I love you, Daddy, and I'm sorry I ate the last piece of cheese in the fridge! Please, Daddy! I won't never, ever do it again. I promise, it's just that…I was so hungry, Daddy. I'm sorry."

Well, I couldn't keep my arms out straight enough that day for him, so my stepfather proceeded to die out another cigarette in the same burn on my arm. And now, at fifty-six years old, I'm supposed to forgive him? I can't. I hate his guts. I'm so damned angry because he made me into who I have been, what I became.

I'm changing my life now, although the scars remain as harsh reminders. Some days, the burns look as raw and fresh as they were fifty-two years ago, and I'm just a bitter, self-centered person filled with pain and anger. My family consisted of my mother, my stepfather, five sisters, and a brother who died at eighteen months. My sisters are all blondes with blue or green eyes and very fair skin. And from what I have learned about my dead brother—there were no pictures of him—he was, too. And then there is me: dark brown hair, dark olive skin, and hazel eyes. I look like no one in my family. My sister Joyce would make comments like, "You're a different breed than we are, and *that's* why Daddy doesn't love you!" Once she told me that the Rag Man had dropped me off at the door and would be coming back for me. I was terrified he would return in the night to snatch me away. Until years later, I never understood what "different breed" meant: that I was my mother's child by another man.

My sister Nance felt bad for me and tried to protect me from him, to no avail. He was strong, and he even frightened her at times. Cindy, the sister who was most like him, took pleasure in saying through the door, "Watch out for the monster in there! He eats bad girls." I thought my heart would explode from the pounding in my chest as I waited to be gobbled up. Cindy also told me that "slimy things" lived under my bed, so I slept with my Daisy rifle with a cork bullet next to me. Rather than risk getting my feet chewed up, I would pee the bed, hoping my stepfather wouldn't find out. He always did.

This led to more beatings and more burns. He would call me "the dog," and I would have to sit by his chair. If I dared move, he would yank my hair. When he went to the kitchen for a beer, he'd twist my hair around his hand like a leash, lift me off the ground, get his beer, and go back to his chair in the parlor. God help me if I should whimper or make even the slightest sound because if I did, he would kick me, hit me, and die out another cigarette against my flesh. I loved Dad and I hated him. I just wanted him to love me, to stop hurting me. But he didn't. Later, I wanted him to stop breathing, to die, to choke to death—anything that would stop him. Nothing ever did.

What became of me? Weekends of drunken stupors, sick stomach, and sweaty palms, a lifetime of pain and misery. So many poor choices along the way, including two failed marriages. I'd been high most of my life. Through all of this experimenting and searching for meaning, I'd never found "me"—had never found the key to unlock the confusion and make sense of my life.

I left home and never saw Dad again, and when he died, I refused to go to his funeral. My mother and sisters were angry at me for that and couldn't understand why I would "embarrass" them that way. But we had all lived under that same roof. I couldn't understand why they couldn't understand.

Years later, I did visit the bastard's gravesite. I peed and spit on his stone, hoping for relief from my pain. I didn't get it. My stepfather was dead and I couldn't hurt him like he'd hurt me. He'd even had the luxury of dying peacefully in his sleep. I'm still angry about that!

My mother eventually apologized to me for what Dad had done to me all those years while I was growing up. She blamed herself. She and my stepfather had separated for a while, and it was during this estrangement that Mom met my father, had a brief encounter, and became pregnant with me. Then she and my stepfather reconciled. It was only after he was dead that she told me this—after she felt safe. I understood. She had been his victim, too: scared of "or else" and knowing no way out. You see, my stepfather had been a detective for the police department where we lived. I remember him taunting her with, "Go ahead and call the cops, Theresa!" They would have told him to keep his wife and kids in line, patted him on the shoulder, and looked the other way. They would not have gotten involved because he was one of their own. They had a code—a blue wall of silence—when it came to one of their brothers. So my mother had remained silent all those years for survival's sake.

As for me, after forty years of being high in order to escape the pain Dad had inflicted on my heart, my soul, and my mind, I was on my last roll of the dice. I'd numbed myself for so many years because it was the only way I could cope. Living without feeling, I had ended up in prison for being so high that I had gambled away not only my own but also someone else's money. I'd done so without a thought about the consequences, or of how I would embarrass my family. I guess I just didn't care.

I entered York CI three years ago. This has been the first time in forty years that I haven't been high on drugs, alcohol, or gambling. And I'm scared shitless, because I *feel*. I feel hurt, sadness, and sorrow. Mostly, I feel anger about what Dad did.

Maybe if I'd been sober long enough to feel these emotions before now, I could have stopped racing down the destructive path my life took. But I only knew that being numb made me feel safe. I didn't have to think about *him*, or the pain he'd inflicted. I didn't have to think at all when I was high—I could be happy, or at least pretend to be. And in the pursuit of that "happiness," I became an old lady pulling along a trunk full of junk: shame, guilt, distrust, disgust. At fifty-six, I'm just learning how to empty that trunk, little by little. It's getting lighter. I'm no longer afraid of feeling.

It feels good not to worry about how much money I need today for drugs and gambling, and to build and rebuild relationships with my five children and nine grandchildren. I know this will take time, but I am getting my life back and seeing through bright eyes now—no fog, no haze.

This is good. This is real. This is me.

"No" Is Not Just a Word

BY CHRISTINA MACNAUGHTON

Backstage, I feel the weighted silence of audience anticipation deep in my bones. This simple community theater is where life is best; this is where I'm happiest. I wait anxiously for the cue to my main scene in *Jane Eyre*. Suddenly, Shawn comes up and presses himself against the back of my humongous period costume—a nightmare of petticoats, lace, and fleur-de-lis. His dark eyes and deep voice send shock waves through my already overheated body. "You look enchanting," he tells me. "Brontë couldn't have imagined a lovelier Blanche."

This was how Shawn spoke, not in the condescending tone many adults used with me. I was thirteen years and ten months, as adult as I was ever going to be. Obviously, Shawn saw it, too. He had a small part in our production, and we had become friendly over the months of rehearsals. Even though he was twenty, I felt that he could see I was mature beyond my years.

Over the past year I had come into a brand-new body, one with curves and mannerisms that were just dying to be tried out. On Shawn I practiced my first clumsy attempts at flirting. I told him about my struggles with my backward parents and their desire to keep me a child. Shawn completely indulged my tantrums, as well as my innocent, fumbling tries at coyness. He was my first real guy friend. I knew he was sincerely interested in my thoughts and feelings.

After the play ran its course, we continued to hang out. On a night I knew my mother was working, I invited Shawn to my house to watch "intellectual" movies. I answered the door with overdone hair, makeup, and an outfit my sister had used the previous Halloween when she dressed as a slutty female pirate. I was sure that by the end of the evening he would think I was the most alluring, most interesting creature in the universe.

We never kissed, not even once. When *On the Waterfront* ended, I ran to the kitchen to get juice I'd spiked with wine, Shawn following. We sipped our "cocktails" for a while and I felt him come up behind me like he had at the theater, his large hands clutching my hips. He leaned into my ear. "What would happen if your mom walked through the door right now?" I giggled and squirmed out of his grasp.

"Stop!" I laughed. "We're going to miss the start of the next movie." I flipped my hair and batted my eyelashes. The moment was thrilling. None of my friends could get alone with a guy, no parents around. They would be dead jealous when I told them.

Back in the den, *Raging Bull* exploded on the TV screen. Shawn seemed absorbed in watching Joe Pesci pound the crap out of some poor slob, so I took a long swig of the doctored juice and lit one of my mother's cigarettes. Without warning, Shawn grabbed me, holding me terribly close. "You didn't invite me here just for movies and juice, right?" he said. It sounded more like a statement than a question. Again I attempted giggling, but my high-pitched laugh died in my throat. "Come on, Shawn. Let me up." I was trying to sound casual, but inside I was the baby gazelle who's just realized she's been picked off of the herd. I felt scared, but I couldn't freak out. He'd think I was a baby.

As he continued, Shawn took my silence as consent. I squeezed my eyes closed. His weight on top of me pressed my face into the sofa cushion, leaving lines that would last hours after he left me. He whispered while he did it. I didn't hear what he said; I tried to concentrate on Robert De Niro on the TV across the room. I remember I cried, but most importantly, I remember I never said the word "no." I'd been bluffing the whole night, but still I refused to show my empty hand.

Later, I told myself I must have wanted this; it must've been my choice. I'd dressed that way for a purpose. I had wanted to flirt and tease and be an adult, and this was what I'd gotten. I felt embarrassed and ashamed, dirty and wrong, but this was what I'd asked for.

Years later, Connie, my therapist, heard the story of "my first time." I didn't cry or become emotional; in fact, I joked that I didn't relish admitting I'd been "easy" so young. "Honey," she explained. "You were raped."

"No chance," I sputtered. "I never said 'no.'" Only after the words left my lips did I realize the absurdity of that statement.

The *R* word floored me. I had never considered it as something relating to *me*. Still, my stomach lurched in agreement with Connie's assessment, even as my mind rejected the idea. How was it that my digestive system had a better sense of reality than my cerebral cortex?

I always thought rape was a guy jumping out of the bushes or the drunken football player at the homecoming dance. It involved kicking and screaming, black eyes and ripped dresses. You had George Clooney to comfort you as you shivered small and sad on an ER exam table, the *Law & Order* cops to ask you the questions that would lead them to the evil stranger. I never realized rape happens while you're doing what you thought you wanted to do.

I have no idea what I will tell my young daughter when she asks about my first experiences with boys. I guess I'll try to teach her that no girl earns her own violation, and that "no" is a concept, not just a word.

Wishes

BY CHARISSA WILLETTE

I. Prince Charming—1994

I stop by the wishing fountain and check my watch—four o'clock. Mom's not picking me up until nine thirty when the mall closes. My friend Jenn is *supposed* to be meeting me here, but, as usual, she's late. Jenn and I, fifteen and fourteen, respectively, come to the mall once a week to hang out, shop, check out hot guys, and experience what we consider grown-up freedom. I pull a penny from my change purse, close my eyes, and make a wish that I'll meet Prince Charming. Let him be cute, tall, funny, and smart, I think. Oh, and money—he *must* have money. I let my penny fly and watch it sink to the bottom with the others. So many coins, I think. So many wishes.

Jenn's an hour late. When I call her, she says she'll be here in a little while; she's still trying to convince her mom to give her a ride. I walk around some more, looking at things I've already looked at. The mall's pretty empty—it *is* a Wednesday. If anyone from school sees me all by myself, I'll never let Jenn live it down.

I pass a really hot guy. He's noticeably older, at least eighteen. He's about five-foot-nine with curly brown shoulder-length hair, hazel eyes, and a mischievous smile. He's dressed grunge: ripped jeans, tattered sweater, crumpled golfer's hat, dusty green Adidas. I look back toward the wishing fountain. Wouldn't it be nice...

In Filene's, I head for the juniors department, grab some clothes, and enter the dressing room. I pull a brown bodysuit over my head and try to snap it. Damn it, I think, why do I have to be so chubby? I wrestle with it and finally declare the bodysuit the winner. I'm exhausted and sweaty. Why are dressing rooms always so hot?

I try on the jeans. Perfect around the waist but a little too long. I take them off. Standing before the mirror in just my bra and panties, I suck in my stomach, lift things, pull things. I should've wished to be tall and thin instead of wasting my wish on some guy. I get dressed, stick my tongue out at myself, and leave.

Hours later, I collapse on a bench by the pay phones and wait for 9:30 to come. I'm pissed at Jenn because she never showed. She and I haven't always been friends. In middle school, as I sat by myself in the cafeteria, she used to make fun of me and yank my hair. My protests would invite further taunts. "Aw, Little Miss Perfect doesn't want messy hair. Every hair in place, everything from your scrunchie to your shoe-laces matching. Christ, who the hell is *this* perfect?"

Perfect? If I were perfect, wouldn't I have friends?

One day, I decided I'd had enough. When Jenn pulled my hair, Little Miss Perfect punched her in the face. After that, she stopped making fun of me, and over time we became friends.

I look up from my watch and see *him* again. And, oh my God, he's coming my way. Is he checking me out? Is that possible? My heart races.... Oh. Hottie's only coming to use the phone. Still, I'm just a couple of feet from him, biting my lip, hoping he talks to me. Pleeease talk to me.

Is it luck? Fate? The wishing fountain? Reaching into the bag he's holding, he accidentally drops it. Coins roll every which way, some toward me. He's going to talk to me! Yes!

These are the first gloriously romantic words out of his mouth: "Boy, I must look like an ass."

"N-no," I stutter. My only task is to look cute, so I giggle the cutest giggle I can muster, then stoop to help him pick up his money. He tries again to fish a dime from his bag and again he drops it. "Well, now you look like an ass." I say it flirtatiously.

His smile could melt those runaway coins of his. "Hi. I'm Kevin."

"Hi, Kevin. I'm…" Oh no—what's my name? Think quick. "Charissa," I finally spit out. Thank god I'm wearing my favorite outfit: light blue Bongo jeans, a white, fluffy knit sweater, and white Keds sneakers. My hair looks pretty good, too—curly, shoulder-length. I wear very little makeup, only lip gloss and a light blush.

We talk for a few minutes about nothing in particular, until he realizes the security gate to McDonald's is closing. "Excuse me, Dollface. Gotta get something to eat. I'm starving!" Running past me, he hops a bench and slides under the gate.

That's when it hits me: this really hot older guy is talking to me. *Me*, who no guy has ever noticed before. Damn, why aren't any of the popular girls here to witness this? Mom always tells me that the teasers are just jealous of me, but I don't believe her. Mothers are supposed to say things like that. If the popular girls saw me talking to Kevin, though, they'd envy me.

He reappears, heading my way with a bag full of food. "I love how you just slid under the security gate!" Did I really just say something that dorky?

"I actually surprised myself," he says as we laugh. He's modest, too. I look at my watch: 9:42. I'm reluctant to leave, but I tell Kevin my mom's waiting outside.

"Your mom? You don't have a car?"

"I'm fourteen." I say it nonchalantly, trying to appear mature.

"Oh. You look older than that."

"How old are you?" I ask. Please don't be too old.

"Nineteen. Anyway, Dollface, can I get your number?" Yes! He doesn't care that I'm only fourteen. Because I don't have a pen, I take out my lipstick and write my number on his arm. "I'll definitely call you," he assures me with a smile. "Oh, before you go, can I get a kiss?"

I've never kissed a guy before, but I can't tell him that. He'll think I'm a prude. "I've never kissed a girl before," he confesses. "And your lips look so soft. I'd just like to know what it feels like to kiss them." His eyes plead. My heart flutters. I want to give in but I don't.

"We don't even know each other," I remind him. "You'll have to wait until we do." Walking away, I wave, remembering my wish. Is Kevin my Prince Charming?

The next day, when the phone rings, I lunge for it. "Charissa? It's Kevin. Whatcha doing?"

I may pass out. "Nothing, really. What are *you* doing?"

"Thinking about you," he says. "When I saw you sitting by the phones last night, you looked like an angel. I never imagined love at first sight would happen to me."

I manage a brilliant reply. "Uhhh."

"So why were you alone at the mall?" he asks. I tell him how Jenn stood me up. "That sucks," he says. "But if she hadn't, we might never have met."

For the next three hours, we talk about everything from music and movies to religion and politics. I start to believe he could be the one!

"Listen, Dollface, why don't we meet at the arcade tomorrow?" he asks.

"Sure, that'd be great."

"Okay. See you tomorrow then. I'll be thinking about you all night."

I'm so excited about seeing Kevin today. What to wear, what to wear? I try on every shirt I own and settle for a cream bodysuit. Turning sideways in the mirror, I realize I have to cover up the little chub hanging out. I decide on the new Aztec design vest Mom bought me at County Seat. Jean skirt? No, jeans. I'll pull my hair back with an Aztec design hair clip—thanks for matching, Mom! Very little makeup; a squirt of my favorite perfume, Love's Baby Soft; my cream ballerina shoes.

Our moms drop us off at the mall. As Jenn and I walk toward the arcade, my eyes find Kevin. His legs are spread, his whole body focused on Mortal Kombat. He's wearing his baggy faded jeans, torn at the knees, and his dingy green sneakers. The green in his T-shirt and cardigan bring out the green in his eyes. His hair is unruly—the way I like it. When his game is finished, I approach him, Jenn in tow. "Hey, Kev. This is Jenn."

"Hey," he says, smiling at me. I blush. After a little small talk, Kev says, "Charissa, I have to run to my place real quick and throw a load of laundry in the wash. I live right near here. You wanna come?"

Hesitant to go with him alone, I stall. "I don't want to leave Jenn by herself," I say. Jenn keeps quiet, looking back and forth between Kevin and me as if she's watching a tennis match.

"We won't be more than fifteen minutes—I promise."

"It's no big deal," Jenn says. "I'll wait here. Go."

"Come on, Dollface," Kevin says. "I don't bite. It'll be quick and it'll be with me—what more could you want?" His eyes sparkle, and after a few more minutes of sweet-talk, I go with him. He's only doing laundry, I think. What could be the harm?

His apartment is a studio. There's a hallway with a horizontal coat-rack to my right—the kind in motels—and to my left, a little bathroom. The main room has a small kitchen area and a living-bedroom combo with a twin bed, a nightstand, a TV, a stereo system, and a cheap folding table. The walls are institutional off-white. The only personal touch is a psychedelic poster tacked crookedly above the bed.

"Have a seat," he says, pointing to the bed.

I sit at the edge, uneasy about being alone with a strange older boy.

Kevin sits down next to me and begins kissing me. Startled by his slimy tongue probing my mouth, I put my hand on his mattress to stabilize myself, catching it in his sweater. My weight accidentally rips the buttonhole. I'm mortified, but Kevin gives me a boyish grin.

He gets off the bed, takes off his sweater. He pulls his T-shirt over his head and removes his pants. Shocked at his nakedness, my eyes bulge. I've never seen a guy's thing before, and I'm both disgusted and curious. He notices my staring and smiles. "I need to wash these, too."

I expect him to put on another set of clothes, but instead, he makes himself a bowl of cereal and turns on the stereo, singing and dancing to Pearl Jam's "Black." As I take glimpses of his bouncing penis, I feel a stir in my groin. He finishes eating, sits back down on the bed next to me, and leers.

"Aren't you supposed to be doing your laundry?" I ask. Where's his laundry basket? Where's the washing machine?

"In a couple of minutes," he responds.

"Oh. I better get back to Jenn before she sends the cavalry after me."

Kevin leans into me. "Can I have a hug?" His voice sounds husky now. I'm getting a bad feeling about this, but I give him what he wants—anything to get out of this suffocating room. Midhug, he pushes me down on the bed and starts wrestling playfully with me. I laugh and try to wriggle away. Am I being paranoid?

The playing stops. Kevin lowers himself onto me and kisses me. Oh God, all the date-rape stories I've been warned about in sex-ed flash through my mind. He gropes my breasts. I push him away. I have to get out of here.

"I won't hurt you, Charissa. Just relax. If you weren't so beautiful, I wouldn't be so excited—so hard…. Touch him. Feel how hard he is? He won't bite."

I thought he had to do laundry. Why is this happening to me? "I want you to stop!" I say. "I want to go back to the arcade!" I try to make it sound as if I'm in charge, but it comes out shaky.

"You're going to tease me and then leave me like this?" He's shouting now. "Don't you know what blue balls are?" Alert to everything around me, I shake my head no. "When a guy gets this hard, his balls fill up with blood. And if he doesn't get some release, they explode. He'll never be able to have kids. Is that what you want to have happen to me?"

I shake my head no.

He becomes nice Kevin again. "I just love you so much, Dollface. I want to lose my virginity to you. Don't you want to share something special with me?"

"I guess," I whisper. It *could* be romantic to sacrifice our virginity to each other.

"Lie down," he says.

I kick off my ballerina slippers and scootch up toward the headboard. He gets on top of me, kissing me, fondling me. Oh God, I'm not ready for this. Kevin removes my vest, my jeans. He unsnaps the crotch of my bodysuit and raises it over my head. He pulls off my white Hanes underwear and undoes my Playtex eighteen-hour bra. I curse Mom for buying me such granny-looking underwear. I don't like being naked before him. Is he staring at my fat?

After he's finished, he pushes me aside and examines his sheets. "If you were a virgin, why didn't you bleed more?" he asks, annoyed. I shrug. How much was I supposed to bleed? And anyway, who wants blood on their sheets? He goes to the kitchen, refills his cereal bowl, and sits down to eat it.

After people make love in the movies, they're mushy with each other. And we're in love, right? I walk over to him and do what I think I'm *supposed* to do—sit in his lap.

"Could you please get off me?" he says.

⁂

It's nine o'clock by the time we get back to the arcade. Jenn's nowhere around. I spot my mom's car near the mall entrance, and we stop so she won't see us.

"Call you later, Dollface," Kevin whispers. "I love you." His good-bye kiss warms my heart.

Getting into the car, I'm nervous. Do I look different? Will Mom smell the sex on me? "Hi," she says, smiling.

"Hi," I say, smiling back.

"Did you and Jenn have fun?"

"It was okay."

Between the mall and home, I start feeling giddy. I've just lost my virginity. I can't wait to tell Jenn.

II. Torn Pants, Empty Sky
—1998

The weight of someone else on the bed wakes me from my nap. "Kev?"

"Let's do it." He starts unzipping my black velvet pants. This is nothing new. Kevin always wants sex and I always give in. If I resist, he'll threaten to get it elsewhere. Today, though, I'm nauseous and exhausted.

"Kevin, please. I don't feel good. Let me sleep." I grab the open flaps of my pants and try to roll onto my side, but he stops me.

"Come on. You can go back to sleep when I'm done." He yanks at my pants, but I hold on. "Charissa, don't think I won't cut them off of you if I have to."

"Please, Kevin. I just don't—" Before I can finish, he grabs the material of my pants and pulls, ripping them from zipper to ankle. He yanks the pants off. When I try to sit up, he grabs my arms and raises them above my head. He crosses my wrists, holding them in his grip with one hand as he pulls off his boxers with the other. I feel like prey.

"Stop!" I demand.

Instead, he straddles me and pushes aside my panties. When I buck, trying to prevent his entering, he squeezes my wrists harder.

"Get off of me!"

His hand clamps down on my mouth. I whip my head from side to side in a useless attempt to get loose. My struggling seems to excite him more. My eyes light on the gap between his front teeth that, four years earlier, I had found so cute. Looking away, I stop fighting and go limp. During the rape, I stare at the ceiling, counting his thrusts, screaming the numbers in silence to distract myself until he finally collapses.

"See? That wasn't so bad," he says, rolling off of me.

I scramble off the bed and run down the hallway. I'm not surprised that he forced me to have sex, but he's never ruined my clothes before. Replaying the scene in my head, I become furious. I go to the kitchen and grab the scissors from the drawer.

Charging back into the bedroom, I glare at him. "Those were my favorite pants!"

He shrugs. "So we'll get you another pair."

I show him the scissors. "I don't want another pair. You ruined mine so now I'm going to ruin yours." Grabbing his favorite jeans, I begin cutting.

He lies naked on the bed, looking amused. "That make you feel better?" he goads. "Why do you need scissors? You too weak to rip 'em with your hands?"

I drop the scissors and put all my strength into the jeans, imagining that it's Kevin I'm ripping apart. My palms throb as I fight the stubborn material. When I can't rip anymore, I throw the jeans to the floor and stand there, sweaty and out of breath.

"Look at you with just a shirt and panties on," he says. "Why don't you come over here." He's leering, stroking his renewed hard-on.

"Go to hell!" I say. Grabbing a pair of sweatpants, I leave the room, snatch up my cigarettes, and go outside.

In tears, I stare up at the night sky. "Hi. It's me." I am speaking aloud. "If anyone's up there, I need your help. I love him, but I'm not strong enough. It's been bad for months and it keeps getting worse. So I'm asking for a favor. Please let me die. I don't want it to be painful. Just let me go to sleep and not wake up."

I hear footsteps. The door opens. I wipe the tears from my face.

"Hey, Dollface, you still pissed?" He lights a cigarette. I stub mine out and get up off the porch floor. He takes a drag, watching me. "They're just a stupid pair of pants," he says.

"That's not the point. You *ripped* them off." My anger surges again.

"What? Don't you like it rough?" This is his attempt to charm me.

I mean to say it calmly, but blurt it out instead. "I can't do this anymore, Kevin. I have to leave."

"That's fine. You try it. But the thing is, I'll *never let* you go. I'm always going to know where you are and what you're doing." He inches closer. "And I'll kill anyone else you ever love. Process of elimination. There'll be no one left but me." He puts his arms around me and kisses my cheek. "You look tired, Dollface. Go get some sleep."

Before I walk inside, I glance once more at the starry, indifferent sky. It's hopeless. There's nothing I can do but stay.

III. My Hair Story
—1999

I hold my hair up to my nose and breathe in deeply, smelling all the memories that have just been severed. I want them back. I wish I could reverse what I've done. Gently, I place my hair back in its new home—a brown paper bag. I long for what it symbolizes: my happiness, my self-discovery, and most of all, my freedom.

My hair has been cut at the insistence of my lawyer, who thinks it's too long and makes me look too "goth." "Charissa," she said, "when we go to trial, you're going to have to make some changes to your look. The piercings have to go, and the black nail polish. The tattoo on your wrist has to be covered up with a scrunchie. No black clothes—we'll have to go shopping for appropriate outfits. And one more thing: we have to cut your hair. We want you to look as sweet as possible. It was self-defense; you and I know that. But it's going to be hard for a jury to believe you're innocent with that long black hair. It makes you look too hard. Too sexy."

And so, a month before my trial, I go to the salon. They want to give me a pixie cut, but I refuse. I have to keep *something*. So we settle on a bob. It's just long enough to put in a ponytail, but no match for the foot and a half that has been cut off. I gather up the loose hair, secure it with a rubber band, and place it in a paper bag. Then they start tackling the four years' worth of black dye. They bleach the color out twice, then highlight it to get it as close as possible to my natural dirty blond. After the several hours it takes, I'm lucky I have any hair left. When I finally look in the mirror, I think, okay, I don't look slutty anymore. Now I look like a calico cat.

My lawyer is pleased with the outcome. Unfortunately, it doesn't make a difference. I end up taking a plea bargain.

In the four months between my guilty plea and my sentencing, I think a lot about my hair. How it went to every party, did every drug, was there with me each time I had sex. It went with me to my prom, my graduation. It was there when, at fourteen, I lost my virginity to Kevin, and at eighteen when I stabbed and accidentally killed him while he was beating me. When the police arrived that night, I used my hair to hide my face.

Six months after my sentence begins, my mom decides to move. "Did you pack the bag with my hair in it?" I ask her when she comes to visit me.

"Of course I did," she says. "You know me. I'll keep it forever."

I'm relieved to know that, even when I come home fifteen years later, my hair and my memories will be waiting for me. The day I let the stylist separate my hair and me, I didn't realize how life-altering a moment it was. By cutting my hair, I was cutting myself off from my life before prison.

All my happiness and all my history wait for me inside a brown bag in a home I've never seen.

The Marionette

BY LYNNE M. FRIEND

To love, honor, and cherish
Till death do us part

The week had started out so hopefully. My sister Andrea was flying in from Connecticut to visit my first husband, Paul, and me in Colorado. I hadn't seen her for over a year, so I was excited that she was coming. Andrea was a couple of years younger than I, twenty-three, and we'd always had a close and special relationship. I'd lived out in Colorado for seven years by then. Most of my family lived in Connecticut.

I picked up Andrea at the airport on Monday afternoon. I had taken time off from work so we could spend the whole week together. I was eager to show my sister the new house we'd bought the year before and to spend time just catching up. Paul was looking forward to Andrea's visit, too, as they'd always gotten along well. That weekend, we would celebrate Paul's birthday and mine, two days apart.

Andrea and I spent the week together, sleeping late, going shopping and to the movies, eating at restaurants and visiting the Denver zoo. We took a couple of day trips up to Pikes Peak in Colorado Springs, and to Grand Lake, one of the most beautiful areas I've ever seen. We talked and laughed more that week than ever before.

Paul, who owned his own painting and wall-covering business, worked all week while my sister and I played. He came home in a good mood most of the time, but at night, after Andrea had gone to her room, he'd complain that I hadn't cooked dinner or that I was behind in the laundry. I was in my fifth year of marriage and had become used to Paul's complaints and tirades. Our home life pretty much ran parallel to whatever mood he was in at any given moment. I tried hard to manage everything, but between working full-time and taking care of a four-bedroom house, I often fell short of my husband's expectations. Paul didn't believe a man should have to help with housework. Once in a while, he wouldn't notice when things weren't done, or weren't done to his specifications, but most of the time he did. I often felt like Paul's puppet: he pulled the strings and I danced to whatever tune he dictated. I made his happiness my number one concern.

Our courtship had been wonderful. Paul was a good listener, considerate of my feelings, and fun to be with. Everyone thought so; my girlfriends were always reminding me how lucky I was. Once when we were dating, Paul had lost control and hit me, but later, he was so apologetic and hard on himself that I forgave him and we moved on. I believed that once I became his wife, he would show me nothing but love and respect.

The first year of our marriage was okay, except for Paul's domineering personality. He began to tell me what to do and when to do it, and because I wanted to please him, I did as I was told. During the second year, his bossiness graduated to physical violence. The first time he slapped me across the face, I was in disbelief. I locked myself in the bedroom and cried for hours. I didn't know what I'd done to deserve this treatment. Paul apologized through the door and I believed his promises that it would not happen again. Now, five years into our married life, Paul was often violent. I kept telling myself that if I tried harder, he wouldn't get so angry. His rage was my fault and my responsibility; if I wanted a more peaceful marriage, then I had to improve myself.

When Paul complained to me during the week of Andrea's visit, I assured him things would get back on track after she left. This did little to console him, but I knew he wouldn't force any big confrontations or get physical with me while my sister was there. He cared too much about what other people thought of him. To the rest of the world, Paul was Mr. Personality, drawing people to him with his charm and his sense of humor. But now whenever my friends told me how lucky I was to have Paul, I'd get a pain in my stomach that would last for hours. If only they knew, I'd think.

He was careful to avoid hitting me in the face; instead he'd punch me and kick me in the stomach, pull my hair, spit on me. I'd broken fingers and toes trying to block his assaults. I worked at a small real estate company and would make up stories to explain these injuries to my coworkers. Sometimes I'd see them give each other concerned or disbelieving looks as I made my excuses. I wasn't sure how many of them I'd truly fooled. I only knew I couldn't tell anyone the truth. I was afraid of the repercussions. So instead, I convinced myself that if I could only unlock the riddle of how to be a better wife, things would work out.

Andrea and I had a wonderful four days together. We made plans to take Paul out to dinner for his birthday on Friday. From there we'd go to a dance club with some of our friends. Paul had okayed this itinerary, so I made reservations at his favorite restaurant. Andrea and I bought new sundresses for our big night out.

On Friday, I made a german chocolate cake, Paul's favorite. Andrea and I got ready, drank some wine, and listened to music while we waited. Paul had agreed to be home by five o'clock to get ready for our night out. When Paul's father called from Connecticut to wish his son a happy birthday, I told him Paul was running late and that he should call back at six o'clock. But Paul still wasn't home when his father called again. "I'll have him call you," I told his dad.

At seven thirty, I heard a crash out in the driveway. Paul's van had collided with the empty trash cans I'd forgotten to bring around back. If he wasn't already in a bad mood, this would trigger it, but if we could get his birthday celebration underway, maybe it would pass. He stormed into the kitchen looking disheveled, blue paint in his hair and on his work clothes. "How the hell many times do I have to remind you about those garbage cans, you stupid ass?" he screamed. He was carrying a half-empty six-pack by its plastic ring.

"I'm sorry," I said. "I was busy and I forgot. I'll get them right now." Ignoring the incredulous look on my sister's face, I rushed out the door. We lived on a cul-de-sac, and a couple of the cans had rolled across the street. Waving to the neighbors, I gathered them up quickly and ran as fast as I could to the back of the house.

When I came back in, Andrea was sitting at the kitchen table, sipping her wine and looking confused. Paul was in the upstairs bathroom, muttering to himself. "What the hell is his problem?" Andrea asked.

I shrugged. "Probably stressed from work." Oh, God, I thought, please don't pull any crazy stunts in front of my sister.

When he came downstairs, he was wearing clean clothes and looking for trouble. He grabbed a beer from the fridge, took a long sip, then stared at Andrea and me. "What the hell are you two dressed up for?" He was slurring his words.

With as much calm as I could muster, I said, "We're taking you out for dinner on your birthday, remember? You're late. Where have you been?"

"Guys at work took me out for some beers. You got a problem with that, dumb-ass?" Glaring at me, he took a step closer.

"Excuse me," my sister said. Clearly uncomfortable with what was happening between Paul and me, she went downstairs to the guest room and closed the door.

"Your father called," I said. "I changed our reservation to eight thirty, so you have time to call him back if you want."

"Yeah? Well, fuck your reservation. I made plans and they sure as hell don't include you two."

"Paul, please," I said. "My sister and I have been waiting for you for over two hours. What do you think you're doing?"

"Listen, bitch. I'll spend my birthday however the fuck I want to!"

I could hear Andrea downstairs, on the phone with her husband. "Corey, they're fighting. I don't know what to do. . . . Okay, I'll stay down here."

Heading for the front door, Paul yelled, "Fuck you guys! And don't wait up for me either!" In a sudden fit of uncharacteristic bravery, I walked over to him and put my hand over his on the doorknob. "You are *not* going to do this to me," I said. "Not with my sister here. What's wrong with you? Why are you being like this?"

"This is what's wrong with me," he said, and he struck me hard across the face. He must *really* be angry, I thought. Well, I was pissed now, too.

"Fine! Go!" I screamed, heading for the kitchen phone. "I'll just call your father back for you and tell him what you did." His fist landed in the small of my back and sent me staggering. "He's hitting her!" I heard Andrea saying. "What should I do? . . . Yeah, okay. It's locked." When Paul realized Andrea was on the phone, he left without another word. I heard his engine turn over, his van back down the driveway and drive away.

When Andrea came out of the bedroom, she looked terrified. "Oh my God, Lynne. What the hell's going on here? Is this how you live?" I'm not sure if I was crying more from the pain or from the fact that the secret was out.

"I don't know what's wrong with me," I sobbed. "I try everything I can think of to be a good wife, but he's always so mad at me!"

Over the next few hours, I poured my heart out to my sister, describing my marriage: the harsh words, the constant "orders," the spitting and bruises and broken bones. I let out every secret I'd been holding in for seven years. Andrea was less shocked than I imagined she'd be. "I've heard the way he talks to you sometimes, but I had no idea things were this bad," she said.

We were both exhausted. Andrea went back to the guest room and I tried to sleep on the couch in the family room, which was adjacent to

Andrea's. I was hoping nothing would happen if and when Paul came home, but I wanted to be close to my sister, just in case. The last time I looked at the clock, it was 1:00 A.M. and still no Paul. I must have dozed off, though, because it was after 2:00 A.M. when I sat up, startled by the crashing noises in the kitchen.

"Nothing to eat in this goddamn fucking house!" he screamed. "Didn't you go to the fucking store? What the hell is *this* shit?" From my position on the couch, I watched him pull food from the refrigerator and throw it onto the kitchen floor, including the steaks I'd bought for the following day.

Afraid to move a muscle, I said a silent prayer that Paul would go upstairs and pass out without noticing me. Instead, he opened himself a beer, grabbed a large kitchen knife, and sliced into his german chocolate cake. I watched as he gorged himself on cake, hoping he'd find some momentary satisfaction and leave me alone. When he finished his beer, he went to the refrigerator and got another. I'd taken most of the beer out to the garage earlier so that he wouldn't drink another six-pack, but I'd left a couple in the fridge so that he wouldn't fly into a rage; it was the kind of planning and second-guessing I had come to learn. He sliced himself more cake, then began playing with the knife, pushing it with his finger and watching it spin around and around on the table. I prayed to the Lord that he wouldn't notice me.

After a few minutes, Paul climbed the stairs to our bedroom. When he discovered I wasn't there, he screamed, "Where the fuck are you, you little bitch?" My throat was dry and constricted. I had to pee, but I didn't dare move. When his footsteps pounded back down the stairs, I shut my eyes and pretended to sleep, hoping my thundering heart wouldn't give me away.

Paul entered the kitchen again, kicking the food he'd littered the floor with earlier. He went into the living room—to lie down on our couch and go to sleep, I hoped. Then I heard his grunting and heaving; he was vomiting up his beer and cake.

He walked down into the family room, mumbling as he approached me. Three blows, in rapid succession, landed against my chest. "Get up *now!*" he screamed, but he'd knocked the wind out of me and I couldn't. He sat on top of me and spat in my face, smearing the spittle with his hand. Then he pulled me up by my hair and forced me to crawl across the floor and up the stairs to the kitchen. I sat on the floor, dazed and wheezing, as he fired plates of food at my head, and when I held up my hands to protect myself, I felt a painful stinging in my fingers from the impact. When I tried to crawl away, he took hold of my hair again and forced me into the living room, dragging me across the floor until we'd gotten to the place where he'd thrown up. Grabbing both sides of my head, he forced my face into his vomit. "Clean it up! Clean it up *now!*" he kept screaming. I gagged and gasped for breath as he pushed my face into the mess again and again.

When he finally let me go, I stumbled to my feet and into the kitchen. My chest felt like it was on fire and my fingers were so swollen I couldn't bend them. My throat was parched from crying. I grabbed a roll of paper towels and staggered back into the living room, trying as best I could to obey him. I got down on all fours and tried to clean up the mess, but I guess I wasn't working to his satisfaction. He began kicking me in my rib cage and on my behind. "Fuck you. I'm going to bed!" he shouted. He stumbled up the stairs, disappearing down the hallway.

I lay there on my back on the living room floor, staring up at the ceiling. Even after all this time, all the previous attacks, I felt stunned that he'd done this to me. It had been his most vicious assault. Tears streamed down my puffy face, and when I tried to move, my body wouldn't let me.

After a while, I made my way back to the kitchen. I could hear him snoring upstairs, so I knew I was safe, at least for the time being. I grabbed the large knife he'd been spinning and eased my bruised body back down to the family room. I slipped the knife under the couch cushion, wondering if I'd have the guts to use it if I had no other choice. After I'd collapsed on the couch, my sister whispered to me from behind the guest room door. "Lynne, are you okay?"

"I'll live."

"I was so scared for you, Lynne, but Corey told me not to call the police. We thought Paul might hurt you worse if I did."

"We need to keep quiet," I said, careful to keep my voice low. "Go back to sleep, and I'll see you in the morning."

In too much pain to fall deeply into sleep, I kept drifting in and out as I tried to figure out why all of this had happened. I didn't want Andrea to see me so badly beaten, so early in the morning, I went into the downstairs bathroom and washed up. Looking in the mirror, I felt ashamed. I hadn't wanted my sister to see the brutality I lived with, but the evidence was all over my face. My nose was bloody and crooked, my eyes and jaw were puffy, and a large bruise discolored my swollen left cheek. I hoped I could use makeup to conceal the damage. With my broken fingers, I could hardly hold the washcloth, but I did the best I could. My chest felt like it had a thousand-pound weight on it, and my right side was tender to the touch. As I made my way up to the kitchen, my toes screamed in pain.

I cleaned up all of the food and dishes as best I could—and as quietly as I could, so as not to awaken either of them. Maybe if I cleaned up the evidence, we could all pretend it had been a nightmare. After finishing up in the kitchen, I went back downstairs, sat on the couch, and cried. Andrea got up at around eight o'clock and cautiously came out of her room. She took one look at me and said, "Oh my God."

We drank coffee and talked quietly. I kept repeating, "Why do I make him so angry? What am I doing wrong?"

"You don't do *anything* wrong," Andrea said. "It's not your fault, Lynne."

At around ten, Paul came down the stairs with a sheepish look on his face. I knew if I looked at him, I'd start to cry. He sat down next to me and began his familiar soft-spoken apologies. "I'm so sorry about last night, honey. I was a real drunken jackass. And Andrea, I'm sorry you had to hear all that." When he caressed my face, I flinched. "I'm so sorry if I hurt you, honey. I was so drunk, I didn't know what I was doing. But it won't ever happen again. I swear to God."

I couldn't respond—couldn't even look at him.

While Paul napped that afternoon, my sister and I sat on lounge chairs in the backyard, trying to absorb some sun. "Famous last words: it won't ever happen again. Ha!" Andrea said. "You can't keep living like this. I'm serious, Lynne. You should leave him and come back to Connecticut."

Every breath I took resulted in sharp pain, but I tried to hide how badly I was hurting. I didn't want her to worry. I kept apologizing to her for ruining her vacation.

The next day was Sunday, June 30, my birthday. Paul talked us into going out for brunch. I put on a lot of makeup to cover my bruises. I was hoping I looked normal, or at least presentable. After we ate, we took a drive up into the mountains. I barely spoke to Paul all afternoon. I didn't feel much like celebrating—another year of pain, I thought. "Up there on the right is Idaho Springs," Paul told Andrea, pointing to the place he meant. He'd been chatting with my sister all morning, trying to charm himself back into her good graces. "They have the caves and mineral baths and natural springs there. Remember what a good time we had there, Lynne?"

"Yeah," I said, staring out the opposite window. I was thinking about what Andrea had said: that I should leave him and move home.

We took Andrea to the airport the next day. Paul waved to her with one hand, his other hand around my waist. We watched until her plane took off.

We drove home in silence. I went downstairs and slept for several hours. When I got up around 10:00 P.M., Paul was already asleep in our bed.

The next day he brought me roses and began another round of apologies. I hated myself, because I knew I was weakening. I wasn't going to leave him. I loved him, and I was afraid of what he'd do to me if I tried to leave. Besides, I thought, he does seem genuinely sorry. I was sorry, too.

That night, in bed, when he tried to touch me and kiss me, I felt nauseous. When I didn't respond, he whispered, "I love you," and left me alone. I cried softly, listening to his slow, shallow breathing as he slept.

Without Paul knowing, I went to the medical clinic the next day to get my fingers wrapped. When the doctor accidentally touched my side, I winced. He took an X-ray: three broken ribs. He wrapped my fingers, wrapped my ribs. I had never been to this doctor before, but he urged me to extricate myself from my relationship.

I cried in the car on the way home. I knew I was not going to follow that doctor's advice and I hated myself for my failures, my weaknesses. Another small piece of my soul had died during my sister's visit. I was more Paul's discarded toy than his wife. I was his broken marionette.

Falling

BY ROBIN LEDBETTER

A drop falls in slow motion.
Breath, heavy from anger, hurt, confusion.
Another drop
Tears blur my vision.
A faster drop
Why do you do this to me?
Drip drop
I hate you!
And then a rain storm falls, blood red
What have I done?
I'm sorry. I'm so sorry.
I love you.
Please forgive me.
Panic assaults me as blood falls like perfect rain.
What the fuck? What the fuck? What did I do?
I am afraid, but not because life spills.
I am afraid of being alone.
Please don't leave me.
The tears that have been threatening break free as

I drop to my knees, towel in hand, and try to rub away my
  felony.
I cannot be alone.
I rub harder. Can't breathe. Can't keep up.
Another wave of panic paralyzes me, forces me still,
and I remember our first kiss,
the falling head-over-heels in love.
The joy. The peace.
Finally, I'm complete.
Then I remember each blow, every punch,
every venom-soaked accusation.
Every scratch, bruise, and scar.
Every tear 'til now.
I remember falling again, this time out of love.
Yet as the floor grows redder, I am afraid only of being alone.
It is I who have fallen.

IV.
Crime and Punishment

*Killer movies, violent television, and political hot
air about "getting tough" on crime create heat and smoke
that obscure the fact that prisons warehouse and destroy the
lives of our most poverty-stricken Americans—people who
would never spend a day in jail for the same crimes if
they had economic resources.*

—KATHRYN WATTERSON

*Nothing lovely flourishes here. Little that is good is
nourished here. What grows here is hypocrisy, obscenity,
illness, illegality, ignorance, confusion, waste, hopelessness.
Life in prison is a garden of dross, cultivated by those who
never check to see what their crop is.*

—JEAN HARRIS

*People who treat other people as less than human must not
be surprised when the bread they have cast on the waters
comes floating back to them, poisoned.*

—JAMES BALDWIN

Lost and Found

BY ROBERTA SCHWARTZ

The last time I slept over at my mother's house was the night before my sentencing. In the morning, my mother got up early with me. I remember her standing in the doorway wearing her lavender velour bathrobe, even though it was July. She liked velour bathrobes with zippers down the front and pockets for tissues. The bathrobe was old, stained, and comfortable. "What can I make you for breakfast?" she asked.

"Nothing," I said, "I'm not hungry."

"How about a glass of juice?"

The orange juice she gave me was freshly squeezed, the way she'd always squeezed it when I was a child. She hugged me as I left her house to go to court with my brothers, Mike and Joe. "Okay, so we'll have a cookout tonight," she said.

"Fine," I said, though I think that, intuitively, neither of us believed that cookout would happen.

In spite of his faith, my boyfriend Alex also must have known I was going to prison. All the other times I had traveled back from Texas to Connecticut for court dates, he'd let me wear his watch so I would have something close to me that was his. The morning he was to drive me to the airport, I had sat on the edge of his bed, watching him brush his teeth. He had come and sat beside me, had held my hands, and looked into my eyes. Alex is such a sweet man and has the most beautiful, soulful eyes. When he asks me why I love him, I tell him, "Because when I look into your eyes, I can see into your good heart."

"I'm proud of you," he'd said that morning.

"I don't want to go."

"You'll be back in a week." He'd held my head to his chest to reassure me. But he hadn't reminded me to take his watch with me and I hadn't asked.

I didn't call Alex the morning before I left my mother's house for the sentencing hearing. I was afraid it might show a lack of faith—that if I called, I would go to jail. I drank the orange juice, took a shower. I had the TV on, the YES Network. An avid Yankees fan, I was watching the rebroadcast of a Paul O'Neill "Yankeeography." Joe, the older of my two brothers, came in and turned off the television. "What do you want me to tell Alison and Laura?" he asked.

"Tell them I'm in Texas," I said. "Tell them whatever you think is best."

I turned the television back on. Paul O'Neill and Yankees broadcaster Michael Kay were my friends. They'd been with me almost daily since 1998, and I felt safer with them there. Joe left the room. He'd have to figure out for himself what to tell his daughters.

Joe was dressed for court in a navy blazer, khakis, a yellow dress shirt, and a tie. Mike, my younger brother, wore a pinstriped suit, still looking like a lawyer though he wasn't practicing at the time; his health problems and my legal entanglements were about all Mike could handle. Joe drove. His willingness to go with me to court had surprised me, but I knew he was really there more for my mother and Mike. We didn't argue in the car, or about the parking space on Main Street, a few blocks from the courthouse. This was unusual because we were a bickering family. We picked at each other, little nits.

I was wearing a black sleeveless shell dress to the knee and a long-sleeve long jacket, about an inch longer than the dress. My mother and I had found this suit in Lord & Taylor at the Trumbull Shopping Park, and it had been my favorite outfit until I'd worn it over the previous six months to my arrest, my arraignment, my divorce, and my presentencing conferences. I knew I was wearing these clothes for the last time today. I'd bought my black suede pumps at Wal-Mart the previous January for a wedding. I wore them all the time because they made me feel more confident. Shoes can sometimes do that for me: make me feel better about myself. Because it was July, I wasn't wearing stockings. I was about fifteen pounds overweight so the dress felt tight. As I'd gotten older, I'd gained weight around my stomach, and it had made me angry and self-critical. I'd pulled my shoulder-length hair into a ponytail and had not put on makeup or jewelry. This is why, in spite of the faith I proclaimed that God would send me a miracle, I think I must have known I was going to prison: no jewelry. Still, I hoped the sad, tired, pudgy, middle-aged, no-makeup look would show who I was: a woman who deeply regretted all she had done.

As I walked down the block between my brothers, everything looked different. But it was I who'd changed; I was a different person heading to court as a criminal than I had been as a lawyer working in Bridgeport. I'd become like the city itself: scandal-ridden, stumbling along, trying to rebuild. Walking through the courthouse doors, I felt like everyone could see the words branded across my chest: *liar, cheat, drug addict, thief.* I was relieved when we got into the empty elevator that would take us to the third floor, but just before the doors closed, a woman I knew stepped in. "How are you?" Liza asked.

"Fine, thanks." My brother pushed three and the elevator rose.

Liza's husband was the son of my father's best friend. When she'd gotten married and moved to town, she'd come to my father's law firm because she couldn't find a job. She hadn't been very happy then, and I'd felt badly for her. My father had asked me to teach her how to do real estate closings. Now she was successful, the mother of twins, and I was a fat convicted felon about to be sentenced. During that endless thirty-second elevator ride, my humiliation was nearly unbearable. "Good luck today," Liza said. She knew, of course. Everyone knew.

My lawyer was waiting by the courtroom door. We went in and I sat on a hard wooden bench in the second row. A few moments later, Bernie Green walked in. Bernie was a well-respected lawyer and a personal friend of my uncle, and he had been a business friend of my late father. He was also the father of a man I'd once loved—a man who'd liked me well enough but had not been able to love me back. Tears came to my eyes when Bernie sat down beside me and patted my shoulder. He had come out of the kindness of his heart.

The man I'd stolen from was also there, and though this sounds strange, I believe he, too, had come out of the kindness of his heart. I'd written a twenty-page sentencing statement to explain what had happened to me; how my father's death had overwhelmed me with grief and depression; how I'd continued to work in his office trying to save everything he had worked on; how I'd gone forward with marriage plans that should have been postponed or canceled. My statement explained how I'd begun writing checks, how I had taken drugs until they'd taken over my life. I suspect my victim felt both anger and pity toward me. We had known each other as children. Now he was president of his father's company, my father was dead, and I was probably going to prison.

I think the scariest thing I ever did was the thing that may have saved me. I'd been writing checks for fees to myself for about four years, and because I was using cocaine round the clock at that point, I was just barely functioning and covering up. At first, I'd been getting the legal work done but not the paperwork—the keeping track of time and billing. Near the end, I'd been managing to work only the bare minimum, covering the real estate closings, returning phone calls haphazardly. I needed money for the drugs, or for whatever my husband,

Denny, wanted money for, or to keep my mortgage afloat and pay my office expenses. It had started innocently enough: I'd written a check for fees I was owed. It was a Friday and I had to pay my secretary, so I told myself I would bill on Monday. But Monday never came. It had been a slow thing—never a plan, never anything I'd meant to do. Yet I'd done it over and over. If there wasn't enough money during the week from real estate closings, I'd write checks for more fees due from other matters, intending to bill later. Then I'd started inventing matters that needed to be billed. There'd been other things as well: a bank had mistakenly sent me closing proceeds twice and I'd neglected to return the second payment. I'd failed to put the funds from an estate settlement into an interest-bearing account. When finally I was pressed to return the loan proceeds and closing funds, there was the escrow from the condominium development to draw from. The reason I hadn't sent the money back at first, or set up the interest-bearing account right away, was because I'd kept telling myself I would do it the next day. "I'm going to do it" became my mantra of denial when, in truth, I was rushing through whatever I had to do to get through each day so that I could go home, walk my dog, lie on my bed, watch sports, smoke cigarettes, and keep myself medicated with cocaine, and, later, OxyContin. When I was drugged, I didn't have to think about my deceased father, or the mess of my marriage, or how I had not been able to save everyone and fix everything.

Here's how I was finally caught. Darren, a company vice president, met me at my office early in the morning to pick up a check for money I owed his firm for the sale of three houses. I knew this was it, but I didn't know how to confess. Darren accompanied me to the bank but waited outside while I went in for the money, half-hoping the funds would miraculously appear in my account. Telling this now, I feel again the horror and fear in my chest as I went back outside to face him. "I don't have the money," I said. We returned to my office. When he picked up the phone to call the man I'd stolen from, I asked if I could speak to him in person. Darren agreed, so I got in my car and followed him from my office in Bridgeport to the company offices in New York. The day was bright and sunny. I weighed about ninety pounds and looked like a concentration camp victim. I chain-smoked cigarettes and snorted cocaine the entire ride. I was still doing coke, but I had begun detoxing from the pills. My heart was pounding; I could hear its thump in my ears. I was such a mess that I didn't fully understand the consequences, but I remember wondering if I would be arrested then and there. Seated in the company's conference room, I told my victim how I'd written checks on his escrow money. He was shocked, both by what I'd done and the amount of money involved. After he'd sufficiently recovered, we made a plan: I would give him all the money left in my business escrow account, sell my house, give him a mortgage on a share of a building that was to have been part of my inheritance, and resign from the bar immediately. In return, he would not have me arrested. But I'd been arrested after all, six months later, by the state; I was a lawyer who had become a thief and I had to be punished. The weekend I was arrested and arraigned, I was also divorced. Denny had left me while I was in rehab and I had moved to Texas and gone into recovery.

My victim and I spoke briefly before the proceedings began. I think my written statement may have given him some understanding because he didn't ask the judge to send me away. What was most important to him and his company, he said, was restitution. I was, at that point, a year into my recovery, and I hoped that having stayed clean and worked hard to confront the "whys" of what I'd done would show that I had begun to make amends. I hoped, as well, that my newfound faith would bring me a miracle. God was there with me in that courtroom; I felt his presence without a doubt. But when the judge spoke, he compared me to the men whose greed had brought down Enron and MCI-WorldCom. It was as if a dark curtain was being drawn between me and the life I'd begun to rebuild.

I turned in disbelief to my lawyer. "Four years?" He nodded. Before

I could even glance back at my brothers, I was led from the courtroom to a holding cell on a lower floor.

"Stand facing the wall, feet apart, hands palm against the wall," the female marshal said. She patted me down, then clanked the cell door closed between us. I was behind bars—the kind you see in made-for-TV movies. I held a crumpled tissue in my hand, squeezing and squeezing it. The walls of the three-foot-by-eight-foot cell, dull gray cinderblock, reminded me of the walls of my college dormitory. I paced my cage, banged my head against those gray walls. A cement bench ran the length of the cell. I tried sitting. Tried lying down. The dress I was wearing only went to my knees so there was no way to curl up into a ball and disappear. "Four years," I kept repeating. Why had my judge hardened his heart against me?

I was worried about Alex—how badly this would hurt him. I saw his face before me, his brown eyes so open and sweet. Alex. I shook my head, as if doing so might give me a clearer picture. Four years. I cried and cried.

They had allowed me to return to Texas between my arrest and my sentencing because my recovery had been going well and because I was the kind of person who did what she was told—except for the eight years of illegal drugs and the embezzling of large sums of money. I recalled how I'd stand in line at the bank during those lost years, listening to the silent, scolding voices in my head: *Drug addict! Thief!* Then I'd step up to the window, chatting amiably with the girls behind the counter. I was dressed professionally. I was pleasant and funny—one of the customers they liked, even though I was always overdrawn and always cashing large checks. I never arrived at that bank without excuses for why I needed the cash. When lying becomes integral to your lifestyle, you offer people reasons before they can think to ask you for them. Mostly, I was cashing checks so I could meet Victor and buy the coke I needed to get through the next few days. At that point, I was buying three eight-balls at a time—$250 a bag, but I'd usually run a tab, paying

Victor $1,500 at a time. Victor and I would talk sports: the Knicks and the Giants sometimes, but mostly the Yankees. The day David Cone pitched his perfect game, Victor had come by with a delivery in the seventh inning. He had stayed and watched with me. At that point, my friends had pretty much given up on me. Now Victor was my friend. I didn't understand why he wouldn't talk to me after I confessed to my client and was preparing to go to rehab. Years later, I realized he'd been afraid I was wearing a wire. I hadn't been, but would I have if I'd been asked? Definitely. Once I'd been liberated from my lying and stealing, I reverted to being the good girl who did everything she was told.

The marshal was nice enough; she kept unlocking the holding cell and letting me use the bathroom. But the female marshal who relieved her for lunch was hard and cold. "You don't have stockings on?" she asked. I shook my head. "Give me your hair elastic." I stared at her for a few seconds. Did she think I was going to strangle myself with a ponytail elastic? My hair was shoulder-length, brown fading to gray. I should have colored it one more time before the hearing, but I hadn't wanted to jinx myself by doing anything that seemed like preparation for prison. The ponytail elastic was the only thing I had with me that was Alex's. I pictured him in his long-hair days, his hair pulled back as he did yard work or rode his bike. I saw his beautiful tan face, his sculpted cheekbones and broad smile. I pulled the elastic free and passed it through the bars to the marshal. She pulled out a form. She was actually going to write a property sheet for my hair elastic. "Just throw it away," I said.

Through all my months of flying back and forth from Texas to Connecticut for preliminary court appearances, Alex had kept telling me we were just going to live "as if."

"Do you *want* to go to jail?" he had asked.

"Of course I don't."

"Okay, then. Think positively. Stop assuming it's going to happen."

I had a friend who advised me to "walk it through with God." I hadn't really understood what she meant, but the truth was, whenever I tried "walking it through," I would imagine myself being led down a long dark hallway to a jail cell. I knew that God had forgiven me, but I worried that my having been born again to his grace was not necessarily going to let me off the hook. For the past year, God had been coming to me at odd moments. One time, after my confession but before my arrest, I'd been peeing in the ladies' room at work. I was now a temp doing data entry. Seated on that toilet, I'd begun thinking about how much I loved Alex and how much I enjoyed this new work, modest as it was. A feeling of peace and well-being enveloped me. Then I thought, *But what if I'm arrested?* My next thought was of an Old Testament passage I'd recently read: how Jacob had waited seven years to marry Rachel. The feeling of calm returned. I'd think about that bathroom meditation every once in a while, usually when I was feeling insecure about Alex. Whenever I'd become scared of losing him, Jacob's faithfulness would give me comfort.

Sometime after 2:00 P.M., two male marshals unlocked my cell, handcuffed me for the first time in my life, and led me out through a freight elevator to an underground garage. I was alone in the back of the transport van—the "ice-cream truck," in jail lingo. It was a short ride; I was driven a block and a half to the Golden Hill Street Courthouse. The Golden Hill facility had once housed the city's main court, but now it was rundown and little-used. As I was driven around back to another underground garage, I saw through the window the number 171 and the stairs leading down to my father's old law office. I told myself not to think about that. My father was dead. I was a prisoner.

When the door clanked shut behind me, the two other women in the cell looked me over carefully. Both were my age, maybe younger; it was hard to tell. Drugs age you. Criminal behavior ages you. Later, at York, I would come to know forty-year-old women who looked sixty. The keys rattled; the officer walked away. This cell was larger than the first, twelve by fifteen maybe, but with the same cinder-block decor, the same cold, uncomfortable bench and iron bars across the front. This cell had a toilet installed behind a half wall in the corner. The other girls told me their names and I told them mine. Elsa, a tall African American, was wearing short shorts and a T-shirt. Periodically, she grabbed the cell bars with both hands, leaned her face between them, and screamed, inexplicably, "Mommy!" Dee was a white woman, smaller than I at five feet. She wore a sleeveless T-shirt, purple sweatpants, and sneakers without laces. "What are you here for?" my cell mates asked. "How long did you get?" When I told them I'd been an attorney, Elsa said, "Don't tell anyone that." Dee nodded in agreement, advising me not to tell anyone anything.

The cell was as cold and damp as a dungeon. It had been several hours since my mother's freshly squeezed orange juice, but I wasn't hungry. Maybe I'll get thin again, I thought—no small consolation because my weight gain seemed tied to my failures. I turned away when Elsa went to the corner and peed in semipublic. To distract myself, I read the graffiti on the walls and stared at the wadded balls of toilet paper stuck to the ceiling. I was grateful that I'd used the toilet at the other facility.

Later that afternoon, other women arrived from the Stamford-Norwalk court run. They talked on and on for hours, comparing cases and checking on each other's friends. Electra, coming in from Norwalk, was still high; she danced and staggered around the cell, her flabby stomach flopping up and down over the top of her hip-huggers, her breasts spilling out of her halter top. Electra had been released from prison a few weeks earlier, stolen a car with a friend, and gone on a joy ride that had ended with a bus-stop crash. She claimed also to have gotten pregnant and lost the baby during her brief period between jail bids. "My girl's gon' be so mad to see me comin' back!" she said.

The afternoon I spent at the Golden Hill lockup was like a live version of *Prison for Dummies*. I listened carefully to whatever advice the women in the holding cell offered. What I would later come to realize is that, if you pay attention and ask the right questions of your fellow prisoners, the advice and information you get is more useful and reliable than whatever the staff might tell you. Eventually, I would become one of those advisers, mentoring new inmates overwhelmed by the system's rules, vocabulary, and myriad inconsistencies.

At afternoon's end, my fellow detainees and I were handcuffed two by two, put back in the ice-cream truck, and driven to the New Haven courthouse. I was handcuffed to Electra, who towered over me and wobbled on her spike heels as she walked. I didn't want her to touch me or sit too close, but inside the crowded transport van, this was unavoidable. Whatever I thought Electra might do, she didn't do it. She just babbled on and on, and I kept nodding in agreement to whatever she said.

In New Haven, we were led to yet another holding cell, where we waited for the last pickup before our final destination, the maximum-security York Correctional Institute, located in the shoreline village of Niantic. The guard in Bridgeport had promised us we'd be fed in New Haven, and an officer did hand us bag dinners and room-temperature orange drinks. A minute later, a second officer burst into the cell and took the bags away. He said he'd redistribute them when we got to York. Why? How could they refuse to let us eat for an entire day? Other than mean-spiritedness, there seemed to be no good reason for this decree. I would come to learn that officers could refuse us just about anything, depending on their moods or whims, and that prisoners were powerless against such inconsistencies. Sometime between 8:00 and 9:00 P.M., we were handcuffed in pairs, marched out into the hot, sticky midsummer night and loaded into vans for the final leg of our journey: the Niantic prison that returnees referred to disparagingly as "Camp York."

At York, the doors were locked behind us and we were herded into a ten-foot-by-ten-foot holding cell. We were told we could eat our dinners now. My stomach was a jangle of nerves and my mouth was parched. I drank the orange drink, but when I unwrapped the soft, squishy sandwich, I felt queasy. What if the meat had gone bad in the heat? Rather than eat it, I threw it away.

They divided us into two groups: new arrivals and court-run returnees. Elsa and Dee wished me luck and we parted company. I was directed with fifteen other women to a large holding area with mint green cinder-block walls and toilet stalls with half doors. We were told to pee in cups so that our urine could be screened for drugs. We filled out paperwork and had our identification pictures taken. We were assigned inmate numbers.

When they turned on the telephone, I was second in line. I tried to be patient as I punched in my Texas phone number and the inmate number they had just given me. Alex's voice made me cry. "I spoke to your brother," he said. "He wants you to call him. There may be some good news—something about a sentence modification." This would turn out to be a false hope to which I'd cling for over a year, but at that moment, my only concern was Alex.

"Are you okay?" I asked.

"Are *you* okay?" he said.

"I am now. I just needed to hear your voice. I never would have left on Sunday if I thought I was going to prison. I would have stayed with you until the last possible minute."

"I know that," he said. "Don't cry. We'll just do letters and phone calls for a while." But I knew four years was too long; he couldn't possibly wait for me that long.

"I'll be okay if you're okay," I said.

"And I'll be okay if you are."

"I love you, Alex."

"I love you, too." We repeated it over and over.

They called us in three at a time for the strip searches and delousing showers. With a squirt of foul-smelling bug shampoo on my palm, I stepped behind the curtain and under the water, relieved that we didn't have to shower in some big, open room. I didn't care about the frayed hospital nightgown and ratty bathrobe, or the fact that there was no comb for my hair. Clutching a clear plastic garbage bag filled with state-assigned property, I was taken with the others to another waiting room. Prison, I would learn, is 10 percent movement and 90 percent waiting. Finally, we were led outside and down a path to the medical building. What would it be like if you arrived in winter, I wondered. Would you still have to walk across the complex in nightclothes with wet hair?

York, the only women's prison in Connecticut, is divided into two sides, East and West. The West Side is maximum-security, which means your movement is restricted and you are confined to your cell for longer portions of the day unless you have a job, a visit, an activity, a medical appointment, or school. On the East Side, except for when you're being counted, you can go to the day room or outside to the fenced-in yard. Housing units are also divided between long-term and short-term prisoners, and by levels of crime or amount of time to be served. On the East Side, if you're not in the Marilyn Baker rehab program or Thompson Hall, you live in the dorms. Dee had told me I should sign up for Marilyn Baker because the building and food were better. She and Elsa had both predicted I'd go to the less restrictive East Side because this was my first time. But on my first night in prison, I was assigned to the medical building.

When my last name was called, I was directed to a room where three other inmates were already in bed asleep. As quietly as I could, I placed my plastic bag of belongings in the corner, pulled out the two blankets I'd been assigned, and climbed onto the top bunk. The room was frigid with air-conditioning. I wrapped myself between the blankets and faced the wall. "Dear God, I know you were with me in the courtroom today," I whispered. "And I know you're with me now. Thank you for all my blessings, even though I may be blind to them at the moment. The Lord is my shepherd; I shall not want. The Lord is my shepherd; I shall not want." I prayed and cried myself to sleep.

The lights flashed on and off a couple of times during the night. At some point, someone came into the room and woke the girl in the bottom bunk for court. A few minutes later, I heard rustling around where I had dropped my plastic bag. I told myself I was just being paranoid.

When the breakfast wake-up call came at about 4:30 A.M., I rose quickly. I still had no appetite, but I was afraid I'd get in trouble if I didn't go to breakfast. I pulled prison clothes from my garbage bag: shapeless blue cotton pants with a slack elastic waistband, a maroon T-shirt, a padded bra, used underwear. I looked through my toiletries; if you arrive at prison with no money, they issue you an "indigent bag" that contains a crappy little toothbrush, travel-size toothpaste, soap, deodorant, and shampoo. There was a hole in my bag. The toothbrush was missing. My prison-issue sneakers—laceless imitation Keds—were missing, too. In their place was a much bigger pair. So it hadn't been paranoia after all; the girl who'd left for court had stolen my toothbrush and taken my sneakers. When I reported this to the officer in charge, he told me indifferently that he was sure she'd bring them back.

I brushed my teeth with my finger, then followed the faceless crowd to the chow hall in my oversized sneakers. I remember glimpsing my own and others' reflections in the window glass and noting that we were all dressed the same and wore the same early-morning faces. *Of course you're all alike,* a new voice in my head scoffed. *You're all criminals.*

Breakfast was watery juice, watered-down coffee, tasteless hot cereal, and bruised fruit. We were required to leave the table and return to our units as soon as we finished our meal; this was not a social club. I would later learn how to eat slowly and keep pushing something around my plate if I wanted to stay longer, but that morning, I was happy to rush back to an empty room because I had to go to the bathroom. This toilet thing was going to be a problem; I couldn't go to the bathroom in front of other people, men or women, not even to pee.

With the sun coming up, I finally had a chance to look at my surroundings: two sets of iron bunk beds, one chair, a toilet with a half wall, a walk-in shower. I liked the fact that I could hide in the shower for a few minutes and wash myself unwatched. By the time the other girls came back, I was done and back on my top bunk. It was about 5:30 A.M. There was nothing to do but lie down and go back to sleep.

Orientation took an hour and was held in a common room equipped with tables, plastic chairs, and a television. Guards were "corrections officers," we were told—COs for short. When speaking with COs, you addressed them as Officer or Mr. or Mrs. So-and-So. The phone policies were explained. We were given commissary slips, a visitor-list form, and a phone-list form. Our visitor list and phone list were limited to seven names at any given time. I filled out the phone list but at that point did not want visitors.

Commissary was just about the most important thing in prison. Once a week, you chose items from a two-sided list, filling in a form similar to a standardized test: two Honey Buns, three soups, five bagels, one sweatshirt, etc. If you had money in your account, you could buy fifty dollars' worth of food and an unlimited amount of toiletries or prison-approved clothing. You could get a television set—black-and-white or color—or a radio, a tape cassette, art supplies, board games. You could buy sneakers, a rain poncho, underwear, socks. I had heard about commissary from Elsa and Dee, so I had already asked my mother to send money. I had hated to make that request, but I had made it anyway.

We were given inmate request forms. Elsa and Dee had told me about these, too. "You have to write about *everything*," Elsa had said. "You can't just walk into the CO's office and tell them you need something. You need to write a request for an appointment." It was unclear to me what you did if there was an emergency.

Inmates were not allowed on anyone else's bed under any circumstances, we were told; nor were we allowed in anyone else's room. If we were caught in a room where we didn't belong, we would get a ticket. Tickets were classified; some would get us sent straight to "seg" (the segregation unit, a kind of jail in jail); others would require us to appear before the review board for punishment. If we were issued an informal ticket, we would be assigned extra duty—maintenance jobs, most likely. After I was there a while, I would observe that COs gave out lots of informals when they were preparing for some kind of visit or inspection and needed to get the girls to paint, wax the floors, or spruce up the place in some other way.

From orientation, we were taken in groups to the doctors' offices. My blood was drawn by a loud red-haired nurse who seemed to think it was hip to talk trash to the girls. I was given a chest X-ray to make sure I didn't have tuberculosis, or worse. As I sat waiting between stations, I felt like a sexless, formless, useless nothing. In front of me were girls of all shapes, sizes, and ages, from seventeen to seventy. They were talking and laughing, joking with the guards, yelling. Everyone looked either ugly and mean or sad and scared; I saw no in-between. I saw no one who looked like me.

Wendy, my cell mate in the other top bunk, had been sent to prison on a fifty-dollar trespassing charge. She was slow—possibly retarded. She kept lapsing into baby talk. Clearly, Wendy needed social service help, not prison. My other cell mate, Red, was an old hand at incarceration. She described how to cook in a clear plastic trash bag—the size used for a small bathroom garbage pail—and advised me on recipes using hot water, squeeze-cheese, noodles, and potato chips. She had received a letter from her husband. Did I want to hear it? As she read aloud, a hard, tough inmate changed into an insecure wife trapped in a bad marriage. Her husband had hit her and run away, leaving her alone for the police to find, with their drugs. He had not shown up in court the day she was arraigned because he hadn't wanted to get arrested himself. "Does it sound like he really loves me?" Red asked. "Do you think he'll wait for me?"

"I'm sure he loves you," I said. What I thought was: why would you *want* him to wait for you? It would be like me wanting Denny back.

Shortly before lunch, a guard came by and handed Red two large garbage bags. She was being moved.

In the afternoon, we were sent to see a physician's assistant pretending to be a doctor. There were about forty women in this group. I talked to a few of them during the hours of waiting and testing. Kat had returned to prison for having violated probation. Rosalie from Colorado was waiting to be extradited because her ex-husband had gotten a warrant on her for sixty dollars' worth of back child support. Audrey was an embezzler like me. Lynn, a drug addict, had been arrested at the courthouse on her way to a hearing to have her ex-husband jailed for his failure to pay child support. When the guard at the entrance had searched her purse, he'd found eight baggies of heroin. Most of the women I met in the early days insisted, "It wasn't my fault." Guilty as charged, I was the only real criminal, living in a prison of innocents.

When I was called in to see the so-called doctor, I refused the Pap test. All I wanted was something for my splitting headache so that I could get some sleep. At Golden Hill, Dee had advised me to tell them I was drinking a quart of vodka a day. "That way, they'll give you Librium and you can just sleep your days away," she'd said. I couldn't do that, though; I was too proud of the year I'd completed living clean and sober. The doctor said he would have some Motrin ready for me at med line. Med line, the prison's three-times-per-day medicine call, was a big social hour. You got out of your room and, walking back and forth to the medical unit, could hook up with your friends. Med line was a time and an opportunity to pass notes and commissary, hopefully without getting caught. Many women, I would learn, tongued their meds and saved them to barter for food and toiletries. They gave good drugs in prison if you had the right ailments, and good drugs were marketable. I didn't want drugs, though; I wanted to remain sober and to be left alone.

After dinner on my first full day in prison, it was back to my locked room in the medical unit. At 6:00 P.M., however, we were allowed thirty minutes out of our rooms. I waited anxiously by the door, hoping to get to one of two available phones. At forty-one years of age, I needed my mother.

I was so relieved to hear her voice. The length of my sentence had shocked her, she said. It had shocked my whole family. They had believed I would be sentenced to prison, but not for so long. Was that why I was here, I wondered—because my family had had no faith? "Please call Alex," I said. "Let him know I can't talk to him tonight. There won't be time."

My mother and Alex had never met. When I had told her I was moving to Texas, she'd assumed it was another of my crazy decisions, like taking drugs and stealing. Why would I move all the way across the country to a place I'd never been when I was in such a big fat mess here at home? Alex and I were just friends, I'd told her, which was true then. I wasn't running away to be with him. To stay in Connecticut and live with my mother would be the worst possible thing – sitting around chain-smoking, wallowing in depression, waiting to be arrested. Going to Texas was choosing life. My mother wasn't stupid, of course; Alex and I *were* just friends, but I had fallen in love with him almost from the moment we'd met while he was visiting friends in Connecticut. (He says that's crazy.) When my mother had objected to my relocating, I'd presented her with a whole list of reasons why I needed to move to Texas. As with everything else in my life, I'd built a good case. But even Alex had had his reservations. "Tell me you're not moving here just for me," he'd said. "Of course not," I'd said, citing my list of reasons to him, too: I'd gotten healthy again at the sober house in Texas; I'd started to recover; I'd begun putting my life back together. And it *had* worked out. Alex and I had begun to build something good. My mother could see the changes in me. If only I could have been the person I became in Texas without the ugly history—the drugs, the stealing, the disastrous marriage.

My mother and I said our good-byes and I hung up the phone. At 6:30 P.M., we were locked down for the night. I tried to write a letter, pressing down so hard on the small pencil stub I'd been issued that my hand hurt. I could barely see my own writing on the back of the blank inmate request form I used for stationery. I put on my aqua hospital nightgown and climbed up onto my bunk. The girl who'd taken my stuff returned from court around 8:00 P.M. "Boy, your feet must hurt, wearing my sneakers all day," I said.

"Oh yeah," she said, with a laugh. She took them off and put them by my stuff. I don't remember her name now, but I recall how she cried later when she talked about losing her kids. I said nothing about the toothbrush; it hadn't been that important after all.

They count you all the time in prison, even in the middle of the night when you're behind locked doors. Some officers just shine a flashlight on you; others turn the lights on and wake you up. Is it for spite that they do that? For sport? I slept in fits and starts those first few nights, reciting scripture I had memorized until I fell back to sleep. I daydreamed about my return to Texas, picturing myself at the airport, with long hair pulled back in a French braid. I saw myself walking down the long corridor, thin again, and falling into Alex's waiting arms. Sometimes I skipped past our reunion into the life I wanted to lead – married to Alex and a new mother of twins. I saw myself in my white princess nightgown, the one I'd bought for my first trip to Texas, back when I was petite and thin. I was seated in a chair, nursing one of our babies, while Alex smiled and watched. In my daydream, he loved me so much that he had waited. On the third or fourth day of my prison life, I gave up that daydream. I would be forty-five by the time I was released—too old to have a baby. Admitting that to myself hurt like a punch in the stomach. I returned to the vision of the happy girl just off the plane. Later, the daydream switched: I walk into the house, crying with relief to be home, and Alex proposes on the spot. The reality of my eventual homecoming years later would be nothing like that, of course. It's just that the first time I'd gone to Texas—when I barely knew Alex but was forming my plan to live there—everything about getting off the plane and being hugged by him had turned out exactly as I'd imagined. It had been the first and only time in my life that my reality had dovetailed with my daydreams.

The girl who'd stolen my toothbrush moved on my second day. I was left with Wendy, whose constant crying was a cry for psychiatric help. I was too miserable myself to help her. On day number three, Wendy and I got two new roommates—one was African American, the other a Latina. The new arrivals took an instant dislike to each other and spoke only through me. "Tell your friend she stinks." "Tell your friend to stop banging on the window." Lourdes had returned to York after thirteen days on the street and acted happy to be back. She pounded on the window and screamed in Spanish to her friends when she saw them walking to med line or on their way to school. When Lourdes wasn't screaming, she was asleep and snoring so loudly that it sounded like the honking geese who roamed the compound. Sandra, quiet and withdrawn, had terrible gas. I hid my face in my blanket whenever she used the toilet. Sandra sat next to me at each meal, not for my company but for the food I didn't eat.

I was sure I would be moved—that seemed to be the third-day pattern—but when no CO opened the door and threw a garbage bag at me by Friday morning, I knew I was stuck in there for the weekend. I continued to try to write letters with the dull pencil stub. My words to Alex were filled with hope and God. I clung to my faith like the life raft it was, and continued to hope against hope for my miracle. On Saturday afternoon, we were taken to the library for half an hour. I found Doris Lessing's *The Golden Notebook* and a couple of baseball books, *The Bronx Zoo* by Sparky Lyle and one about the 1986 Mets. On the "keep" rack I spotted a copy of the New Testament—a huge find for me because it also included the Psalms and Proverbs. Back in our room, Sandra and Lourdes's war of words escalated. I had to quiet them somehow. I opened the Bible and began reading aloud from Matthew. *When Mary his mother had been betrothed to Joseph, before they came together, she was found*

CRIME AND PUNISHMENT

to be with child by the Holy Spirit. Reading scripture to my cell mates felt strange, but, miraculously, it quieted the room. Even Wendy stopped crying long enough to listen.

I read aloud through that weekend and on into Monday morning, when finally the garbage bag was tossed my way. I was packed and ready to go an hour before the CO unlocked the door.

"Where to?" I asked her.

"The gym."

"The gym?"

There were almost fifteen hundred women in York that summer, about three hundred too many. Because of the overflow, the gym had been converted into an eighty-six-bed, four-toilet dormitory. We slept in boat-shaped gray plastic beds with mattresses stuffed inside. After five nights locked down, I felt relieved to be in an open space. But four or five days later, my little nest was torn apart. A state inspection had been scheduled because of complaints about the overcrowding. Our dorm had to be turned back into a gymnasium and all evidence that eighty-six women had been living there had to be eliminated.

Because my crime was nonviolent and because I'd remained discipline-free, I assumed I would be moved to the less restrictive East Side. Rumors circulated that a new building called "the Fenwicks" was opening. I thought "new" meant brand-new—clean, modern, air-conditioned; I was sure I would be relocated there. Instead, I learned that I was assigned to Zero North, G Tier, on the highly restrictive West Side—a unit that housed long-term violent offenders. When I asked why, I was told that, though mine was a victimless white-collar crime and I had no prior criminal history, these facts were irrelevant. I had been assigned to a maximum-security unit because of the length of my sentence. At the moment, this felt to me like the worst and scariest of scenarios.

The housing units on the West Side were cement modules. There were two levels of rooms called tiers on each side of the command center. Each tier had twelve eight-foot-by-ten foot cells, two showers, two telephones, and a glass-encased common area with a green plastic couch and matching chairs. The pay phones were situated in the common room, where you couldn't hear yourself think, let alone hear the voice of the person you had called. The TV was the center of activity in the common room, of course. It was activated at certain times of the day by the officer at the desk, but inmates controlled the volume. Whenever the chatter in the room became loud, someone would make the TV louder. That made people raise their voices, which made whoever was trying to watch TV—cartoons or BET videos, mostly—jack up the volume some more. I learned to talk on the phone with my finger in my ear.

The behavior of the women at Zero North was horrifying. We were in jail. Why was everyone acting like we were at a party? Why didn't anyone seem remorseful? Because I was still thinking like someone who'd just finished rehab, I wanted to talk about amends and recovery. *You're a drug addict and a thief*, my voice reminded me. *You're no better than anyone else.*

I settled in unhappily at Zero North, but not for long. A few days after I'd moved there, the intercom buzzed. "Come get garbage bags and pack up," the CO said. My door clicked open. I jumped up, heart pounding, and hurried downstairs. "Where am I going?" I asked.

"A & D." I must have looked confused. "Admissions and Departures," he said. I couldn't believe it—was my miracle happening? It was 10:30 A.M. on Monday morning, the beginning of my second full week in prison.

"Am I going home?" I asked.

"No," he said. "You're moving to the Fenwicks."

The Fenwicks is an old redbrick building, built around 1920 when the prison was called the State Farm for Women. There was a men's prison across the lake from us and the Fenwicks, between the two facilities, had been being used by the men. Now, because of the overcrowding, York had reclaimed it.

When I got off the bus and dragged my bag up the cement steps, an officer unlocked the gate. The heat outside was almost unbearable that day; inside, a noisy industrial-sized fan blew warm air across the floor of the musty hallway. Someone directed me to an air-conditioned office. I stood inside the door, happy for the cold, waiting for someone to tell me where to go and what to do. I was unfailingly polite in prison, and with some guards this made a difference. CTO DeLucia was a tall blonde, probably around my age. She had a kind voice and a pleasant smile. "You're in 19B," she said. "Just go up the stairs." "B" meant bottom bunk.

An inmate behind me in the doorway said, "Uh-uh. That's Lenora's room. Lenora needs the bottom bunk."

The smile dropped off the CTO's face. "I'm not speaking to you."

Fenwicks North had been my fourth move in less than two weeks. I didn't have much of anything except my state clothes and my library books. I dragged my bag up the stairs and to the end of the hall. 19B. Nineteen had always been one of my favorite numbers, so I told myself this was a good omen.

Two black women stood in the hall, watching me. The door to room 19 was closed. When I opened it and walked inside, a blast of hot air and an unpleasant musty smell hit me in the face. The room was barely wide enough for the bunk beds and two chairs. I sat down on the bottom bunk and felt tears behind my eyes. "This is not acceptable," I said aloud. "This is disgusting." When I walked back into the hallway, the two women were still standing there. The mannish one wore her hair in dreadlocks. The other, pretty and slim, had kind eyes. The dreadlocks woman laughed at me. "You gonna cry?" She turned to her friend. "Aw, she gonna cry."

"No, I'm not," I said, and I wasn't—not in front of her.

I went back in the room and sat on my flat unmade mattress. The other woman came to the doorway. "Keisha don't mean nothing," she said. "Just make your bed and take a shower. You'll feel better." Because

I didn't know what else to do, I did as she suggested, but I felt no better.

I was sitting on my bed when Lenora returned. Her three hundred pounds filled the room. "That bottom bunk's mine," she said, by way of greeting me. As far as I was concerned, she could have the bottom bunk, except it wasn't up to me. There was no free choice or free will in prison; if I wasn't sleeping in the bed assigned to me, I'd get in trouble. I didn't want to fight with Lenora, but I didn't want to get a ticket either. Would she be mean to me until we switched?

Lenora's girth and her booming voice intimidated me at first. It was clearly her room, even though she'd only moved there three days earlier. I stayed on my bed, out of her way, as she dragged the chair from the corner by the window to the bunk bed ladder. It was scary watching her hoist herself up to the top bunk. At about five-foot-eight, she carried her weight around her like a barrel. She stood up on the chair, put one foot on the ladder, then threw her body onto the bunk as if she were mounting a horse. Luckily, the next day, Lenora went out to the rec yard and fell off the picnic bench. She was sent to medical where they filled out an incident report, gave her a bag of ice, and classified her as a bottom bunk. "They gave it to me because of my obesity," she said proudly. Lenora wore her weight as a mark of distinction.

You could see Lenora's dimples when she grinned; beneath the layers of skin and the missing teeth, she had a pretty face and a nice smile. She had been at York for two years when I first met her and her parole hearing was coming near. She told me parts of her story but not the whole story in one sitting. She'd been incarcerated for knifing her cousin. "We were in the kitchen. I was smoking pot and he was doing crystal meth," she said. "He got sort of crazy and tried to rape me. I told him to stop, and I pushed him and screamed at him. Then I cut him." When I tried to picture the kitchen where the assault had happened, I saw the kitchen of the little house in Trumbull, Connecticut, where I'd lived as a child—a kitchen of earlier times and less money, before our big house on Hollydale Road with the fire alarm and the intercom system. "So I called the ambulance and the police. Then I got me a beer and went out on the front porch and waited. I thought he was dead." Thankfully, he hadn't been, and Lenora had gotten five years. If she made parole, she would only have to serve two and a half of those years before relocating to a halfway house for her final six months. Lenora had all her paperwork ready. "These are my certificates," she said proudly, showing me a folder of awards and commendations.

Lenora taught me practical stuff, like how to tie your bottom sheet down so it wouldn't slip off the bed, how to write for packages from home, and why it was important to sign up for groups and apply for jobs. I was funny to Lenore—naïve about prison, and, in a way, about life. It took me a few days to realize why she looked familiar: Lenora had served the oatmeal at breakfast on the West Side. She had always smiled and said hello.

Lenora was the leader of the black women in Fenwick North, who shouted as they came down the hallway, "Nora, you goin' outside?" "Wanna play cards, Lenore?" "Nora, you got somethin' to eat?" She was "Ma" to the eighteen-year-old across the hall. She answered every query, except when she instructed me to tell them she was sleeping. My name was "Lenora's roommate" and because of that, they were nice to me, too. Lenora's metal bin beneath the bunk bed was filled to overflowing with food and candy. She always offered me stuff to eat, but I usually said no. She rose at three-thirty each morning to get ready for work. If my snoring had kept her awake the night before, she was angry with me and would open her metal bin and let the cover clatter to the floor, tit for tat. Sometimes she would bang around without meaning to wake me, like the time she saw ants by her kitchen boots and whacked the boots against the floor in an effort to kill "the animals."

The nice thing about Lenora's kitchen job was that she was gone before I had to get up. I'd fall back asleep until I heard the five thirty wake-up shout for breakfast. There was no intercom in the Fenwicks, so announcements were made by guards standing at the bottom of the stairs and bellowing. "Breakfast wake-up! Thirty minutes to chow!" Breakfast at the Fenwicks was easier than at other units because we didn't have to leave the building. When the next scream, "Chow!" was heard, we just walked downstairs. Because I had no job assignment for the first month or so, I would go back to sleep after breakfast until they shouted "Count clear!" at 8:00 A.M. When Lenora returned from work at 10:30 A.M., she would take off her kitchen clothes and rush into the shower. Then she'd put on her shorts and T-shirt, get on her bed, eat something—usually potato chips—and go to sleep. Sometimes she brought stuff back from the kitchen to eat, like grilled cheese sandwiches. That was one of the perks of working in the kitchen: after cleanup, inmates could make themselves breakfast. Lenora also brought back huge bags of ice so all the girls could stop in and fill their travel mugs with ice for ice water. Bringing back the ice or the sandwiches wasn't authorized, but no one ever stopped her. When all the commotion settled down and count began, Lenora would turn on her two fans, lie down on the bed, and go to sleep again. She would sometimes stay asleep until dinnertime. She would be back in bed by 8:00 P.M., retired for the night.

I didn't have a problem with Lenora's schedule because I had the room to myself in the morning and I liked going to bed early. The only problem I had was in the afternoon. Before I got a job, I was just as happy to stay on my bed and read or write or just lie there because that was all I could handle. But Lenora wanted the door closed and I didn't have a fan. Also, because she never washed her washcloth with her laundry, it had a pungent odor that permeated our room. Lenora wanted the door closed to the noise and I wanted it open to the air. That and my snoring were our issues. After I got a job and a fan, and Lenora got rid of the washcloth, the door thing no longer mattered.

I can still remember so clearly the girls who lived on our short hall. Little Tammy lived with Tanya in the end room. Some of the girls called Tammy "the Smurf" because she was four-foot-ten and weighed about

170 pounds. Tammy was a drug addict who couldn't stay out of prison. It was just as well; at least in prison she could see the doctor and have her hepatitis C treated. I knew Tammy the whole time I was in and wrote to her a couple of times after I went home. We were friends in a way, although our friendship was based mostly on my helping her and giving her stuff from my commissary. But on one of my first days in prison, Tammy had given me half a tube of toothpaste because I'd run out of indigent supplies, and I've never forgotten that kindness.

Across from Tammy and Tanya lived Keisha and Kyra. Kyra was a middle-aged white woman trying to act like a twenty-something black girl. After a couple of months, she became really sick. That was when I found out she had HIV and hepatitis C. Kyra, who'd dropped out of school in eighth grade, told me all about the prison school where she worked as a teacher's aide. One afternoon, against all odds, she talked the guards into letting me out of my unit so that I could meet with a teacher at the school who was looking for an aide. I got the job, and finding useful work grounded me for the rest of my stay at York. This is going to sound sappy, but looking back, I now realize that Kyra's intervention was a gift from God. Inmates could not sign out of a unit for another destination if they were not on a list, but somehow Kyra and the Lord had made it happen.

Brenda and Gwen lived across the hall from me. Brenda was a twenty-year-old Puerto Rican girl with large brown eyes and a big mouth. She was in the nurse's aide class at school and sat on the bus every morning with her girlfriend "Brown," who lived on the first floor and went to cosmetology. Using my nail clippers, Brown gave me the best haircut I ever got in prison. It cost me a package of cappuccino and two Honey Buns. Brenda and I had a huge screaming fight one morning. It was a daily thing with her: as soon as the wake-up call came, she would start talking and yelling down the hall. After about a week of this, I asked her nicely to be more quiet. She began mocking me. When I asked her again, she began yelling. I told her to shut up. Then my next-door neighbor, Diane, entered the fray. "This is prison!" she screamed. "If you don't like the noise, go to mental health!" I told Diane to shut up, too. Downstairs in the dining room over breakfast, Diane continued to taunt me from another table. I finally turned around and said, "Diane, shut the fuck up." The room went silent as I walked out. A guard, waiting in the hallway, summoned me to the office. I was so angry that I burst into tears. I can picture him—an older man with white hair and a mustache. He'd been around. He wrote about the incident in the logbook and suggested I keep my room door shut to avoid further trouble. I was still so clueless about how things worked that it didn't occur to me until years later that he could have given me a ticket and sent me to seg for fighting. That was pretty much the last time I went to breakfast at the Fenwicks.

Diane lived with Teresa. Teresa came from Hartford, like Lenora, and they worked in the kitchen together. I don't remember why Teresa was in prison—something to do with drugs. She had boyfriend issues. Lenora used to tell me that Teresa was always waiting for her man to send her money, but that he was running around with another woman now and Teresa was living in a fantasy world. Teresa and I had our skirmishes, too. One day, she and another girl were talking in the bathroom about a movie I'd seen. Getting out of the shower, I joined the conversation. "Shut up, Mrs. Kravitz," Teresa said. "No one's talking to you." I said I didn't realize it was a private conversation. "Well, it is, so butt out."

"If you want to have a private conversation, don't have it in the bathroom," I snapped back. Teresa responded by informing me that no one at Fenwicks North liked me, which hurt my feelings.

"She's just stupid," Lenora said later. "No one likes *her*. Why you even talk to her?"

Later, Teresa and I made amends. "Hey, Roberta, what's up?" she'd say. She was one of the few girls at the Fenwicks who called me by my first name.

Next to Brenda and Gwen were Alicia and Nadesha. Alicia was a twenty-eight-year-old white woman who also did the let's-pretend-I'm-black-or-Hispanic-or-a-lesbian-in-prison thing. She had a couple of tattoos and would get the girls to braid her hair in cornrows. She and Diane were good friends for a while. I used to hear them talking in fake Jewish accents when they passed my room. Diane would walk by my door and shout, "Gefilte fish!" Then the two would burst out laughing. I'm slow on things like that, so it took me a while to figure out that Diane was trying to insult me with anti-Semitic remarks. Alicia just wanted attention and would try to get it any way she could. Mostly, when no one was looking, she was a sad little girl who missed her baby and her mother. After Lenora made parole, Alicia and I became roommates.

Finally, in the room at the end of the hall, were Rita and Lynda. Lynda was a Latina in her late thirties who was always singing, or talking loudly in Spanish with her friends down the hall, or on the phone with her family. Rita was another middle-aged white woman—malnourished and forever complaining about her low blood sugar. She had dull eyes and a bulbous nose, and her thin hair fell across her waif-like face. Rita was a drug addict like me, in prison this time on a parole violation. She had left the state without permission and then been extradited back from Arizona. There was a husband somewhere, also a drug addict, and a lot of crying and moping around. At first I took Rita for granted. I could always sit with her for a meal if there was no other seat available. She was always good for a conversation or a cup of coffee. One day Rita came by, sat in the chair by the door, and began to cry. She said she was so lonely she didn't know what to do—that she had to find herself a girlfriend because she couldn't bear to be alone anymore. She was unfriendly to me after that confession. A lot of it had to do with my friend Maureen who lived at the other end of the hall. Rita decided she liked Maureen and would follow her around like a puppy dog. Maureen, also a middle-aged white drug addict with no money in her account, would take anything she could get from Rita. In exchange, she'd sometimes hang out with her in the rec yard or sit with her in the dining room. Maureen was from Bridgeport, and her lawyer was an attorney I had worked with in my former life. At first I found her to be abrasive, the way she would shout out anything that popped into her head. But one day while I was sitting on the steps waiting for the guard to unlock the door, Maureen sat down next to me and started asking me about the book I was reading. That's how we became friends. Eventually, Lynda convinced Rita to stop chasing after Maureen and fixed her up with someone else. As I walked into the bathroom one evening, I saw Rita on her bed kissing Lynda's friend. This was the beginning of a series of failed attempts for Rita to find love in prison.

The thing was: every one of my companions at Fenwick North had a story, a need to be listened to, and a longing to be loved. In that respect, we were all the same. I was one of the fortunate ones in that I didn't have to go through prison alone. Although there was always that one heart-stopping second before Alex, on the other end of the line in Texas, accepted the charges for my collect calls, he would inevitably say yes. Then we would talk, and my loneliness would subside.

My mother and I have the same hands. I stretch mine across the visiting room table and we touch fingertips. "My nails are all broken," I say.

"My nails are growing because I can't do anything," my mother says with a sigh.

When I put on my slippers that night, I notice my mother and I have the same feet, too. It is the act of slipping my foot inside the soft blue shoe that reminds me of her. My mother is so little now. We used to be the same size, a smidgen taller than five feet. She used to weigh five or ten pounds more than my 115. I am always telling people we are built exactly alike from the neck down. "I look like my father and my father's mother," I say, "but I'm built like my mother." This isn't a bad thing. My mother is thinner than I am now. Her hair is colored a reddish blonde. My hair is brown, gray, and coppery red—a combination of natural color and hair dye long faded. My mother's hair is short. Mine is too long. My mother is still able to go to the hairdresser every Friday. I cut my bangs with my nail clippers and have not had my hair colored since December.

I'm on the telephone in the hall when she tells me. I'm seated on the floor with my finger in my ear so I can hear. The girls are loud-talking as they walk back and forth. Most don't even notice I'm here. "I was hoping you would call back yesterday," my mother says. I had called in the evening but no one picked up the phone. I don't get upset anymore when I hear the voice say, "Your call has not been accepted." I just wait to call her the next day.

"I wanted to know if you were feeling better," I tell her.

She gets that funny sound in her voice. "I have something to tell you," she says. "I have lung cancer."

I don't say anything at first. I try taking a breath. "I don't understand what you mean," I say. And I truly *don't* understand. Just this afternoon, my friend Amy came to see me. In another life, Amy's mother and my mother were best friends—before my father left my mother and took their friends with him. Amy and I have played together since we were babies. When she asked me this afternoon how my mother is, I said she couldn't seem to shake her pneumonia. "I'm not worried though," I told Amy. "My grandmother lived to be almost ninety-five and my mother's grandmother lived to be ninety. My mother will be just fine."

"What don't you understand?" my mother asks. She has tears in her voice, but I don't cry. I can't.

"I don't understand what you mean," I repeat.

"I didn't want to tell you like this," my mother says.

I take deep breaths. I remember to ask some medical-type questions. I am reaching inside of me for something from God—a word, a phrase. "You'll be fine," I say. "You have to think positively. You have to have faith." I'm sorry for every moment I have wasted, for every time I didn't call because I took for granted she would be there the next time I did. I love my mother. I can picture her clearly. What will I do if something happens to her while I'm in prison?

No, it *won't* happen. My mother will not die.

Roberta Schwartz's mother died in 2003 while her daughter was still in prison. In May 2005, Schwartz married Alex and returned to Austin, Texas. —Ed.

The Chase

BY BRENDALIS MEDINA

Barbara and I were on our way back to Fenwick North from the medical unit when CO Andrus stopped to give us a ride. Barbara saw it first. "Hey, y'all—there's a car on the compound," she announced. I thought she was crazy until I looked out the window and saw the red Toyota myself.

"What the hell?" Andrus muttered.

"Why do you think they're here?" I asked him.

"I don't know, but I'm sure gonna find out." With that, he hit the gas. I don't know if the people in the car noticed us behind them or if they were scared, but they picked up speed. Andrus looked over his shoulder at us. "Hold on girls," he said. "I'm going after them." The chase was on.

Giddy with excitement, I held tight to the armrest. "Wow, I've never been on this end of a car chase before," I said. The DOC van took a sharp turn.

"Faster! Faster!" Barbara yelled.

Caught up in the moment, I yelled, too. "Catch them, Andrus! Don't let 'em get away!" Nothing like this had ever happened at boring York

CI before, and for a moment, I was back home—fifteen again, and sipping that old familiar cocktail of danger and excitement.

It was a summer night and I was on the block with some of the brothers and sisters. I'd only been in the gang for about five or six months. There wasn't much going on that night. Gang life was like that: long stretches of boredom punctuated by sudden bursts of drama: run-ins with the cops or with rival gangs. I was talking with Lisa, one of the sisters, and Maria, a friend of ours who wasn't in the gang but for some reason was always around us. We were in the middle of a heated dispute over whether or not a bandanna looks better with straight or curly hair. Wearing baggy black jeans and a tight little white shirt, Lisa swung her long brown hair. "See?" she said. "You have to have curly hair like this to rock a bandanna right."

"You don't even have curly hair," I said, rolling my eyes. "You have a bunch of dead waves." Laughing, I held out a strand of my own hair. "If you want to rock a bandanna right, you have to straighten out your hair like this."

"Your hair *is* straight today, so why aren't you rocking one?" Lisa said.

"Because I don't have one that matches my outfit." I stepped back to model my black, fitted shirt and my brand-new blue jeans.

Maria, a dark-skinned Dominican, stood there laughing but didn't say a word. Like most Dominican women, she had short, nappy hair that wouldn't look right no matter how many bandannas she threw on it.

The argument was in high gear when one of the brothers, Junebug, pulled up. A short kid with mousy hair and beady eyes, he was seated behind the wheel of a black Saturn. "Whatcha doin'?" he asked.

"Nothing. Just talking," Lisa answered, leaning forward to check out his wheels. "We're bored. Take us for a ride."

"Okay. Get in." He swung open the passenger door. I was hesitant. I knew Junebug didn't own a set of wheels, and I also knew that he liked doing crazy things, like hot-wiring cars.

"June, whose car is this?" I asked, eyeing him suspiciously. "You steal it?"

"Come on, Bren," he said, smirking. "I wouldn't let you girls get in a stolen car without telling you. It's Krissy's car. She let me borrow it."

Krissy, June's new girlfriend, was a friend of mine. She came from a pretty wealthy family and they were always driving different cars, so the claim was credible. Still, I had a weird feeling. "Come on," Junebug said, nudging his head toward the back seat of the car. Ignoring my gut feeling, I climbed in.

Maria hopped in the front and Lisa got in back with me. Junebug peeled out from the curb and our joyride began. He had the music blasting, Stevie B's voice thundering through the speaker. Gang sisters but true romantics, Lisa and I sang along: *Spring love, come back to me.* We rode around for a while with no particular destination, talking, singing, and laughing. Then Junebug hung a right onto the highway entrance.

Everything was fine until I saw the flashing red and blue lights. Up ahead, two state troopers were stopping cars for what looked like a routine inspection. My stomach lurched as we crept forward, but when one of the troopers motioned for Junebug to pull over to the side and he obeyed, I let out a sigh of relief. I shouldn't have. Just as the trooper approached, June stomped his foot on the gas pedal and the Saturn shot forward. "What the hell you *doing*?" Lisa yelled. Without answering her, Junebug drove faster and faster.

Three cruisers chased us, their sirens wailing. I'd never been in a situation like this before, and my emotions ricocheted between excitement and fear. Then, my anger kicked in. "June! You fucking lied to me!" I screamed, punching the back of the seat. Everything was happening so quickly, it didn't seem real. I had no idea where we were or where we were headed.

The sirens were drowned out by the noise inside the car: Maria's hysterical crying and Lisa's wailing that she was going to jail. "I can't believe you have us in a stolen car!" I kept yelling.

Junebug wasn't listening to us; he was too busy talking to himself. "I'm *not* going back to jail! I'm *not!*" He veered toward a wooded area, slammed on the brakes, threw open the door, and ran. "Haul ass!" he screamed over his shoulder.

Lisa and I looked at each other and, without saying a word, leapt from the car. Entering the dark woods, I ran faster and harder than I'd ever run before. We couldn't see where we were going, but it really didn't make much difference because I had no idea where I was. I didn't know which way Maria had run—or even if she *had* run—but Lisa was just a few steps ahead of me. I didn't dare look back, but I could hear the cops gaining on us, and the barking dogs. "Oh, shit! They have dogs," I yelled to Lisa. When I looked back, I couldn't see them. I didn't see the big tree stump either, until after I had slammed into it. When I let out a cry, Lisa stopped and yelled to me, "Bren, what happened? You okay?"

"I hurt my leg!" I could hear the cops coming closer and realized running was pointless. "Fuck it. I give up. I'm going back." To my surprise, Lisa walked over to me.

"If you turn yourself in, then so will I," she said.

Within seconds, we were face-to-face with the cops. A bright light flashed in my eyes and a booming voice commanded, "Put your hands on your head and get on your knees!" My eyes were on the two dogs pulling against their handlers' chains. I knelt in the mud in my brand-new jeans and placed my hands on my head. From the corner of my eye, I could see Lisa in the same position. When I looked up, I saw six cops, their guns and flashlights pointing at us. My heart raced and I was trembling badly. I was afraid they were either going to shoot us or let their dogs attack.

One of the cops standing behind me grabbed hold of my arms. I felt cold metal on my wrist. Before I knew it, I was being pulled onto my feet like a rag doll. He pushed me forward and I stumbled toward the clearing.

Maria was there, standing beside a cop and crying hysterically. A female officer approached me. "Do you have anything sharp in your pockets?" she asked, her eyes scanning me up and down.

"No!" I yelled.

"You better be telling me the truth, because if I get pricked with something, you'll be in more trouble than what you're in now."

"I don't have anything sharp."

She noticed the beads around my neck and took them in her hand. Her smirk said she recognized the gang colors. "So you're a tough girl," she said, letting the beads drop back on my chest. I clenched but didn't say a word.

She made me turn around, lean against the cop car, and spread my legs. I knew the routine; I'd been pat-searched before. Whenever the cops would try to bust one of the brothers on Baldwin Street, they'd line us all up and have a female officer search the girls. When she was done with the search, a male officer began the interrogation. "Where did you steal this car?"

"I didn't steal anything. I didn't even know it was stolen."

"So, where's the driver?"

"I don't know."

"Well, he took off and left you girls here to take the fall."

"We didn't do anything wrong. We just went for a ride."

"Why'd you run then?"

"Because I was scared, that's why."

"What's his name?"

He stared at me, waiting. They were questioning Lisa nearby, and she was speaking loudly enough so I could hear. "I don't know him that good—he's just a kid from the neighborhood," she said. When she shot me a look, I knew what to do. So I jacked up the volume, too.

"I don't know his real name. I only know his nickname."

With his finger in my face, the cop started yelling, "Is he in your gang? Is that why you're protecting him?"

"I don't know him. I've only seen him around the neighborhood. They call him Big T."

"Why would you girls get in a car with a guy you don't know?"

"We've talked to him a couple of times," I said, looking toward the woods. "He seemed nice." I could tell by his expression that he wasn't buying it, but he stopped with the questions and put me into the back of a cruiser with Lisa and Maria.

At the police barracks, I felt numb as they fingerprinted us and took our mug shots. We were put in a cell. The three state troopers who questioned us were decent, bullshitting with us rather than yelling or trying to intimidate us. The younger one did most of the talking.

"So you didn't know that car was stolen?"

Maria, still crying, shook her head.

He gave us a little smile. "You know, you girls should be more careful about who you hang out with. Now, what we're going to do is let you go on a PTA, so if you give me your parents' number, we'll call them and they can come pick you up."

"I can't call my mother," Maria sobbed. "We don't have a phone."

Lisa looked scared. She couldn't call home either. Her mother was too sickly to pick her up, and her stepfather was probably out drunk somewhere. It was up to me, but I knew what to do. With just one phone call, I could get all three of us out. All it would cost me was my pride. Reluctantly, I gave the trooper my brother Ricky's number and explained that he was a Waterbury police officer. As he walked away to call my brother, I felt sick. I wasn't scared of Ricky, but I didn't want to let him down or embarrass him.

About an hour and a half later, Ricky walked in, dressed in a pair of blue jeans and a black T-shirt. I stared at him, trying to figure out how mad and disappointed he was, but his face was stoic, his emotions unreadable. He talked to the officers for a few minutes, signed some papers, and we were free to go. When we got outside, I couldn't bring myself to look my brother in the eye. "I'm sorry, Ricky," I said, my eyes focused on the ground. He put his hand on my back and gently nudged me forward.

On the ride home, the subject came up only once. "It was stupid that you girls wouldn't give them that boy's name," Ricky said. "Why would you protect some jerk who put you in a situation like that?" Then he looked directly at me. "When you go to court, you need to tell them his name." He ended the conversation there. I looked down at my new jeans, muddy and torn at the knees. Wavy-haired or straight-haired, I was never going to rock a bandanna with *these* jeans. I was never going to have Ricky's respect anymore either.

The next day, I went out to the block to look for Junebug, but he was nowhere around. Lisa had already told the other brothers and sisters what had happened, and the president of the gang had let it be known that he would take care of June for what he'd done to us. But Junebug never got what was coming to him, and I never got the chance to tell him what I thought of him. Two days after our big chase, he was arrested in another stolen car and sent to juvie. It was a relief in a way—I no longer had to worry about giving up a brother to the cops like Ricky had wanted me to do.

When my court date arrived, my father went with me. I didn't see a judge. Instead, a prosecutor talked to my father in her office while I waited slumped outside. After a while, I was called in to join them. I was surprised when the prosecutor smiled at me. "Because you've never been in trouble before, I'm going to release you to your father, and this incident won't stay on your record. You're getting a second chance here." She paused briefly, then continued. "Ms. Medina, your father is a good man who loves you very much. You should wise up and listen to him. I don't want to see you in here again."

"Yes, ma'am," I answered, my eyes fixed on the floor. I didn't want to see *her* again either.

Outside the prosecutor's office, my father muttered angry words under his breath. He was furious that he'd had to miss a day's work—a day's pay—because of me. It was usually my brother David giving him headaches. Whenever Daddy was home from work, David would get the yells and punishments; I always got the smiles and crazy stories about when he was a kid. I had never gotten into trouble before I turned fourteen and started hanging out on Baldwin Street. It didn't feel good knowing I had caused his anger. I forced myself to look him in the eye. "Daddy, I'm sorry," I said.

"You think that an 'I'm sorry' fixes everything? Well, it doesn't." He stormed out of the courthouse ahead of me, and I had to run to catch up.

A long, sad chase of another kind had begun.

Prom Queen

BY JENNIFER RICH

I bolted upright in bed, groping for my plastic garbage can. I felt it and put it in front of my face. Mornings were the worst. When I retched, it felt like I was puking up a kidney. I peered into the little blue can expecting to see a vital organ but saw only a stew of bile and trash. As the wave of nausea subsided, I took a few breaths to get my bearings. Was my stepfather awake? Had he heard me getting sick? I checked my watch. It was only 7:00 A.M. and I was withdrawing already. Sonofabitch.

I realized that I was still dressed from the night before and was grateful that I didn't have to go through that rough process. I rolled out of bed, careful not to trigger another vomiting session, and pulled on a hooded sweatshirt with dried bloodstains on the cuffs. I covered my greasy brown hair with a green winter hat, located my hiking boots amid the junk on my floor, and laced them up. I used to wear my boots on trails, but now I wore them as a precaution since I never knew what sort of ground I'd be covering.

Grabbing my backpack, I inched into the hallway. Mom was at work and when I heard my stepdad snoring in the next room, I knew leaving this early would be a cakewalk. John was generally laid back but he'd become suspicious lately. I looked under couch cushions and swiped loose change from the coffee table in case I needed gas money. Eighty-three cents wouldn't get me far, but it would get me back home. I passed my dog, Bailey, snoozing in the ancient recliner. She peered up at me from under half-raised lids, realized I wasn't going to invite her to come for a ride, and went back to chasing bunnies in her dreams. Soundlessly, I closed the front door behind me and began mentally preparing myself for what lay ahead.

The frigid air seared my lungs, creating a cloud of moisture on its way back out. Even the tiny hairs inside my nose were frozen. I cleared a thin layer of snow from my car, fished the keys from my bag, and hit the button to unlock the doors. When the car's panic alarm blared instead, I nearly peed my corduroys before I could turn the damn thing off. I imagined my wealthy neighbors at their windows, staring out at the girl and her green Volkswagen plastered with Grateful Dead decals. Did they realize they were parking their Audis and Volvos next to a space reserved for a criminal? I scrambled into my car and drove out of the parking lot.

Icy air pushed its way through the vents, and I let the rpm indicator climb into the red before shifting gears to force the engine to warm up faster. I couldn't tell if I was shaking from the cold or from the heroin withdrawal. When I caught a glimpse of my eyes in the rearview mirror, I looked away. The whites had turned pink, bordering on red. The once brilliant irises were a muted shade of mud. I drove over Avon Mountain and into Hartford as fast as I dared on snowy streets, silently praying that the cops weren't running radar.

A small bell chimed as I opened the front door and stepped into a pawnshop that, miraculously, was open. The air was heavy with stale incense smoke. I made my way through a maze of glass cases displaying items that had seen better days, noting with relief that I was the shop's only customer. As I approached the counter, Herman emerged from the storage room to greet me.

CRIME AND PUNISHMENT

"Hello dare." Herman's accent was a mix: Manhattan by way of Jamaica. He was dressed in a baggy black jogging suit and a red knit hat that appeared to entrap dreadlocks.

"Hi," I said. "I have some stuff for you." I reached into my pocket and pulled out a fistful of jewelry. I began arranging it on the countertop, trying to make it look nice. Some of the pieces were my own, passed down from great-grandmothers or given to me in celebration of high school graduation, but most of it had been stolen during my most recent string of burglaries.

"Pawn or sell outright?" Herman asked.

"Sell these," I answered, pointing to the stolen goods. "Pawn these." To hell with the stolen stuff; I was only concerned with buying back my own things. He fiddled with the items for a few minutes. When he frowned, I knew what was coming next.

"I can't do much fer you," he said. "How much are you looking fer?"

I always hated this part. I was inexperienced in the art of negotiation and too shy to ask for the amount I wanted. I gave the standard answer. "What can you give me?"

"How 'bout dis?" he began. "Why don't we do eighty-five and you come with me to my place fer a minute. You like ta smoke?"

I told him that the amount was fine and I could go to his house, but just for a few minutes. Although I was feeling worse by the second, I found the prospect of sparking up a joint with Herman not altogether unpleasant. We completed our business transaction, he closed his shop, and we left.

Herman unlocked his SUV and gestured for me to climb in. He lived five minutes away from his store on the upper floor of a two-family home. The kitchen was filthy and brought on a fresh case of chills, but the rest of the place appeared clean enough. I sat down at his dining room table and waited for him to get situated. He took off his jacket and sneakers, then lifted up the back of his T-shirt. I thought he was going to take the shirt off too, but he was only removing the 9-milli-meter he kept in a holster at the small of his back. He placed the gun in an empty ceramic bowl at the center of the table, directly between us. Then he pulled off his hat. No dreadlocks. I felt duped. When he went to get his weed, I was tempted to hide the gun on him but thought better of it.

He came back with a Ziploc bag full of marijuana, reinforcing my stereotypical perception of Jamaicans. The plastic seams of the bag were bulging with deep green nuggets. He handed me the bag and told me to break apart the weed so he could roll it into a blunt. He sat down in the chair next to me and began gutting a cigar.

We were silent as we passed the blunt back and forth. I watched Herman's eyes scan my lanky body, returning each time to my chest. He waited until my brain was swimming in THC before he made his play. "I tought dat maybe we could have some sex now."

I'd known that was coming. I didn't reply right away. This was a deli-cate situation and I felt I should weigh my options. Herman had been fencing stolen goods for me for a few weeks and I didn't want to lose the great deal we had going. On the other hand, he definitely wasn't my type and I knew the dope sickness wouldn't be kept at bay much longer. If I didn't score something soon, it was going to get ugly. When in doubt, I thought, be honest.

"Um, Herman," I began. "I'm kinda dope-sick right now. So I really think it would be best if I just took off." The muscles in his face shifted expression at the term "dope-sick" and I knew that my clothes would remain on.

He replaced his gun in its holster and gathered up his things. We left the apartment. It was an awkward ride back to his pawnshop. I thanked him for taking me to his place, got out of his SUV, and hightailed it to my car.

It didn't look like there was anyone on the streets. The dealers had recently developed the irritating habit of keeping bankers' hours. I was making a second sweep through the usual neighborhoods and past the twenty-four-hour corner stores when I saw Ant's tall figure trudging through the snow toward me. He'd probably seen me before I'd spotted him. I was pretty conspicuous. I leaned over to push open the passenger door.

"Get in," I said.

Ant was huge—about 6-foot-four, with hands the size of bear paws and shoulders broad enough to carry an El Camino. His skin was such a dark brown that when he smiled, the contrast against his white teeth took my breath away. I would've considered him attractive had I not known what a scumbag he was.

He climbed in foot first without knocking the snow from his boots and slid into the passenger seat. The first words out of his mouth were, "Do you have any money, Jen?"

"Yeah," I said. "A little. I haven't seen anyone out in the usual spots."

"I know. Too fucking cold," he complained. "Let's go to my boy's house. He'll serve us if we have at least fifty." I despised having to rely on someone else to get my drugs—especially another junkie because they don't do anything out of the goodness of their hearts. I had dealt with Ant many times before and he had yet to rip me off, but all addicts have their desperate days.

I pulled away from the curb and allowed Ant to guide me deeper into the ghetto. He repeatedly asked to drive, said it would be quicker, but that was one point on which I refused to budge. No way in hell was I going to allow this butthead to drive a car that was insured in my mom's name. We reached the dealer's home a few minutes later, and I gave Ant three twenty-dollar bills. He hopped out of the car and told me to wait, that he'd be right back.

So I waited . . . and waited. He emerged from the house looking as if all was right with the world. He had taken his sweet time to make the deal and gotten his fix before coming back out. He slumped in the seat with a dopey grin on his face and said, "Drive." I eased up on the clutch and started rolling forward, watching him out of the corner of my eye. He dug around in his pocket, then extended his open hand to me, offering the remaining eight bags of heroin. Good boy, Anthony, I thought. He'd stuck to our normal arrangement: a two-bag commission for getting my dope when I couldn't do it myself.

The dope sickness was getting worse now that I had the drugs in my sweaty hand. All I wanted to do was pull over and set up a shot. My body was aching with the need to get high—to feel better. I drove the car into an empty lot by a brick building and parked next to a rusty Dumpster. Ant sat looking out the window, making sure no one sneaked up on us. After rummaging in my purse for what felt like an eternity, I found my needle and set it on my thigh. I grabbed a bottle of water and undid my brown leather belt to tie around my arm. I opened five of the wax paper bags. Never was I more careful than when I poured heroin into a water bottle cap.

It took me a couple of tries, but I finally struck a vein and jammed the plunger down. I slipped the needle from beneath my skin and tugged my sleeves back into place, adding to the collection of blood smears on the cuff. Seconds later, I was feeling like the prom queen ready to dance the Spotlight Dance. I reached under my seat and pulled the lever that popped the trunk. I walked around to the back of the car and hid my syringe and the remaining dope in the compartment of my six-disc CD changer. I was being pulled over and searched by the cops on a regular basis these days, so I'd begun covering my ass in preparation for their harassment.

My next task was to ditch Anthony. He had a tendency to latch on to anyone with wheels and I didn't feel like becoming his personal chauffeur.

"I have to get back home," I said. "I'm working today." This was only half of the truth. I had planned to go back home to take a shower and put on clean clothes, but I definitely wasn't going to work; I hadn't had

CRIME AND PUNISHMENT

a job in months. It didn't matter whether Ant believed me or not. He took the hint.

"Could you drop me on Center Street?" he asked. I nodded and told him it wouldn't be a problem.

When I got home, I was pleased to see that my stepfather's parking space was empty. Not having to deal with the parental units was always a bonus. I parked my car and retrieved the remaining heroin from its hiding place in the trunk, stashing it in the front pouch of my sweatshirt. I climbed the two flights of stairs to the apartment and unlocked the front door. When I pushed it open, I was welcomed by Bailey, doing her I'm-so-glad-you're-back dance. Life sucked, but for the moment, life was good. I wasn't sick and I had the place to myself, except for Bailey, who loved me anyway.

Down on the Farm*

BY KELLY DONNELLY

The cock barks his raspy caw
 through a metallic voice box.

A woman below blows reveille
from her ass—a porcelain bowl
her instrument.

All of this: just another call
to awaken, here, down on the farm.

Then, grunting, snorting, she says:
Time to slop the pigs.
Breakfast is served…. So.
Did I deserve to get what I got?

---

* The East Side of York CI was, during the early days of the prison, the Connecticut State Farm for Women. The facility employed a farm manager and engaged inmates in animal husbandry and the growing of fruits and vegetables, the philosophy being that fresh air and hard work in a rural setting would encourage their rehabilitation.

Throughout each day, the barnyard's hens
Cluckity-cluck and peckity-peck
at each other's eyes.

Just a chick,
I can't fly.

A mellow yellow chick
not canary yellow—
yellow bellied,
yellow jacket...
Yellow, yellow, kiss a fellow:
years and years from now.

No fellows here,
down on the farm.
Just cocks and cats
to keep watch over
hens and chicks.

Cluckity-cluck—
again and again.
Just a chick,
I can't fly away.

Big Girl Jail

BY ROBIN LEDBETTER

Shit, if a dyke come after me, I'ma mess that bitch up f'real!"

"Hell yeah!"

"Yo, Big Bertha ain't gone take my shit—fuck that!"

"Yo, we need a plan. If a bitch come at one of us, we gotta watch each other back f'real. Yo, I'ma hit the bitch high an' you hit the bitch low, ah-ight?"

"Ah-ight."

"Jeannie, you gone have to fend for y'self, word up. I don't know you well 'nough to take out no butch kneecaps for you."

I laughed at this. Sleepy had just met Jeannie on the transport to Niantic, and she'd taken an instant dislike to her.

"Chill, Sleepy. Yo, if a real, true-to-life dyke roll up on one of us, six hands is better than four. Shit, I'm gon' bust a bitch so bad that I ain't never gone be tried again. F'real."

Sleepy, Jeannie, and I were all being transferred from juvie to big-girl jail. With the passing of a new law, we three were the first under-age females to be incarcerated at the maximum-security facility. I was coming from a Hartford lockup, charged with robbery and murder. Sleepy—robbery, drugs, and guns—was from New Haven, and Jeannie, charged with attempted murder, had been housed in Bridgeport. We'd all known we were being transferred, though I alone, thanks to some real cool staff, knew when. So, mentally, I'd had time to prepare for the transfer, but I was still nervous—especially about the dykes. Unfortunately, Jeannie and Sleepy hadn't had the same privilege I had. So when I started telling all the stories I'd heard about Big Bertha, it sent them into the same panic that had been sitting in my stomach since I'd learned I was leaving.

"Whatever," Jeannie said. "She ain't got to do shit for me. I can hold my own."

LaToya—also known as "Sleepy"—started laughing. She got a kick out of this. "Ah-ight, Jeannie," Sleepy said. "Stop playin', 'cause when Big Bertha takin' yo panties off wit' her teeth, yo ass gone be beggin' for some help." That made me laugh, too.

"Damn, Robin!" Jeannie said. "You gon' let her play me like that? We s'pose to be peoples!"

"You *is* my peoples, Jeannie," I said. "I'm just fuckin' with you. An' so is Sleepy. Chill. Can't you take a joke?"

"Peoples? Man, me and Robin was wilding *out* up in New Haven detention," Sleepy said. "When she was up there, we had that shit on lock. She *my* peoples more than she yours. Just 'cause you from Hartford don't make you her peoples all like that."

"Yo," Jeannie said. "You don't even know *what* you talkin' 'bout. I grew *up* with Robin, an' she the reason they put me in Bridgeport 'cause they ain't want us both in the same place. They *knew* we was gone be actin' up."

They were both right. I'd grown up with Jeannie, gone to school with her, knew her crazy-ass mama, all that. She used to pick me up every morning for school and we'd walk together. We was cool, but as we got older we rolled in different circles, so we was peoples, but not all like that. Sleepy and I had only met in New Haven detention. They'd sent me there after I "wilded out" up in Hartford, thinking that if I was around different people, I couldn't be influenced and maybe I'd behave. It hadn't worked. I was straight-up terrible. There was too much on my plate, and my way of dealing with things was to be as bad as I possibly could. I'd hooked up with Sleepy—the resident "bad girl"—and had behaved plain-ass off-the-hook. I'd stayed in New Haven until the night I jumped two of the staff for changing the TV channel from *Xena: Warrior Princess*. They'd known that show was my shit, so they should've known better than that. I think it was a setup. Well, anyway, after that, they'd sent me back to Hartford.

I sat back and looked at my two friends as they continued to bicker. Sleepy had on blue Tommy Hilfiger jeans and a blue-and-white striped Tommy shirt. Her shoulder-length hair was down in a fresh wrap. She was a pretty black girl. Everyone called her Sleepy because of her eyes, which were almost closed all of the time. Jeannie, too—half black, half Puerto Rican—was pretty. Even though her mother was dark as midnight, you couldn't tell Jeannie had a trace of black in her. Her straight black hair was in a side ponytail and she wore a pair of blue jeans and a Lakers jersey. I was wearing black Polo jeans and a white Polo button-up with a black Polo sweatshirt over it. My hair was up in goddess braids. Yeah, we were some ah-ight-looking chicks, I remember thinking. Them dykes was gonna be all over us.

As the van pulled into the prison, we made a pact that we wasn't gone let no lesbian make us they bitch. After being stripped, showered, and given ID numbers, we were escorted to our housing unit. When we walked in, I was surprised at how un-prison-like it looked. From what I could see, all four tiers were made of glass and had tables, couches, and televisions.

"We've got three juvies," said our escort, a tall, square white man in a corrections uniform.

"Yo, Robin!" I heard someone yelling and banging. I turned and looked up. My friend Cookie was pressed up against the glass, her platinum-dyed hair sticking straight up in the air.

"Whassup, Cookie?" I yelled.

"Hey! No yelling," barked the CO "You want a ticket?"

"What the hell's a ticket?" I asked.

"Something you're going to get if you don't shut your mouth."

"Man, whatever," I grumbled. "Where we goin', anyway?"

The CO assigned us our cells and bunks, and then we headed down the tier. As soon as I got on the steps, I saw at least five familiar faces—people I'd met along the way from juvie. "Whassup, Robin?" one of them said.

"Whassup, Tonya? What you doin' up in here?"

"Drug charges," she replied.

"Damn."

"Hey," Tonya said. "Go put your stuff away and come back out, ah-ight?"

"Ah-ight," I said. And as I walked past her to put my stuff in my cell, I noticed a girl sitting on the couch with her hands in her pants.

"My name is Huggie-Bear," she mumbled. "I get all in your underwear."

Another girl, to no one in particular, was saying, "Just call me Daddy-Long-Stroke. Why? 'Cause Daddy-Long-Stroke make you choke."

It's starting, I thought to myself. They're testing us. "Y'all heard that?" I asked Sleepy and Jeannie, who were already returning from dropping their stuff off in their cells.

"Hell, yeah, I heard that shit," Sleepy said. "Y'all 'member what we said, ah-ight?"

When I returned from dropping off my things in my room, I sat down next to my friend Tonya. Jeannie and Sleepy were off talking to different people. They'd already started going off on their own, which was all good so long as they were there when it came down to the come-down. F'real.

"Hey, Robin." It was Stacia, another friend from juvie. I knew she would be here because she was seventeen when we met, and I also knew she was looking at some time for assaulting her boyfriend. "Here," she said, handing me a plastic bag with all the cosmetics I needed. Soap, deodorant, hair grease—the whole nine. The bag had food in it, too: noodles, cakes, juice, candy.

"When I saw you come in, I put together a bag for you," Stacia said. "I'll get more stuff on commissary day and hook you up with more until your money comes."

"Good lookin' out, Stacia. I really appreciate it," I said.

"Yeah, you're welcome." And with that, Stacia walked away. I liked her, and I wanted to hook her up with my cousin when she got out of here. Stacia was a nice girl, and pretty—Polish, with wavy strawberry-blond hair and bright blue eyes. She also had a tough-ass shape and flawless skin. Although she looked innocent, Stacia didn't take shit from no one, which was one of the reasons I liked her so much. I thought about that while I watched her sit in the corner with a Spanish girl.

"Yo," Tonya's voice brought me back from my thoughts. "Give me one of them noodles, Robin."

"What? Get out of here," I pushed her playfully.

"Come on, Robin. I swear I'll pay you back!" And for the next few minutes, Tonya begged me for a soup, which reminded me why she got on my nerves. I really only spoke to her 'cause she was my homeboy's wifey.

I looked around me. If this was jail, it wasn't half as bad as I thought it was going to be, at least as far as appearances went.

"Come on, Freaky Ty! Play with us," someone was saying to the girl sitting on the couch with her hands in her pants.

"I'm *already* playin'," the girl responded.

"Yo, you a nasty ho!" another girl yelled. That's when I realized the girl wasn't just sitting there with her hands in her pants to keep them warm. I felt sick. I couldn't believe it.

As my mind whirled, I heard someone say, "Hell, yeah—I be lickin' that clit!" My head shot up. "I be blowing that bitch back out with my ten-inch dildo, too!"

"She take all that?" a girl asked in amazement.

"Hell, yeah!" the first girl said. "I *make* her take all that! I know chicks that take more. Nikki? Upstairs? She be taking a whole shampoo bottle up in her."

"Tonya," I whispered. "Them chicks is trying to be funny, right? 'Cause we fresh meat?"

"Naw, they serious," Tonya said. "She just talkin' 'bout her girl." I looked at her like she was stupid, then turned my attention to the small Spanish girl who'd been talking. She had long, curly hair—blond with black roots. She was an all right looking girl—not manly at all. They must be just playing, I thought.

"When me and my wife be at home, I be bangin' her out on my gold and black satin sheets. I be leavin' her crying, I wear it out so much." Tonya had joined the others' conversation. I think my eyes bugged straight out of my head.

"What you talkin' about, Tonya?" I said.

"I'm talking about my wife."

"Now I know y'all playing 'cause you my boy Kareem's wifey. Y'all got me good," I laughed. Now they was looking at me like I was crazy.

"Girl," Tonya said. "I'm serious. I been with my girl for a minute. I ain't with Kareem no more."

"Yo, they got you, Tonya? They turned you dyke up in here?"

"Girl, I was with my wife on the street," she answered. I shook my head, needing to get this bullshit out of my ears because I couldn't believe all that was going on. Tonya a follower? I didn't believe her. She was lying or trying to be funny. When I collected myself, I looked up—and nearly had a coronary.

The girl that had asked Freaky Ty to come play cards with her had joined her on the couch and was helping her finish her sex act. She had her hands in Ty's pants, and Ty had her head and eyes rolled back. Where the fuck was I? What planet was this?

"Yo!" I yelled. "What the fuck you doing?"

"Getting mine, 'cause I'm horny. Why you think they call me Freaky Ty?"

"Yeah, but you gotta do that shit in front of everybody?" I might've been afraid of Big Bertha, but Freaky Ty was four-ten, four-eleven at the most.

"You in Niantic, now," Freaky Ty laughed. "This how we get *down* in here. You ain't in no baby jail now."

It was too much for me. I went and sat in the corner. Jeannie came up to me a minute later. Neither of us spoke. I watched Sleepy, who looked totally comfortable in this environment. As if reading my thoughts, Jeannie said, "You know Sleepy gone be the first one to turn gay, right?"

"What you mean, 'first one'?" I said. "I ain't no dyke. Fuck what you talkin' 'bou'?" The nerve, I thought: the first one—is she crazy? "I don't know 'bout you, but I ain't *never* gone be gay. F'real!" Jeannie didn't say another word.

The next day, I learned that my friend Stacia was also a lesbian when I found her kissing her Spanish friend from the night before. After she stopped laughing at me for saying, "Oh, my God—they got you, too?" she explained that she'd been in jail for five months. She *had* to be gay, she said, because she *had* to get hers—as if that was the simple answer to a simple question. I soon found out that everyone was gay up in Niantic. *Everyone.* People I'd known my whole life. Married women. Women with ten kids. There was an insane number of butch women in Niantic—none of them the "Big Berthas" of my imagination. And after I stopped mistaking them for male staff, I got adjusted. I really didn't have much choice, especially since, as Jeannie'd predicted, Sleepy turned into a full-fledged lesbian by week two of our incarceration at Camp Ni-Ni.

When I think back at my naïveté upon first coming to Niantic, I have to laugh. I was prejudiced against something I didn't know about or understand. I am still mortified by that first day there, but I now know that not all gay women act like that, and not all butch women are Big Berthas. I swore I would never turn gay, but ten years after riding through that gate, I myself have turned into a full-fledged lesbian. I have been with my girlfriend for three years now and could not imagine my life without her.

Wasted Time

BY LISA WHITE

Now it's just me and my hard-driven guilt
behind these empty walls I've built.
I'm trapped in my body and want to run
back to my youth, to its laughter and fun.

But the chase is over, there's no place to hide—
Everything's gone, including my pride.
I'm scared, alone, and stuck in this place
with reality staring me right in my face.

Serpents

BY ROBIN LEDBETTER

Serpents hiss in low drools.
Snakes—
dressed in nameless jeans
and shapeless tees—
disguised as you or me.
You're a friend of mine.
And best believe I'm on for a lifetime.
I shine, you shine, shine.
Combined, we form a united front.
I ain't gonna let no one hurt you or treat you like no punk.
Someone once told me,
"Time tells the truth of everyone's tale."
A tongue twister,
twisted in my mind in such a way, as common as cliché:
I can now see the forest for the trees.
You see, as time goes on, reality rears its head, and now
I feel your scales as we embrace,
I see the yellow-rimmed eyes in your face,
I notice the swagger in your walk—

a slithering as you pace.
For a long time faint echoes haunt me. Hissing,
"Hey girl, come here." I squint at you,
your fangs retract as you approach.
"I love you, Robin."
I grab my throat, choke
on your words, still sugar-soaked.
Your venom is not transferred through a bite,
you snatch life with your words, stop hearts with no fight.
I can still smell my name, rancid on your breath.
My nostrils fill:
gossip, rumors poison my blood;
envy, back-biting paralyze my mind.
I seize in disillusionment.
You were my friend.
In one last act, you shed your skin,
The basilisk inside stares me in the eye
And I die another death from your betrayal.

The Lights Are Flickering, Again

BY SUSAN BUDLONG COLE*

The lights in the classroom flickered off and back on, the overhead bulbs dimming to amber then returning to normal. The boy across the aisle leaned over to me, grinned, and said, "Betcha don't know they're testing the electric chair down at the prison. They do that before killin' somebody in it."

I can't backtrack over time to the origins of all my core convictions, but I'm confident my abhorrence of the death penalty goes back to the terror created by a local children's myth about flickering lights. I was a committed opponent of capital punishment by the time I was seven.

When I was a child, the state prison was in Old Wethersfield, Connecticut, about where a motor vehicle office is today. First occupied in 1827, the massive stone building dominated Wethersfield Cove, a section of the Connecticut River just south of Hartford. To a kid it was a nightmare of a place—a foreboding medieval fortress. Indeed, the prison housed first the gallows, then its 1937 successor, the electric

---

* Susan Cole, a retired drug and alcohol counselor, is a cofacilitator of the writing workshop.

chair. If the inquisitors had had access to electricity, they would have built an electric chair. The oak-and-leather contraption with its metal head plate would have fit right in with the rack. During my childhood —from the midforties to the late fifties—the People of the state of Connecticut used that chair to kill eleven men.

In September of 2004, the date was set for the People of Connecticut's first execution since electrocuting Joseph "Mad Dog" Taborsky on May 17, 1960. Serial killer Michael Ross was scheduled to die by lethal injection at 2:01 A.M. on January 26. Ross had been convicted and sentenced to death in 1987, and again in 2000 following a second penalty hearing based on a diagnosis of mental illness. Ross admitted to being a sexual sadist who had raped and murdered eight young women, beginning in the early 1980s while a student at Cornell. Two of his victims were from New York and six were killed after Ross returned to Connecticut. He was sentenced to die for four of the murders and to concurrent life sentences for the other four. Either way he would never leave prison alive.

No one questioned the heinous nature of Ross's crimes—nor his guilt, as he readily admitted it. Nor were there questions raised regarding the quality of his representation. In his case there were no accusations of racial or social bias. Ross was a college-educated middle-class young white man at the time he committed these monstrous crimes: a poster boy for the justification of the death penalty. To make it even easier, he conveniently insisted that the execution proceed; he wanted to die. He said there would be no more appeals. The standard arguments of death penalty opponents appeared to be answered.

The problem for me is that it is not about Michael Ross or "Mad Dog" Taborsky or any of the other 102 white men, 7 black men, 2 Asian men, and 2 women executed in Connecticut since 1662 (the year we stopped hanging witches and "sodomites" and started keeping records). It's about state-sanctioned killing of human beings in the name of the People of Connecticut. I and others of like mind—often

Just Another Death

BY CHRISTINA MACNAUGHTON

I sit on my bunk as the minutes tick by. The count should have cleared half an hour ago. In a place where dictated routine is the axis upon which the world revolves, remaining locked for so long past count time sends an invisible electric current through the heart of every inmate. Something is wrong on the compound.

Unfortunately, right now there's no information. Everyone's locked, so the jail grapevine hasn't had a chance to wrap its tendrils around the latest juicy gossip. I hear the CO tell my neighbor, "Get comfy—we're going to be down for the night." Shit! Whatever's caused this lockdown, it's serious. Resigned to an evening of reading and TV, I'm unaware that what I will hear tomorrow will send me racing to the toilet, puking and crying, and wishing to God that I was a better person.

The next morning it's business as usual. I go about my A.M. routine with no more than a thought or two about last night's mysterious lockdown. Someone's bound to fill me in sooner or later. That's the thing about jail gossip: everyone's dying to get their hands on it, and even more eager to give it away.

My hypothesis proves correct when Marisol, a heavy-set Latina I know mostly by reputation, weasels over to me as I walk through the including victims' family members—are revolted by taking any life in our name. We are the People, too.

Of the industrialized democratic nations of the world, only the United States, Japan, and South Korea continue to have death penalty laws on the books. In sheer numbers of executions the United States stands virtually alone. Once proponents' oft-cited reasons for putting certain criminals to death are debunked—and there is ample evidence to discredit the bulk of their arguments—what's left is vengeance. Not all of the People believe vengeance is theirs to mete out.

In addition to opponents' objections related to lack of deterrent value, risk of killing the innocent, high cost of prosecution of death penalty cases versus a life sentence, and the racial and socioeconomic disparity of most cases, it is the sheer barbarity of both the act of killing and the emotional price paid by the People: by juries asked to condemn, victims' families, witnesses, and executioners. The killings diminish us all. It's no accident that executions occur well out of the public eye in the dead of night. In fact we might reasonably ask: if legal killing is such a good thing, then why not conduct executions at high noon? Think about it: if the death penalty is truly a disincentive as some insist, a public execution would raise the deterrent value exponentially.

Not Michael Ross's death, or any of the killings of those currently residing on Connecticut's death row, will make us any safer. The world won't be a better place. Our society will be diminished by yet another assault on the People's striving for a just and merciful community.

At 2:01 A.M. on January 26, 2005, the People collectively pressed the plunger attached to the needle in Michael Ross's arm. His agony was over.

The People of Connecticut cut another notch in their belt, but many wondered why it didn't feel any better.

medical unit—the prison's Grand Central Station. "Can you believe it?" she says. "That girl used a damn *garbage bag* to kill herself with. Ain't that shit *crazy*?"

Marisol's made a career of ferreting out every morsel of jailhouse scandal and circulating it with Internet speed. Now she scrabbles over the wretched details of the previous night's tragedy with the excitement of a carnival rat in the popcorn machine. Her beady, black eyes search my face, hungry for my reaction.

"Wow," I stammer, trying to push the awful visualization from my mind: self-suffocation inside a garbage bag. "Who was it?"

Marisol leans in conspiratorially but, for the benefit of all around, raises her voice fifty or sixty decibels. "Zoë."

My heart crumples like a wad of used tissue. The hot, salty pressure throbbing behind my eyes warns me that I've got about seven seconds to hightail it out of here before I'm guilty of a jail misdemeanor—crying in public. In this world of masterful manipulators, public tears are almost always accompanied by an ulterior motive. True grief and pain are experienced in seclusion, usually within the confines of a shower stall or one's own cell. Far away from my housing unit, I bolt instead to the nearest bathroom. But before the tears have a chance, my stomach bullet-trains in reverse.

I'm not able to reach the toilet in time, so my uniform is suddenly covered in lunch's corn chowder. I kneel on the dank bathroom floor, cradling my sweaty forehead in the crook of my elbow. Snot, spit, and tears swirl together in the bowl and my hair becomes stuck in the slimy condensation on the toilet's outer rim. At any other moment, this would send me reeling in disgust, but now I don't bother to lift my head. Why save my hair when I didn't save my friend?

Three years ago, I had been in the middle of a malaise I called "not any-where." Not quite halfway through my eight-year bid, I was no longer friends with the clique I'd spent the past three years with—but not *not* friends with them either. Jail routine had sucked away my vitality and left me listless and numb. On a rainy gray afternoon, a bony, stray girl had slinked up to me.

"So how's it going?" mumbled the girl, a good head shorter than me. She shifted ungracefully from foot to foot, scratching at her rhubarb-and-custard acne. Her Coke-bottle glasses magnified hungry, dark blue eyes that darted around the room, searching for something to suck up and spit out as conversation. Looking through rather than at her, I murmured something noncommittal. Resigned to my loneliness, I wasn't looking to be engaged by anyone, and I certainly didn't feel like hanging out with someone so unbearably geeky. But before I could walk away, she dashed in front of me and made a second stab at dialogue. Did I have any good books she could borrow? When I mentioned that my books were on Eastern philosophy, her spotty face lit up.

We chatted away the afternoon. Talking with her was instantly easy and comfortable, and hours of conversation soon became our standard. Without the normal jail pretenses, we discussed everything from politics to our kids. We developed a game, My Mom's Worse than Your Mom, going back and forth until we were both rolling with laughter. As we talked one afternoon, I began styling her long, blond hair.

"Why don't you take better care of yourself in here, Zoë? Your hair's just awful." She looked like she'd spent the better part of the afternoon curled up beneath a car engine. "Maybe we could try a little makeup sometime."

"I want to look nice, but I know I'm not pretty. Do you know how to do makeup?" I pulled out different colored pencils, eyeliners, and hair products. The apathy of three years melted away as I made this girl my pet project. We experimented every day for weeks, trying to find ways to brighten her shabby appearance. We bonded over eye shadow and hair gel. Giddy from the interest I took in her, Zoë basked in the attention of being my Eliza Dolittle.

One morning, while trying an up-do on Zoë I'd seen in a magazine, I noticed a gruesome burn on the back of her neck. "Jesus Christ, Zoë! How the hell did you get burned like this?" My fingers touched the ghastly purple and peach scar. The welt was the size of a silver dollar.

"Oh," she tittered, pushing my hand away. "I had a tattoo—my girl's name. Then I found out she was cheating on me, so I burned it off with a curling iron. I had to leave the iron on for a long time before her name came all the way off. I put it back on when we got back together. See?" Zoë yanked up her pant leg, exposing the ugly, amateur jail tattoo on her ankle.

Zoë participated in one of prison's most popular pastimes—the jail relationship. Relationships in jail are almost never about attraction, affection, or love. They're about control, manipulation, and loneliness. Women who have spent years trading their bodies for drugs, alcohol, clothes, and cars have a hard time stopping a behavior that has worked so well. Other women fall into jail relationships out of boredom, or because facing this life alone is too bleak to bear.

Zoë fell into the latter group. She'd struck up a friendship with another inmate, and their involvement had quickly escalated into a typical dysfunctional jail relationship. Zoë's girl was a regular in the mental health unit, known for stunts like trying to slice the arteries of her wrists with a pair of nail clippers and smashing TVs to cut herself on the shards of glass. Their roller coaster relationship was a constant source of drama, and thus a remedy to the daily ennui. Three times a day Zoë dashed to the dining hall as fast as walkway rules would allow. Repeatedly, she risked serious trouble by entering buildings without permission to meet up with her girlfriend. In passionate letters and fleeting encounters, the two would declare their undying love for each other. A few days later, they would curse each other to the ends of the earth. During off periods, Zoë often enlisted me to help rankle her girlfriend.

Zoë had dropped her girl for cheating on her, again. Many times a day we passed the housing unit where Zoë's partner lived. The girl's cell window looked straight out onto the walkway.

"Please, Chris, when we go past, pretend I'm saying something really funny, really great, okay? You know, start laughing and stuff. I want her to know I don't need her, that I've got other people in my life now."

"Oh, Zoë, you've got to be kidding me! How junior high can you possibly get?" Annoyed at her foolishness, I walked ahead of her, then looked back to see her teary, pleading face.

"Please," she whispered, "I just want her to see I've got friends." So we laughed like lunatics at nothing, five or six times a day.

The last real day of our friendship was a Sunday. Zoë purred as I fixed her hair for church. "When she sees me, my girl's gonna drop that other chick—I know it. She's gonna come back to me for good this time." She checked and rechecked her appearance in the mirror—something she normally avoided doing. For extra luck, I lent her my nicest pair of jeans and best sweatshirt. "Knock 'em dead!" I cheered as she left for services. Strutting out the door, she threw me a Cheshire cat smile.

An hour later the CO called a lockdown, and we all shuffled into our assigned cells. From my tiny window, I strained to see what was going on. Finally someone with a better view called out that Zoë was handcuffed and being dragged away backwards, surrounded by guards. My heart plummeted. I learned that at church she'd jumped her rival and smashed her skull open against a metal pillar. "Oh, man, why'd you do that, Zoë?" I muttered.

"Yeah," my cellmate smirked. "You're never going to get your clothes back now."

"Oh, shut up!" I snapped, aggravated that I'd been caught thinking exactly that.

Zoë's assault earned her a two-week trip to seg, and a smattering of fame. Suddenly, everyone on the compound knew about the scrappy blonde. She became drunk off the shot of notoriety she'd received. Although she had jumped the girl from behind, Zoë suddenly fancied herself a "thug." She and I didn't see each other very often after that. I'd spot her in passing, surrounded by a swarm of parasitic people who'd hookwormed themselves to her and her newfound "rep." Zoë didn't want to talk about Buddhism anymore; she now only read *The Source.* No longer did my friend hum Nickelback songs to herself while lost in thought. Her vocabulary had shrunk to words like "hos," "yo," and "dap." Eliza Dolittle had become Li'l Kim.

At one point, Zoë left jail, only to return a few months later, having earned her "frequent flyer" status. I had moved on, both literally and figuratively. Our final conversation happened in the medical unit. Zoë was alone, stripped of her former celebrity status. She was grotesquely thin, a dead giveaway as to her activities while on the ouside. All the former bravado was gone. In this sad state, she seemed again like the Zoë I'd first befriended. But I was still furious with her. "Welcome back," I sneered. "What are you in for *this* time?"

"Ohmigod, Chris, I missed you *so* much. I'm telling you, I was *so* good out there. Honest. Then I ran into some old friends and one thing led to another." She slumped against the cold concrete wall. "I really tried this time."

"Yeah, well, I hope your 'old friends' take care of you while you're here. When you came in, you were all about recovery and getting your life together. Then you left and totally forgot about the people who took care of you—*before* you were cool. You never even wrote to me when you left. I know you wrote your girl even though she's been seeing somebody else for months. How do you think that makes me feel?"

Zoë's mouth started to form words, but no sound accompanied them. Her eyes fell to the floor. When I realized no explanation was forthcoming, I stomped off, my rage vented. She left prison again a short while later. I found out she was back the afternoon Marisol told me she'd died. We had never made amends.

Zoë killed herself on the evening of June 21, 2006—a Wednesday, the longest day of the year. Life here hasn't changed because of her violent death. I still do my dishes in the sink above my toilet. I still worry about the next shakedown. I wear the same clothes I wore when I met Zoë; they are the same clothes I wore the day she died. The compound is no different either. The day after Zoë's death, a new girl was sleeping in her bed and wearing her uniform. There was a memorial service, but I couldn't bring myself to go. From what I heard, my friend's life was reduced to a three-sentence eulogy, squeezed in between announcements for an upcoming Bible study and a reminder to please pick up our candy wrappers from the chapel floor. It was standard DOC.

Zoë's girlfriend is long gone, as is most of the crew she hooked up with during her thug phase. There is no one left to speak for her or remember her. Like a vast, black ocean, the prison swallowed her up. Zoë is just another death. Two weeks later, the memory of her has vanished as well. Still, she is part of every woman here.

I walk her path every single day. I stand in the same chow hall line, order the same commissary, look out on the same compound. I am herded like a sheep from one area to another, just as she was, just as every inmate is. I've owned her despair and her loneliness. There are days when I avoid the mirror just as she did. At night when I sit alone and face myself, it's sometimes more than I can take. I know what her desperate thoughts were in the moments leading up to her death—I've been there too many times to count. I've choked back the same hopeless sobs at two in the morning. So what made her do it, and not me? What desperate thought pushed her hand that night? Will it one day push mine?

V.
I'll Fly Away

*Holding on to anger is like grasping a
hot coal with the intent of throwing it at someone else.
You are the one who gets burned.*

—THE BUDDHA

*When I stand before thee at the day's end,
thou shalt see my scars and know that I had my
wounds and also my healing.*

—RABINDRANATH TAGORE

*Another world is not only possible, she is on her way.
On a quiet day, I can hear her breathing.*

—ARUNDHATI ROY

My Three Fates

BY CHASITY C. WEST

The sound of shuffling paper broke the silence that engulfed the room. The door leading from the hallway into the courtroom opened with a hollow, woody swoosh. In filed the jury, exhausted and solemn. Juror number eleven—white male, retired electrician—nervously polished his bifocals with the hem of his shirt. Alternate juror number two—musician—took a seat, raked hand through dark hair, and sighed. The foreman—midforties, dirty-blond hair, cable technician—had flushed cheeks and a furrowed brow, but his face was otherwise expressionless. He handed a folded sheet of paper to the sheriff. This single sheet of paper would reveal the results of two weeks' worth of deliberations that would either emancipate or condemn me.

Before the verdict was read aloud, the judge scanned the sheet of paper. Peering over his reading spectacles, his eyes cut across the courtroom and fell upon me. I could read little from his expression; I saw only his eyebrows rise, heard only his deep sigh. But I felt the news could not be good. Was I just being negative and pessimistic, somehow demonized by my own trial? Maybe the judge, a former prosecutor, was disappointed with a *favorable* return, displeased with the result of a case that he had practically handed to the state with his rulings? In another moment, I would know.

The jury—had even one member looked at me when they walked in and took their seats? If they had, I hadn't noticed. I couldn't look up from the tabletop. I was too afraid. Instead, I saw a blue fountain pen, a stack of papers, a box of tissues, a white binder with the words *State of Connecticut v. Chasity West* printed in bold black letters.

I forced myself to look up from the table and face my jurors—the twelve who had determined my fate. *Look at me! Look at me!* I thought as I stole swift, tortured glances. I looked only long enough to notice that some of my jurors were crying. Juror number five—student, black female, thirty-one years old—was holding wadded tissues to her face, her shoulders rising and falling. Jurors number seven, one, and three: all crying. What do tears mean? If the jury looks at the defendant, that's good, right? If they don't, it's bad? But tears? No one had prepared me for tears.

Bracing myself, I gripped Faith's hand; my lawyer was now my closest friend. The foreman cleared his throat and read the verdict. The two prosecutors—a white woman of retirement age with bleached hair and a masculine woman with a permanent scowl—peered at me through eyeglasses that made their eyes seem as big as cartoon characters. Both wore the same victory smirk.

"Guilty." My knees buckled and I stumbled back. Faith, who'd sat beside me for weeks, arguing for my freedom, held and consoled me as I wept into her shoulder. "Guilty." With a gentle, repetitive pat on the back, she reassured me that this was not over. "It'll be okay, Chas," Faith said, struggling to keep her voice intact. "This is only round one in a fifteen-round fight. Don't give up."

Howie, her partner, stood beside us with a solemn expression on his face, his hands stuffed into his pockets. "We'll appeal, kiddo," he offered.

"I know it's hard, but try to control yourself," Faith whispered. "You

don't want them throwing you into that room when you go back."
I tried to stifle the tears but, instead, cried harder than I'd ever cried in my life. I cried until my voice caught in my throat, until all that remained was a steady flow of tears and a body heaving for air. Despite Faith's words, I knew it would *not* be okay.

The room was packed with reporters, sheriffs, lawyers, family, friends, and foes. Behind me on the wooden bench, my parents cried bitter tears. As I watched them weep over their lost daughter, the disheartening truth was that, if this sentence stood, I would never be able to bring forth life into the world. I would never experience motherhood. I would never make my mother and father grandparents. Instead, I would sit back helplessly over the course of their weekly visits and watch them gradually gray and wrinkle, stoop and shrink. Perhaps over the years, they would begin to forget things until they could no longer make the trip down to Niantic prison or remember me at all. My sister, ten years old when I'd been taken away, would blossom, go off to college, marry, and have children of her own without having the opportunity to really know me or to reap the rewards a big sister could bestow. My older brother had lost his childhood playmate, my younger brother his childhood tormentor. All five had sat behind me, strong and lovingly, throughout my trial. Now they held on to each other, broken, their faces buried in their hands.

The rush of emotions coming at me ranged from self-pity to a rage that swelled every capillary in my throbbing head. My thoughts, fleeting and fragmented, were a patternless patchwork of frayed fabric and loose stitches. But suddenly my mind seized on a thought that seemed more rational than any I'd had in the last six years of my life: suicide. *I* would decide whether to live or die, not this jury. The idea was so beautiful in its simplicity that I almost laughed out loud. Suicide. I repeated the word over and over in my head until an unfamiliar sense of serenity enveloped me. I now knew that I was going to die, but *I* would determine when that would be.

My nose ran over my top lip, and I sniffled and buried my face in the safety of Faith's shoulder. The suspense was over. The dam had finally broken. After the three-year wait in York Prison for Women, the pains-taking four-month process of choosing a jury, the grueling eleven-week trial, and two weeks of waiting for the jury to return a verdict, every-thing up to and including that verdict began to seep out of my body and onto the lapel of Faith's navy blue suit jacket. Whatever "every-thing" was or still is, I'm not quite sure, because if I truly knew, I do not think I would have ever found myself in prison. What I do know, however, is pain. And on that day, my heart bled, flowing from my body in the form of tears.

Why had I chosen the men that I had—the men I'd settled for? Why had I always felt like I didn't deserve better? Why had I bought and stolen love? How was it that I had found myself seated in the defen-dant's chair? I was someone who had never had so much as a speeding ticket. I had given my parents minimal trouble growing up and had finished high school. I'd stayed away from drugs and alcohol. I'd gone to nursing school and tried to be a good citizen, a good daughter, a good sister, cousin, granddaughter, niece, and friend. Now I had nothing to show for that life but a murder conviction and one of two options: a life in prison without the possibility of parole, or a state of Connecticut–sanctioned death by lethal injection.

The judge, whose posture seemed more slumped than usual, exhaled deeply again and continued to shuffle papers as he set a date for the penalty phase. Though my tears had stopped flowing, I continued to cry. My heart ached as it pounded against my chest. I could feel the burn of a buried anger whose roots were embedded deep in the anguish of having been misunderstood my entire life. My face was blank and my mind was oblivious to what was happening around me, but a powerful internal storm was gathering quickly and tearing through everything it touched.

I had taken brief, painful glimpses of my former lover during his testimony. Although his daggerlike words had helped to seal my conviction, it was the hurt that did me in. Now I watched him being comforted by aunts, cousins, and grandparents, blood relatives who had offered me only their scornful judgment. I could no longer recognize them as the people I'd once known. Hadn't I been in enough trouble without their rejection? Hadn't I been troubled enough?

The courtroom was bustling from the verdict. Guilty! Guilty! Guilty on all counts! Sniffling, I blew my nose into a flimsy piece of tissue that Gladys, a stout African American sheriff, had plucked from the tissue box on the table in front of me. "Here, honey," she'd said, then plucked another tissue for herself.

"I'm sorry, Faith," I said

"No, I'm sorry, Chasity. I'm sorry this happened to you. I know that you really wanted to go home. You're a good girl." She was crying now, too, wiping a tear from her cheek with the back of her finger.

"No, no, Faith. I mean I'm sorry about *that*." Her blue eyes followed my pointed finger to where I'd left a smear of tears and slobber on the lapel and down the sleeve of her suit jacket. "I'll have my dad pay for your dry cleaning," I said.

Smiling, she tucked a wayward tuft of her straw-blond hair behind her ear. "Don't worry about that," she said. "Dry cleaning's covered in my fee."

It was five o'clock, Friday the thirteenth. I had hoped to be running into my parents' outstretched arms and heading home to Windsor. Instead I was heading back to prison. Seated in the back of the DOC van—chained, numb, out of my body—I knew that this final blow had left my heart and soul critically wounded. Passing Bushnell Park, I stared out the window at women in business suits and sneakers, power-walking in gossipy bunches. I saw a young woman around my age rollerblading. She had tied her sweatshirt around her waist and become lost somewhere between the music coming from her headphones and the radiant sunshine that beamed down on her. That could have been me, I thought. Instead, I was being returned to the place where I would die. This might be the last time that I'd ever ride in a vehicle anywhere—the last time I would ever leave Niantic Prison for Women alive. All cried out, I sat and listened to the hum of the engine. The police cruiser that had escorted the van with flashing lights had detoured miles earlier, leaving us to find our way back to the prison. The two guards riding up front, normally brimming with small talk and corny jokes, were somber and silent. The quiet settled deep into my belly.

The chains I wore felt heavier than usual as I stepped out of the vehicle. I felt frail and spent—as if the trial had eaten away pieces of my body from the inside out, leaving me hollow and cored. If the wind had risen up at that very second, it might have blown me away like the spores of a dandelion, leaving nothing except a pile of chains. Closing my eyes against the lens of the video camera the guard in Admissions and Processing held, I imagined a huge gust coming to rescue me. If my savior had come at that moment, I would have willingly betrayed my body, separating from the shell that was to be stripped, outfitted in a paper gown, and locked in an isolated cell in the mental health unit for "observation." I had been forced to endure such scrutiny too many times before. But this time, I would have flown away, only to return in the middle of the night and tap gently on the window. My body would awaken easily. Ever since I was a child, I'd been afraid of the dark, but now the arrival of my spirit would interrupt my praying, my questioning and cursing God. Maybe my arrival would save me from saying angry words I really didn't mean—from sealing my own eternal damnation. I wouldn't stay long, just long enough to make my presence known, to reassure that wretched and comely shell of incarcerated bones and skin that I was safe and not alone. I would sit by the window until daybreak. Come morning light, I would fly away again.

Seated on the corner of the cot, I replayed testimony and relived the gory crime-scene photographs. I rewound statements collected by the Windsor police and the major crime squad. I reran the expert medical opinions, the autopsy report. I saw my former lover, sitting exempt in the comfort of family and forgiveness. Everything that had transpired played over and over and over in my head, haunting me. Excerpts from the trial. Excerpts from my life. I crossed my legs and adjusted the flimsy paper gown I wore. It had already ripped, so I slipped it off and pulled the stiff blanket over my body to shield me from the stream of cold air being forced out of the overhead vent. Though I'd been raised to be a lady, my nakedness meant nothing to me now. I resented being trapped in this body sitting cross-legged on the cot. Smiling politely each time a familiar face walked past and waved, I was unsure of what to feel. Having become conditioned to feel nothing at all, I now was forced to sit there with no one but myself and *feel*.

I felt prickly with embarrassment every time a guard or a nurse walked by and peered into the cell. What I call "the process" had begun. The process started with a look. All who passed the cell and looked in wore that same awkward expression on their faces: the look of not knowing what to say or whether to say anything at all. The look of wishing they hadn't looked in because now they were forced to make that decision. Yesterday I'd been sane. Today I was not. I would not regain the right to call myself sane until a doctor who'd met me only minutes earlier scribbled on a sheet of paper that I was. Maybe it would be Monday morning; maybe it wouldn't. Whether Monday or Wednesday or the week after that, I would be released from this cold, locked room to return to another—to be, once again, among the "normal," the "uncrazy." But for now I must sit in this barren room listed as "certifiably crazy." Sanity and insanity were separated by a steel door and a Plexiglass window and the signature of an anonymous doctor. I imagined I must have looked convincingly insane: naked, puffy-eyed, pacing in circles, hair awry, comforting myself by whispering songs my mother had once sung to me as a child. Each time someone peered into the cell, I wanted to scream, "This is all a big misunderstanding! I'm not crazy! I don't belong here! I'm a *good* girl!" Instead, I straightened my posture, smoothed my hair with my hand, and turned away from the door. They're *trying* to make me crazy, I thought. I saw a fleeting image of myself: body hanging limp from a makeshift ceiling noose. I wanted nothing more than to disappear, to fold into myself over and over again until I was nothing.

I stared at the peeling gray walls, at a silhouette of someone who'd tried to trace herself by a shadow cast at midday. "Naynay loves Punkin'," was scribbled in pencil. Below that, "Tiny gives dead-head!" and "Hard hittin' New Britain," scratched on the door jamb. On the adjacent wall, "This place sucks." I concurred. Finally I saw it, etched in the paint in shaky script: "Jesus saves." Does he? Well, where was Jesus now?

As the evening progressed, the narrow beam of light that shone through the cell's only window disappeared with the day. Outside my cell door, I heard a small commotion: jingling keys, squeaky stainless-steel dinner cars, overlapping voices. The trap on the door fell open. A hand and a Styrofoam tray came in through the peek space.

"You get no utensils," the disembodied voice said. "Tear off a corner of the tray and try to scoop up your food, or just eat with your hands." When I didn't respond, I heard the keys again. The door quickly opened and closed. On the floor was a tray and a carton of milk. For what seemed like hours, I sat in my corner of the floor, wrapped in my blanket, tormented by solitude.

The next thing I'm about to tell you could have been a dream. For my own peace of mind, I'd like to believe it was. But whether I dreamt, imagined, or hallucinated the events that took place, I do not know for sure. I know only that the things I saw were and still are very real to me.

As night settled in, I began to hear strange popping noises coming out of nowhere. I recognized it as the crackle of old film feeding through the reel of a projector. A lighted area appeared on the wall opposite me. A spread of black-and-white images appeared. Possibly hundreds of still photographs flipped rapidly, creating the illusion of movement like those grainy, old-fashioned movie snippets from the silent-film era. The first scene was of a cinder-block wall streaked with inky fingerprints. The trail led to a girl lying facedown in a pool of blood. A jagged slice shone on her upturned wrist. My breath caught in my chest. *The year is 2001. The month is July. Today is Friday the thirteenth. The president of the United States is George W. Bush. The governor is John Rowland.*

In the next scene, I saw a blindfolded woman. She was strapped to a gurney while technicians forced poison into her veins with syringes. Her arms abducted from her sides, held in place by restraints. Paralyzed, she ceased to breathe. Her heart stopped. Her twenty-first-century crucifixion was completed. *The year is 2001. The month is July. I was born on the fifth of August. Today is Friday, no, Saturday. Or maybe it is Friday? Friday the thirteenth is a cursed day.*

Another scene flickered by. Again, a woman—but this one was old and senile and had milky eyes and a dimple of a mouth. She sat by a window looking out at razor wire and fence. She was not yet dead, but close. She no longer remembered where she was or who she was. She just sat and waited for death to come and take her home.

I did not recognize this woman, but somehow I knew that she was me. They were all me somehow. So there they were: my three fates, none more attractive than the other. *The year is 2001! Today is August fifth! Mom? Dad? Can you hear me? Can you hear me? Can you hear me, goddammit! Jehovah? Allah? Buddha? Can you hear me? Somebody! Anybody!*

The last image faded and the lighted area dulled, leaving only the popping sound. I sat in the dark cell unable to move, with only the dull, crackling noise to keep me company. . . .

I remained in this state of disquietude for hours, maybe even for days—I'm really not sure. But I continued to be haunted by images and omens. I tried to salvage some of the hope I once had had, to rekindle and renew it. I tried to convince myself that Faith was right. That everything *would* be okay. I imagined her speaking to me with her concerned, beautiful blue eyes, her shoulder-length hair with traditional bangs, wearing her favorite navy blue suit. Maybe if I really put my mind to it, I could gather enough hope to make these walls crumble at my feet, rewind time, change the course of my fate. I began to soothe myself with Faith's words, "It'll be okay, Chas."

I don't think I slept. I don't know if it's possible for a human being to remain awake for days at a time, but I believe I did. But then again, I don't think I was actually human during that time. When I finally tried to sleep, I saw Dr. Sanchez, the house psychiatrist, enter the cell wearing a ruffled shirt and black slacks, his salt-and-pepper hair greased back, the tips of his mustache curled upward. I saw myself leave the cot to join Dr. Sanchez in the middle of the floor.

I was beautiful. My hair was styled into a sophisticated coil that rested slightly off center at the nape of my neck. I wore a long, flowing, red skirt with a deep slit and a ruffled hem. My lips were coated in scarlet lipstick. Secured to my fingertips were castanets. Between my lips, I held a single long-stem red rose.

Dr. Sanchez stood with a smoldering expression on his face, his posture erect. Banging a tambourine against his hip, he stomped curtly in a small circle, his high-polished wing-tipped shoes clicking with every step. With one abrupt and final stomp, he extended his hand, arm poised to receive me. Pointing my toe, I brought myself to him, taking slow, deliberate strides in black stilettos. My breasts spilled over the top of a low-cut, sleeveless lace blouse. Another rose—this one in full bloom—was tucked behind my ear, complementing my black crystal chandelier earrings. Saucy rhythms filled my head until I was no longer able to hear the guards' blaring radios or the screams of the other prisoners. Only tambourines, maracas, bongo and conga drums, and the *click, click, click* of castanets. The music was soft at first but soon grew bold and boomed inside my skull until I thought my eyes would explode.

We danced the flamenco until I could no longer differentiate my own image from Dr. Sanchez's. We were only blurs of color: black, white, and crimson—a blend of doom, nothingness, and blood. I watched my mirage whirl through the room, onto the walls, and up to the ceiling until my eyes grew heavy and the pounding in my head subsided. I could fall asleep now to the blaring of the guards' radios and the screams of other prisoners like myself.

Dance of the Willow

BY KELLY DONNELLY

Willow sways and dances
to the hum of earth and sky.
In her reflection
by the still and quiet water
she waits for the call of her Creator
and the whippoorwill.

I Won't Burn Alone

BY BRENDALIS MEDINA

Sherry decides she's going to put her clothes in the dryer, and it's too much trouble to wait the extra five seconds while they finish the spin cycle. Ignoring the red light that indicates the door is locked, she yanks it open, breaking the washing machine.

"What the hell you do that for?" Tasha screams. "We just got that washer and they're not gonna give us another one."

"I just wanted to dry my clothes!" Sherry screams back.

Alice joins in. "You couldn't wait? Now you broke it, you dumb bitch!" Within seconds, everyone on the tier has become involved, shouting rather than speaking their points. I feel my face getting hot. I know we won't get another machine for a while; the COs don't care if we have clean clothes or not. So now I'm pissed, too. But saying nothing, I retreat to my room, leaving them out there to kill each other.

"I can't stand these bitches!" I scream, landing my fist against the locked cell door. I throw a couple more punches. Later, I'll feel the pain in my hand and regret what I'm doing, but for the moment my anger is all that matters.

"Brenda, what happened?" my roommate asks.

I stand before her and stare, then finally blurt, "I hate this place and all the people in it!" I plop myself on the counter as a way of declaring our conversation is over. I'd been fine one minute, throwing punches the next. It seems like any little thing can set me off whenever I go out on the tier. Why am I so angry?

I've always had a hard time tolerating ignorance, and in this place, it's epidemic. So I often get aggravated and frustrated, and when I do, my aggravation and frustration often turn to rage. I blame my anger on the fact that I've been in jail for so long, and although that's partly true, it isn't the whole truth. Explosive anger lived deep inside me long before I ever came to prison, sometimes erupting through the surface without my understanding why or how.

As I stare out the window, studying the sky, my mind wanders back to my Catholic school years and I think of Sister Rosemary. I can see her standing with her Bible tightly gripped in her hand, frowning as she describes the flames of hell. "Children, if you follow the path of sin, you will burn for eternity." I can't help but wonder what Sister would say if she could see how I turned out: in jail for the long haul, wrestling with one of the seven deadly sins on a daily basis. I imagine her making the sign of the cross and warning me, *Child, the sin of wrath will condemn you to the eternal flames.* Well, if Sister's right, then I'll burn in hell for sure. But I won't be burning alone. The people I used to run with were all guilty of the same sin. And I remember vividly the day the anger consumed us all—the day Ed died. . . .

I trudged up Baldwin Street, wondering why the president of our "family" had called this emergency meeting. Nearing the abandoned building that served as the Unidad's headquarters, I saw the crowd milling around outside. It looked like every member of the family had gathered. People were crying and hugging each other. Whatever had happened was really bad, and I approached with a sense of dread.

I entered the building and headed upstairs without a word. On the second-floor landing, I ran into Juan, one of the brothers. I extended my hands to give him the special handshake, but Juan caught me off guard, pulling me close and hugging me long and hard. When I pulled away, I asked him what had happened. Juan's eyes widened with surprise. "Nobody told you?"

"I have no idea what's going on."

"Ed got killed last night."

Juan fell against me and began to sob, but rather than comfort him, I stood in shock, a chill running through my body. *They killed Ed*: those words kept ringing in my head. I closed my eyes and pictured him: lanky body, brown eyes, soft black hair, caramel skin. And that to-die-for smile. Ed was fun and loving—crazy at times, but in a silly way. I could see him running up and down the street chanting, "Oohroo kakoohroo." The nonsense phrase was something he had made up one night as he played with a toy skull, holding it in his hand and making its jaws open and close. "Oohroo kakoohroo." He'd uttered it so frequently that eventually it had become our warning signal. Whenever a rival gang was near or the cops were about to cruise by, you would hear, "Oohroo kakoohroo." It sounded like a voodoo chant.

As memories of Ed filled my head, I felt my face dampen with tears. The more I spoke to the other brothers and sisters, the crazier it all seemed. It wasn't until Marvin, a young, short brother, came down to the house that everything became clear.

Marvin was Ed's best friend and he'd been with him when everything had gone down. He told the story with a dry tightness in his throat, and I shut my eyes and pictured it unfolding. After Marvin and Ed had come back from celebrating Ed's nineteenth birthday at the bar, they headed up Willow Street, where they ran into Mara, Ed's girlfriend. It was about three in the morning and Mara was furious with Ed for standing her up. Their argument got so loud that the people whose house they were standing in front of were awakened. A guy not much older than Ed stuck his head out his window and yelled for them to

shut up. Ed screamed back. When the guy came outside, the confrontation turned physical. Ed got the best of the guy, who became furious
that he had gotten a beat-down from the guy who'd woken him up.
There was no way he was leaving it like that. He ran inside, coming
back out with a gun in his hand. As Ed moved toward him, he fired four
shots. Ed reached the bottom of the porch stairs and dropped. Three of
those four bullets had hit him. As Mara held her head screaming, Marvin ran to his friend. Ed bled to death in his arms.

I went outside, and that's when the real nightmare began. The sisters stood off to the side, watching the brothers as they drew up the
blueprints of their revenge. They huddled together, some crying, others
cursing and slamming their fists on parked cars and walls as they spoke.
More brothers arrived, armed with bats, knives, and guns. Someone
pulled up in a U-Haul truck and, one by one, Ed's avengers climbed
in. I trembled as I watched. Before Marvin jumped into the truck, he
turned to us girls and made the gang sign. That's when I saw my older
brother, David. My blood was a part of this ugly mission, too, and I felt
sick to my stomach. David's eyes met mine for a few seconds before he
dropped his eyes to the ground and climbed in. When the truck was
filled, the brothers drove off to hunt for Ed's killer, who, by his rage-
filled action, had signed his own death warrant.

The search lasted for hours but was unsuccessful. Apparently, Ed's
killer had learned that his victim had belonged to the Unidad and he
had fled. His father must have known what that meant, too, because
in an attempt to save his son, he had gone to the police and confessed
to the murder. The ploy hadn't worked—too many witnesses had seen
otherwise. The brothers quit for that night, but they vowed they would
not rest until another life was taken.

No one sold their street drugs that night—the shop was closed.
We shared stories about Ed and comforted one another. For a few
rare moments, we were united like the family we had always claimed
to be.

I stood in a corner with Marvin, Juan, and two of the sisters. "It's crazy," I said, shaking my head in disbelief.

"I can't believe he's gone," Marvin mumbled.

Surprisingly, Juan began to laugh. "You guys remember when we went pool-hopping that time?" he said. "Ed was so crazy. He's gonna be missed."

We all fell silent. Marvin pulled out a forty-ounce of Private Stock and held it out in the middle of our small circle. We all knew what that meant. I tapped the bottom of the bottle, then the cap. Everyone followed suit. Marvin twisted off the cap, tilted the bottle, and said, "For Ed." He spilled some beer on the ground. That was one of our rituals for a fallen brother or sister; I had observed the custom before, but it had never carried as much meaning as it did that night.

Juan started telling the pool-hopping story, and as I listened, I, too, remembered a special moment I'd shared with Ed. It was Saturday night and I'd had a bad argument with my mother. I couldn't recall what we'd fought about, but I remembered storming out of our apartment, vowing not to return.

Baldwin Street had been empty that night. No one was at the abandoned building except for a few older brothers who were working on getting drunk. Because I didn't know them well, I didn't feel comfortable staying there. I went back outside and walked up and down Baldwin Street. I had nowhere else to go, but I refused to go back home. Finally, I headed back to the building, dragging my feet. Ed was coming down the stairs. "Brenda, what's up?" he asked, flashing that smile. "Why are you out so late by yourself?"

"I had a fight with my mother," I said. "I'm staying here tonight."

He looked toward the second floor and then back to me. "Not when those guys are drunk, you're not."

"Well, I'll just keep walking around then, because I'm *not* going back home."

"By yourself?"

"Why not?"

Ed stared at me for a second, then grabbed my arm. "Come on," he said. We walked around for a while in silence. It was starting to get chilly and we had no plan, no destination. In front of Manny's Pizza, Ed said, "I'm going to keep you company tonight, but I'm going to have to find us a ride because we can't walk around all night."

"Ed, just go home. I'll be fine," I said.

"No. I'm not leaving you alone. I'd let you come home with me, but my mom would freak."

"Okay, so just stay at the abandoned building with me," I said.

He shook his head. "I sleep heavy." I knew what he was trying to say: if one of the older men tried something stupid with me, he wouldn't hear it.

Ed took off running. A few minutes later, he pulled up in a green Toyota, swung open the passenger-side door, and told me to get in. And because my only other choice was to go home, I did. Ed drove onto the highway and headed for New Britain. He knew some of the brothers from that chapter, so we hung out with them for a few hours. Then we headed for Hartford. We drove around all night and didn't get back to Waterbury until the sun was up. I knew it was wrong for Ed to have stolen that car, but I also knew he'd had a place to go home to that night. He'd done it for me so that I'd be safe. I would always be grateful to Ed for that.

I was roused from that memory when Marvin nudged my arm and passed me the 40-ounce. I could've shared my story with Marvin and the others, but I wanted to keep that special moment just between Ed and me. So I just took a sip of the beer and said, "Ed is going to be missed."

Three days later, I stood in front of the funeral home on Willow Street. Hundreds of people were there—fewer than fifty were Ed's blood relatives. His Unidad family had come from everywhere: the Hartford, Meriden, New Britain, and Middletown chapters were there. The cops were there, too. They knew a gang member had been killed, and that a convergence of gang members from all over Connecticut could mean trouble—maybe even the launch of a street war.

Ed's mom knew who we were, but she accepted that Ed had been a part of us. She had allowed the Unidad to help pay for the funeral arrangements. I greeted those members I knew, met many I hadn't known, and hugged the ones I ran with every day. After everyone had paid their respects and it was nearly time to go, word spread that all members of the Unidad were to get in our circle—a ritual we did at our weekly meetings. Ed's younger brother took his place in the circle that began around Ed's casket and ended outside the funeral home. Other mourners stared at us in silence and the cops held their collective breath. When in place, we grabbed each other's hands and started our other meeting ritual. The Hartford president—the big man—cleared his throat and in a booming voice asked, "Whose father?" We all answered with the Lord's Prayer. After our amens, we made the gang sign and gave the collective shout, "Always united!" Then, without prior planning, many of us in the Waterbury chapter, the majority in tears, started screaming, "Oohroo kakoohroo!" It was sad and strange—beautiful in its own way.

When the spiritual moment was over, the anger returned and the guys went back to their planning. As I watched them curse and vow revenge on the one who had caused us this sorrow, I asked God to save us from our pain, anger, and hatred. I wanted to run far away, or stay and scream to my brothers and sisters, "Enough! How many of us have to die before it stops?" Instead, I sat on the steps of the funeral home and wept. My tears were for Ed, the friend I'd never see again, and for my brothers who were blinded by their thirst for vengeance. Then I cried for myself, who was no different from them because, secretly, I also wanted to see Ed's killer dead.

Click! The popping of the prison doors returns me to reality. "Bren, are you coming out to the tier?" Jen asks. I nod and she props the door open, then disappears. I look out the window once more and remember how I had felt years ago, sitting on those funeral steps, praying that God would save us. It seems he never did hear that prayer. Ed's killer was never found, but we all dealt with our pain in different ways. As time passed, we lost more brothers. Marvin and David both served time for attempted murder. Last I heard of Juan, he was on the run for taking someone's life. As for me, my anger deepened and distilled over the years. It was no longer a simple emotion for me; it had become a way of life that had ended with a twenty-five-year prison sentence.

The next day I find myself at Bible study, for all the wrong reasons. Because I'm only there to meet up with my friend, I pay no attention to the woman who is preaching the word of the Lord. As far as I'm concerned, God evacuated my life long ago. Why should I listen to him now?

After Bible study, I wait for my friend while Sister Shareese prays for her. Then, suddenly, the preacher is looking directly at me. I try to make a run for it, but she touches my arm, then places both hands on my shoulders. "Is there any special request you would like to ask God to grant?"

My anger rises in me and I blurt out, "God abandoned me years ago."

Sister Shareese doesn't try to tell me I'm wrong, or that God loves me and will be my salvation. She just stands there with her hands on my shoulders, her gaze holding me. It is almost as if she knows my story and my pain without my having spoken a word. I stare deeply into her brown eyes. I see an incredible peace in them—a peace I want.

Seasons' Rhythms

BY KELLY DONNELLY

(FOR SHA SHA)

Early spring, she walks
the soft, damp trail,
delicious with the smell
of leaves, decayed by
snow and rain. Soon,
this decay births dark,
fertile earth.

She bathes in the energy
of summer's sun. The tide
guides her, edging along
sapphire waters.
Her spirit soaring,
she feels its rhythm.

Memories of hiking a sun-kissed path—
trees the color of fire—accompany autumn.
Aroma of oak, maple, and birch,

thick and smoky, return.
She celebrates her birth.

Winter quiets her, carrying with it
a companionable silence that warms
her soul like the burning logs
making comfortable
her heart and home.

Flight of the Bumblebee

BY KATHLEEN WYATT

Seated on the overturned bucket, I coax him from the flower to my fingertip. I cannot believe this: I can pick him up and lift him into the air with impunity. I nudge two more from their perches, balancing all three bumblebees on different fingertips. Their plump bodies vibrate ever so slightly against my skin, their bristles vaguely tickling. These bees are drunk on sun-fermented nectar. I return the intoxicated insects to stamen and pistil, leaving them buzzing in the brilliant morning light.

The garden—my sanctuary, my escape—is alive, breathing, bursting with purple phlox, daylilies, and snapdragon. Yellow finches play a game of chase overhead and a cluster of mahogany irises lure the butterflies. A hummingbird drinks from the trumpets of the morning glories. The garden floor is bejeweled with wild petunia and a humble footpath that I fashioned from stones turned out of the soil. Ladybugs, with their appetite for aphids, are always welcome visitors, unlike those twilight gate-crashers, the skunks and cottontails who fancy tender blooms, shoots, and crunchy bulbs for their late-night nibbling, or the slugs who leave long trails of slime across stones and pebbles as evidence of their passage. Tiny toads appear at watering time. I detain one in the cup of my hand, tenderly rubbing its smooth belly, cool from the earth. I feel its tiny heart beating against my palm and loosen my hold, letting it leap free.

A lake glimmers a hundred and fifty yards to the west of where I live. Mature pines frame the water, stretching to the sky and creating choice hunting posts for the osprey. Wild turkeys parade past, the toms showing off their finery. One evening I glimpsed a red fox slipping in and out of the woods, playing hide-and-seek with an unseen opponent. Frequently at sundown, I catch sight of deer darting across the trails heading for a cool drink. Sometimes they stand at the forest edge, staring back at me as I stare at them. Then in a flash they turn, their white hindquarters disappearing into the brush.

As dusk draws near, with the garden tended to, I look to the west. The sky melts into ribbons of oranges, violets, and pinks, lingering at the horizon, then melting into the lake. I stand hypnotized until the last cast of light has vanished.

I close my eyes and draw a deep, inward breath, giving thanks for the favors bestowed upon me. Deliberately, gradually, I exhale, steadying my gaze on the drab ugliness of concrete, steel, and double-pane glass. The homestead that lies before me is my residence: a maximum-security state prison for women. But I have learned to look past the razor wire–crowned fencing and the heartache it surrounds, instead finding peace in nature's arena. While working in the gracious surroundings of the prison garden, I am blind to other inmates, sometimes even to the guards. The thick sweetness of the daylilies perfumes my senses, and I meditate on this dragonfly, its sleek, cobalt frame hovering above the daisies. Like those intoxicated worker bees that have escaped the drones, the queen, and the keepers of the hive, I too am at large, if only in the chambers of my mind.

Reawakening Through Nature:
A Prison Reflection

BY BARBARA PARSONS

I. Falling

After school today, I went directly to Grandma's next door instead of stopping at our house first. Now I find my suitcase on our front steps. The door is locked. It's October 1957. I'm nine. "Mom!" I yell, trying to force the door handle open. "Let me in!"

My mother appears at the door. "You want to spend all your time with your grandmother? Go ahead! Move in with her!" When she walks away, my tummy gets tight. There's a bad taste in my mouth. I pound on the door, crying and screaming useless apologies.

After a while, I drag my suitcase around back and head down the steep hill that levels off to a field surrounding a lone apple tree. I lay the suitcase flat on the ground under the tree and sit on it. The sky through my tears is a blur of blue. I've spent a lot of time down here at this old tree, climbing in it or playing house beneath it. A cool breeze shivers the leaves. I feel safe in this quiet place, where I'm close to home but away from Mom's moods.

I look up at our house, on the hill above the field, and just beyond it, at Grandma and Grandpa's house. Grandpa, my dad's father, died two weeks ago from cancer. Since then, I've gone each day after school to visit Grandma. She is sad lately, but before Grandpa died, she was loud and talkative, giving her opinions all the time or gossiping on the telephone about other people's business. Grandpa was quiet. After work, he liked to sit and watch TV or, when Grandma got going, escape to his garden. I wouldn't be far behind.

"Barbara, if you don't give those peas a chance to grow, there won't be any left for your grandmother to cook," he'd say, smiling. But I loved the sweet taste of the raw baby peas, the smell of tomato vines and rich, sun-warmed dirt. Now Grandpa's dead and no one will tend the garden. No one will give me piggyback rides, or make me smile, or watch out for me when Mom turns mad.

It's getting dark now, and the shadows make everything look spooky. My knees are stiff from squeezing them against my chest; I've been sitting on my suitcase for hours. Up the hill, the lights go on in our house. I feel a lump in my throat and a pull in my chest. Too scared to sit alone in the dark, I gather my belongings. The suitcase seems heavier now and it takes all my strength to drag it back up the steep slope. Why isn't Dad home? Maybe he's not coming home. Maybe no one wants me anymore.

At the back door, I knock and call, "Mom? Can I come home now?" I'm trying hard not to cry. She doesn't like it when we act like babies.

The door is yanked open. "Get in here, Barbara Ann! And stop making a scene." I slink into the house, holding my breath, fear lifting my shoulders almost up to my ears. I'm afraid Mom will crack me over the head with something within her reach: a pan, a cooking spoon. "Go to your room and stay there," she orders. "I don't want to see your face until morning."

My room seems miles away. If I run, I might get Mom madder, so I have to remember to walk at the exact right pace. Both my hands are on the handle so I won't drag my suitcase along the carpet and leave a mark.

When I reach my room, I ease the door shut, set down my suitcase, and crawl onto my bed. Safe!

Black smoke billows from windows shattered by the impact of a jetliner converted by terrorists into a bomb. The flames are hot enough to melt metal, they say. Those trapped on the top floors have a bleak choice: wait to be burned alive or leap to their deaths. Some hold hands as they drop, others fall alone. Later, we will watch in horror as the towers implode and crumble to dust, but it is seeing the desperate descent of the jumpers this day that launches me into a downward spiral in my struggle to live with post-traumatic stress.

Mom believed it was the responsibility of the eldest daughter to assist with the household chores. She also believed that if she spared the rod, she would spoil the child, and I was the child she was least interested in spoiling. She threatened, hit, threw things: a pot of peas, boiling away on the stove; a plastic hairbrush that hit so hard, it broke against my arm.

My mother's first hospitalization at Fairfield Hills Psychiatric Hospital occurred the summer I was seventeen. The nerve-racking drive in fast-moving traffic took over an hour. But if the travel drained me, the visits were worse. I went every day. Mom needed company and no one else would visit her. I dreaded that daily walk down the long corridor to her room, ignoring, as best I could, the stares of the other caged mental patients.

From visit to visit, Mom's moods were unpredictable and subject to abrupt shifts. Sometimes, my getting up to leave at the end of visiting hours would trigger hysteria. "Mom, I *can't* take you home with me," I cried during one such episode. "They won't *let* me." She howled so loudly, resisted my exit so strenuously, that the attendants had to restrain her. "Okay, we got her," they told me. "Go!" On the long drive home, I catalogued a list of reasons why this hospital stay was good for Mom. But my heart wasn't in it. I kept seeing them straijacket her and strong-arm her back to her room. All that summer and into the fall, I kept my feelings in check, pretending to myself and others that I was stronger than I was. It was a pretense I would carry into middle age—a pattern of denial that would eventually land me in prison.

On September 24, 1990, my mother ended her life by jumping from a window of her sister's twelfth-floor apartment. Mom's terrorists were the fear, depression, and paranoia that raged in her head. It wasn't until I watched the World Trade Center victims jump to their deaths eleven years later that the full force of her desperation finally hit me.

Mom had loved the outdoors. She kept a small flower garden but preferred the flowering bushes—lilac, mock orange, bridal wreath, rhododendron—that stood sentry around the border of our property. Squirrels played in the large maple and oak trees in our backyard, and bird feeders swayed from their branches. Twigs, leaves, and acorns littered the ground below, and Mom would bend daily to scoop up the debris. When she was well, my mother was meticulous, and her yard had to be as neat and orderly as the house she kept. When she was not well, chaos took the upper hand.

Often, Mom would pack my younger brother and sister and me into the car and drive us to Macedonia State Park or Kent Falls, where we'd wade in the brook or hike the trails in search of salamanders. In summer, we went almost every afternoon. My siblings and I would try to catch small fish with our plastic pails and nets. "Here's one! Quick! Hand me the bucket!" But the fish were always faster than we were, and the brook water was so clear, you could stand still and watch minnows and baby trout whiz right past your legs.

Today, on this summer day in prison, I close my eyes and hear that brook that's a hundred miles and a lifetime away from here. I see my mother, alive and young again, at peace. She is sitting on the rocks, watching us play. She's taken off the short-sleeve blouse she wore over her navy blue bathing suit but has left on her shorts. There's a contented look on her face as she leans back, tilting her face to the sun. When she arches her neck, her brown hair falls behind her.

Mom was diagnosed with paranoid schizophrenia when she was in her early thirties and, I, the eldest daughter, became her caretaker. I married and had children, but serving my mother's complicated needs remained one of my most important priorities. When I was in my thirties, my seventeen-year marriage began to fail. I had a full-time job, four kids to raise, and friends who kept advising me to stop serving everyone else's needs and take care of myself. And so, instead of checking on Mom every day, I began stopping by once or twice a week. When I did, she'd attack. "Just get out! I don't want you here! You're nothing but a tramp!" I'd leave and try again a few days later.

The final rift came when my mother accused her friend Gladys of telling someone a secret that Mom had told her. Gladys had no idea what Mom was talking about, but there was no reasoning with her. For Christmas, Gladys's daughter Amy had bought her mother and me tickets for a Broadway show, *Me and My Gal*. Mom was furious when she found out I had gone to New York with "those people." She never spoke to me again, except to tell me, "You're no longer my daughter. You are dead to me."

Then *she* was dead. We had never made up. Mom had died hating me, and I felt, once again, like that little girl on the front step with her suitcase, locked out of her life and guilty of something I couldn't quite identify.

In her open casket, Mom looked shrunken and strange. Her dyed blond hair had been neatly arranged in the fluffy style she'd worn during her later years, but the bruises on her face were visible beneath the thick makeup. The white sweater they'd dressed her in covered her broken arms, but her lips, slightly parted, revealed the plastic thread they'd used to cinch her jaw.

In the months after Mom's death, a solitary crow began to perch on the rail of my father's redwood deck outside the back door. It would stay for hours. Dad was convinced it was Mom watching out for us. At first, I dismissed that possibility, but the crow showed up with such frequency that I became a half-believer, too. At work, I would look out the window and see a solitary crow ambling across the parking lot. I began to feel stalked. What were the crow's intentions? Was it watching us to protect us from harm, or to harm us?

Since my incarceration, whenever I see a crow, I wonder if it's my mother, sitting restlessly on the branch nearest my window, cawing, reminding me of a guilt I am not likely to forget.

II. Bird Feeders

Danny, the eleven-month-old golden-Labrador retriever I am training for the York Prison Pup Partnership, looks out the window, his head darting from side to side. I get off my bed and go to the window to see what he sees. At the bird feeder, blue jays bully the other birds, and the squirrels, those thieves, perform acrobatics to try and take what isn't theirs. The feeder hangs from a big oak tree on the side of the building where I live. Thompson Hall is on the minimum-security side of the York Correctional Institution compound.

Danny and I sit side by side on the large gray plastic commissary box I have placed in front of my window. As we watch the daily goings and comings at the feeder, my knowledge of birds grows. The chickadees are well-mannered; the nuthatches and juncos eat daintily. The male cardinal is a dandy in his scarlet coat, his mate a drab and faded counterpart. Ironically, Danny has developed a fascination for crows. As soon as he hears their calls, he is in the window, watching.

Our staff at Thompson Hall keeps the bird feeder filled. Officers toss peanuts, sunflower seeds, and breadcrumbs on the ground beneath the feeder. Inmates have more of an opportunity to converse with the staff on this side of the prison. It is a more humane atmosphere here, and the filled bird feeder becomes a reminder that our own freedom grows closer each day.

For the first four years of my incarceration, I lived on the newer, more punitive maximum-security side of York CI. Occasionally, from the permanently sealed windows, I would notice seagulls sitting along the rooftop—silent, vigilant corrections officers with wings. The thought of a bird feeder hanging in the stark, regimented world of the maximum-security facility is beyond belief, as is the idea that a staff member might take the time to fill a feeder. Danny would have had a hard time surviving the daily fluctuations between chaos and isolation enclosed within those gray cinder-block walls. *Clink. Clang. Jingle. Clank.* Steel doors, locks and keys, recycled air, dark rooms that discourage emotional growth.

After I was moved to the minimum-security side, I could hear the gulls, and their cries reawakened me to the natural world. At Thompson Hall, I had the freedom of choice to open my window, even on the coldest night. Three years later, that window has never been completely closed. In prison, you take freedom in whatever form it is offered you. Unlocked doors. Open windows. Silence instead of shouting. A puppy.

We train our pups to become service dogs for disabled clients, some of whom are wheelchair-bound. The dogs are taught to open doors with a tug rope attached. They learn how to turn light switches on and off, "bark" for help, retrieve telephones and keys. They learn how to tow a wheelchair back to a client after it has rolled away. The dogs arrive at York as eight-week-old pups Each trainer works with her assigned pup for about thirteen months. They leave us at fifteen months, headed off to a National Education for Assistance Dog Services site for their advanced training.

While the dogs are with us, volunteers from a local church take them on outings to acclimate them to sounds, smells, and situations not available at the prison. They may visit a grocery store or a shopping mall, ride on a bus or lie beneath the table at a restaurant filled with wonderful aromas. We rely on these volunteers to help our dogs overcome problems such as car sickness and separation anxiety. It's ironic that the puppies' socialization outside of prison is a high priority, whereas, for us, the inmates, the community outreach excursions that reacquainted us with the outside world were discontinued long ago. Maybe that's part of the reason why the dogs never return once they've left York CI but nearly 70 percent of the women do.

Being a puppy handler is rewarding, but it's stressful, too. Some inmates are jealous. Some officers resent inmates having dogs. "Thompson Hall needs a ride for a seven (inmate) with K-9 to the walk gate." If the transporting officer is resentful of the program, a puppy handler may wait for forty-five minutes

"Those dogs eat better than we do," inmates often complain.

"Yeah, and they get better medical care, too."

In truth, the medical care of a particular dog mirrors the medical care of its trainer. It all depends on who you are—whether, for instance, you are a compliant conformist or a "loose cannon" who questions an unreasonable command or an inappropriate remark. A "troublemaker" and her puppy may both pay a price. A "player" and her pup will reap rewards when she sweet-talks the uniforms, grants them favors, or laughs at their disparaging remarks.

When the puppies we've bonded with are scheduled to leave, we trainers can be given several weeks' notice—or just a day or two. I cried happy and sad tears the day my first dog, Webster, left; the chance of ever seeing him again was slim, but I was proud that he was ready to go. It's like sending your children out into the world. They follow their own paths but carry your imprint. My children and grandchildren love nature as much as I do. I like to think that after Danny leaves prison and I become a fading memory, he will continue to stop and watch the birds.

Sometimes as we sit side by side on the gray box, enjoying the action at the feeder, Danny turns from the window and looks into my eyes. He nudges my cheek, gives me a quick lick. I put my arm around him, grateful. Love of any kind is in short supply at York, and unconditional love is precious.

III. Survivors of Abuse

It's strange. They say women, often without realizing it, marry versions of their fathers. But Mark was more like Mom: sweet and loving at first, and later angry, needy, and unpredictable. Two years into our marriage, he was diagnosed with the same disease Mom had suffered: paranoid schizophrenia. But unlike Mom, he refused to take his prescriptions, medicating himself instead with alcohol.

Mark was my second husband. Our relationship began when my roommate's Amazon parrot landed on his head as he walked out of my cottage with a peanut butter sandwich in his hand. It ended eleven years later with dead chickadees lying on the ground beneath my bird feeder. Mark had grabbed one of his guns and used the birds for shooting practice.

The freedoms I've begun to reclaim on the prison's minimum side have helped my progress in coping with post-traumatic stress disorder. Color is healing for me, and so green vines and pastel blossoms border the window and bulletin board of my room, sunflowers and butterflies adorn the walls. I don't know how old my mother's father was when he first molested her, but I was four when he molested me. After he finished and we left the small storage room where he'd taken me, the trees, the sky, and the neighbors' lawns had all turned gray. The night I shot Mark, our bedroom was awash in yellow. In an out-of-body experience, I watched the woman pick up the gun, unable to help her or stop her.

Now I sit in a circle with other inmates, baffled by what these fellow Survivors of Abuse group members are saying. How could all of our men, strangers to one another, have spoken the same phrases?

I'm going to do whatever I want to do whenever I want to do it.
No one else would ever want you, so you better get used to it.
Sweetie, I'd die without you. I swear it's never going to happen again.
Where could you go where I wouldn't find you?

Hearing Mark's words come out of these women's mouths, I flash back to the night I confronted him about his affair with a fifteen-year-old girl. I see his smirk, hear the way he turns things around so that the problem is my unreasonableness. Why can't I just be patient while he decides whether he wants to stay or leave me? I know I can't win this argument. I never win. He is an imposing, overweight man—six feet one to my five feet five—and he's strong as hell. He has many more guns than he needs and has hinted that someday, if I push him hard enough, he might have to make me disappear. But today, I feel so disoriented and weak, these threats aren't necessary. His look of utter contempt is enough to keep me in my place.

The voices of the women in my group drift back, and I realize we have this fatal error in common: we stayed with our abusers because we both loved and feared them, and because they were talented manipulators—masters of the bait-and-switch who kept us constantly off balance.

As Sandra speaks about the sexual abuse she endured, I remember the pain in my rectum and vagina during and after Mark's violent poundings. Tears blur my vision. How could he have done those things to me and called it love? How could I have allowed him to?

In tears, Ava tells us what her husband did to their four-month-old daughter. "It was hard for me to register what I was seeing. He was bent over her, licking up and down her legs, licking her private area."

Nauseous, I begin to sob. I blame myself—my stupid, uneducated denial—for the fact that my husband molested my granddaughter, as my grandfather had molested me. When my children were growing up, I had tried so hard to keep them safe—to break the cycle of abuse. But I had failed my sweet, beautiful granddaughter. She'd been harmed because I'd stayed with Mark, convincing myself that his failings were my fault and my responsibility. And in the middle of that worst night, the room had gone yellow and I'd taken his life—an irrational and horrible act of last resort in defense of the child of my child. That night, my life as I knew it collapsed. Twenty-four hours later, I'd been processed into a sisterhood of misfits.

I'm brought back to the group by the scraping of chairs. Our hour is over for this week and I return to my cell. But for the rest of the day, and for the next day, and the next week, the soft pastels, the sunflowers and butterflies on my walls, the birds calling outside my open window, offer no comfort at all.

IV. A Visit from the Goons

I subtract each day of my life in prison from my sentence: twenty-five years, suspended after ten. Every day I'm here, I embrace the guilt I feel about my crime and the mess I've made of my life, the hardships I've inflicted upon my children. And because my ID badge identifies me as Barbara Lane, not Barbara Parsons, each day I carry the burden of my husband's—my victim's—surname. Still, I try to move, step-by-step, beyond this debilitating guilt, focusing as best I can on the day when, having served my sentence, I will return to my family. It's not easy. The psychological roller coaster of memory can be triggered by a slamming door, a harsh comment, an inmate's or an officer's invasion of my personal space. For women working to overcome their post-traumatic stress disorder and take healthy charge of their lives, prison can be a defeating environment.

"Jackie, I just put our stuff in the dryer."

"Okay, Mom. I'm almost done here, too." Jackie and I share cell A12 of the Zero South building on the maximum-security side of the compound. She's been cleaning our common space, and I've been doing our laundry in preparation of the anticipated lockdown. Lockdowns are one of the routine interruptions of routine at York CI. My cell mate is twenty years younger than I—the age of my oldest daughter—and her energy is boundless. Each week when we change our sheets, she uses our mattresses as punching bags to fluff them up from pancakes to puffy clouds. They don't stay that way for long, but it makes her feel good to release the energy. The mother-daughter connection Jackie and I have established works for us; we look out for one another without expecting anything more than trust and mutual support.

"I hope they shake down our building first so we can just relax the rest of the time," Jackie says. She and I are both taking courses at the prison school, so we have plenty of homework to get us through the lockdown period. We've also stocked up on commissary: popcorn, potato chips, chocolate pudding, strawberry Pop-Tarts. We never know how many days these compoundwide shakedowns will last, or what kind of misery they will bring.

On Monday morning, at 11:00 A.M., it begins. Our lunches arrive at noon: bologna, cheese, potato salad, and bread on Styrofoam trays, fruit punch in Styrofoam cups. We eat quickly, nervously. As we finish, the intercom voice warns, "I want everyone properly dressed in their uniform! Jeans, maroon shirt and shoes, no exceptions! Step out of your cell and form a single line! No talking, eyes to the ground, and arms on top of your head!"

Click. Our cell door unlocks electronically and Jackie and I join the others, twenty-four women times four tiers, all of us dressed identically, our arms on top of our heads, our eyes cast to the floor. We stream down the stairs to the common area.

Shakedowns are always stressful, but this one is worse because it's being conducted by the Correctional Emergency Response Team— CERT for short. CERT trains at this, Connecticut's only women's prison, to prepare for trouble at one of the men's facilities. They wear black ninja-style uniforms and black helmets with tinted visors. They carry billy clubs. Their K-9 dogs look restless, ready to lunge.

As we leave the building, I'm jarred to see close to a hundred of these helmeted, faceless intimidators. *Thump, thump, thump.* They march to take their positions, five feet apart from each other. Each spreads his legs two feet apart, grips his billy club. "KEEP YOUR EYES ON THE

GROUND!" one of them screams. As we file past, I keep reminding myself not to hold my breath. My upraised arms begin to feel as heavy as lead pipes.

The gym is dimly lit. We're directed to sit facing the wall with our backs to the activity behind us. *POP!* A sound like a gunshot echoes through the room. I try to fend off the familiar symptoms of panic attack: nausea, heart palpitations, shaky stomach, pressure in my bowels and bladder. *POP!* I look over my shoulder to sneak a peek, trying not to let the helmeted officers see me. *POP!* One of them is striking the metal volleyball pole with his billy club.

In groups of five, we are taken to the bathroom to be strip-searched by female counselors and correctional officers. "Take off all your clothes and hand them to me," the CO says. She shakes out each item as I hand it to her. "Lift up your breasts. Open your mouth. Turn around and let me see behind your ears. Bend over. Squat. Pull your cheeks apart. Lift up your right foot. Now your left. Turn around. Pull your vagina apart. Cough." By the time my clothes are handed back, I'm a piece of meat. I dress hastily and leave the small bathroom that stinks from the memory of the hundreds of naked women previously searched here.

Our group is directed to the opposite side of the gym and told to resume our positions on the floor, looking toward the wall. *POP!* Why do they have to keep doing that? An officer shouts, "Cruz! Ward! Harris! Jones! Lane! Come see me!" Oh shit, what's *this* about? Jackie and I have both been called.

We're ordered to take a drug test, but I'm not especially worried. I have no addiction and no history, and Jackie attends NA, AA, and Al-Anon meetings faithfully. There's nothing incriminating in our cell, so this must just be part of the intimidation. We take turns peeing in cups while a female staff member watches, lest something drop from our vaginal cavities into the toilet and get flushed away. I'm embarrassed by this procedure, so it's difficult for me to relax and pee, and the officer's impatience doesn't help matters any.

After the five of us have produced our urine samples, a helmeted officer orders three of the women to go back and sit on the floor. To Jackie and me, he says, "Which one of you wants to go first?"

Jackie must be able to read the panic on my face. "I'll go," she says. Two CERT storm troopers guide her by her elbows to the wall. She is handcuffed, grabbed by her upper arms, and forced to walk backwards toward the exit door. Another officer follows behind with a camcorder; it's policy to videotape the use of force on an inmate, and backwards-walking is considered force. Jackie looks back at me, calling, "It'll be okay, Mom!" Then she's out the door.

A counselor walks over to me and whispers, "Just go with them. Do what they say. Stay calm." But staying calm is impossible, especially when the intimidators return and motion for me to stand. I'm cuffed, grabbed under the arms, and hauled out of the gym backwards, the videotaping officer chasing after us. My legs are killing me and my body feels like it is being twisted in a million directions. They are just about dragging me across the compound because I can't walk backwards fast enough to keep up with them.

When I arrive at the restrictive housing unit—nicknamed "seg," short for segregation—a staff member takes me into custody. I'm uncuffed and escorted to an area where I am strip-searched again. My general population clothes are taken away, replaced by a thin green scrubs outfit. I'm led to a cell on E tier. Jackie is already there. *Click!* "Why are they doing this to us?" I ask, but Jackie doesn't know, either. A small door in the thick heavy cell door opens and sheets and blankets are passed through it. "Thank you," I mumble. *Clank!*

We make our bunks and lie on them, Jackie above, me below. Over-whelmed and scared, I force myself to glance around the cell. There's a sink attached to a wooden counter, a toilet bolted to the wall, a Bible on the tray attached to my bed. The floor is so filthy, I don't want to step on it. This cell is a painful reminder of the one I occupied during my first weeks in prison, and I am suffering a refresher course in despair.

"How long do you think we have to be in here?" I ask Jackie. Ever resourceful, my roommate jumps down from her bunk and heads to the door. Two girls have arrived in the cell across from us. Jackie hollers to them, "Hey! What does it say on our door?"

"A & D pending," one of them shouts back.

Jackie's spent time in seg before, but this is new to me. I ask her what that means. "Means we haven't been charged with anything yet," she says.

We ask every staff person who walks by our door why we've been brought here, but no one will answer us. Down the hall, we hear the unit counselor direct staff to stay away from our room because we're asking too many questions.

My usual coping strategy is to keep busy—to stay in the moment—but here in seg, the idle minutes become hours and my grief overtakes me. I've been on Zoloft the past couple of months, due to my son Adam's death in a traffic accident, but during lockdown, medication is dispensed sporadically. Still, I hold up well enough until the evening of the second day, when hopelessness sets in. I begin to sob so loudly that an officer comes around and asks if I want a request form. "Yes," I tell him. He slides one through the trap door, along with a pencil stub. *Unit Manager, HELP!!* I write. *I don't know what I'm in seg for. Please help me! Barbara Lane.* I slip the request under the door, and the CO picks it up, reads it, and walks away without a word.

As the tiers have filled up, the noise in seg has become deafening. Communication through the ventilation system is constant and loud. "Jackie? That you? It's me, Brenda. What'd you do, girl?"

"Don't know. Barbara's with me, too."

"Barbara? Hey, Barbara! I never thought I'd see the day you was in seg!"

On the third day, they test Jackie's and my urine again. "But I don't use drugs," I say. "I don't have a history." We both pass the drug test again. Why are they doing this to us?

It has to be about eight or nine o'clock that night when we hear footsteps on the stairs, men's voices, the opening and slamming of cell doors. "Oh, Jackie, it's them. We have to go through this *again*?"

Sure enough, the storm troopers are preparing to shake down the seg building. When Jackie and I peek out at the hallway to see what's going on, we see the inmates across from us being strip-searched in their cell by a female officer. We also see the men, supposedly patrolling the hallway, standing there, watching the peep show.

We're next. "Please don't make me strip in front of the window," I beg the CO. But she insists no one can see me, and I can't risk arguing with her. Again, we go through the humiliating routine of exposing our every nook and cavity. After we're dressed again, we're ordered into the hallway. My wrists are bound tightly behind my back with polyurethane cable. Jackie's having her wrists bound, too. We're led to the stairs, then down to the common area. The lights are blinding. Video cameras on stands record our movements, and a large audience of correctional staff in various uniforms watches us. We are herded into a multipurpose room to sit and wait while, upstairs, CERT officers pull apart our cells.

After the tier is shaken down, we are led back up to our cells. An officer pries a pair of cutters between our wrists and the tight cable that binds them together. I'm one of the lucky ones whose wrists aren't scratched or bruised by the cutters. After the storm troopers leave, there is an eerie silence, except for the sobs that travel through the cell block.

On the fourth day, Jackie and I take another pee test. A CO tells us we will be moved back to Zero South as soon as the CERT team leaves, but that they are calling the shots. "You're in seg because your cell smelled like marijuana," we are finally told by a second-shift CO, who's learned this from someone in A & D. Jackie and I look at each other in bewilderment. There is no way. Has someone set us up?

I'm deteriorating badly by now, my mind racing full-speed into scenic flashbacks of my crime. The storm troopers leave around noon.

Jackie and I are released from seg and sent to Admittance and Departure, where we surrender our green scrubs and are reissued gen pop uniforms. As we walk back to our unit, the sunshine disorients me. Our room's been pulled apart and there's a torn teabag lying at the bottom of our toilet bowl. "Is that supposed to be our marijuana?" I ask, my voice rising. "Did those bastards put us through four days of hell so they could give their drug dogs some practice?"

"Come on, Mom," Jackie says, rubbing my back consolingly. "Let's get this room put back together."

Three days later, my son Arthur comes to see me. Sitting across from him in the visiting room, I notice he's flustered and ask him why. "Before they'd let me in here, this officer took me into that cruddy bathroom out in the entrance room and she made me strip down to my boxers," he says.

I'm furious. "A *female* officer made you do this?"

Arthur nods. "Whatever she was looking for, she didn't find it." He reaches across the table and takes my hand. "I'll put up with whatever I have to, to see you, Mom," he says.

This is the first I've heard of anyone's family member being humiliated in this way. Don't they realize that having your mother in prison is hard enough? For weeks, I tried to find out why my son had been singled out for this treatment, but no one would give me an answer.

In the days and weeks following my stay in seg, I spent as much time outdoors as possible. I walked slowly from building to building, lifting my face to the sun, breathing in the fresh air, and trying as best I could to cleanse myself of my fearful experience. In seg, I'd shed five pounds and relinquished my remaining illusions about "innocent until proven guilty," or about the prison's interest in rehabilitating inmates. It is a general conception that convicted felons are liars, cheats, and manipulators—the scum of the earth. That certainly seems to be the attitude of those who run the facilities. How else could they justify treating human beings this way?

It doesn't have to be like this.

It didn't used to be.

V. What We've Lost

Oh, shit! What is it? Help!"

Tork, a wide-shouldered, tough-as-nails inmate from Bridge-port, is screaming like a sissy. Several of us come running to see what's wrong.

There are gasps, whimpers. "Looks like a giant rat," Georgia whis-pers, wide-eyed. I tell them to get me a broom.

A few seconds later, broom in hand, I charge the opossum, shout-ing, "Get away from here! Scat!" It scoots across the yard and under the fence. I turn back to the frightened faces of these girls who, from the time they were small children, witnessed the terrors of the streets.

"What's the matter?" I ask. "No one's ever seen a possum before?"

I push past them, shaking my head. City girls.

It's no accident that our prison is parked in the middle of a kind of nature preserve. Almost ninety years ago, in 1917, a specially appointed committee of sociologists, engineers, and government representatives traveled the state in search of a tract of land on which to build the Con-necticut State Farm for Women. There were specifications: the property was to be no fewer than two hundred acres and was to include wood-lands, tillable pasture, and a natural water supply. It was to be located within reasonable distance from a railroad so that women who had fallen prey to the evils of the state's larger cities could be transported to the new penitentiary. This was to be Connecticut's first prison for females.

Bride Lake Farm, on the outskirts of the coastal village of Niantic, was purchased in the spring of 1918. The site would "secure an adequate separation of groups and sufficient privacy in open air work and play for a population of from five to ten hundred women." The goal of the prison's founders was to foster the rehabilitation of "wayward women" with fresh air, nature's resources, farm labor, and supervision by an all-female custody staff. The institution was to feed itself and give back to the community. Under the direction of a farm manager, inmates would work in the gardens and orchards, the dairy and poultry plants, the barns and kitchens. Surplus meat, eggs, fruit, and vegetables would be donated to the local almshouse and orphanage.

The formula worked successfully for the next several decades. Women healed, reformed themselves, and rejoined the community as productive citizens. Despite the fact that there was no gate to lock them in, few inmates attempted escape. The recidivism rate was so low that the State Farm came to be known as "the prison that cures with kindness."

Eventually, the agricultural operation was declared non-cost-effective and discontinued. By 1993, the grounds were surrounded by security fencing and barbed wire. A large, box-shaped warehouse building now housed the food service preparation for *all* of Connecticut's prisons. Each day, government-surplus goods and foods that had passed minimum standards of quality were freighted in, prepared, and shipped around the state to a cumulative prison population of seventeen thousand.

At York, I worked in "food prep" for twenty-seven months. Carrots, potatoes, onions (and, occasionally, prechopped lettuce), bought in bulk, were the only fresh vegetables, except for the two slices of tomato once a year on our Fourth of July hamburgers. One of the doctors from the medical unit lobbied the administration for years to provide us with fresh fruit. His persistence eventually paid off; in my seventh year at York, we were finally given apples, oranges, and bananas for dessert instead of calorie-laden cake.

The Department of Correction's decision makers do not consider that women might have different nutritional needs than men. Meals consist of whatever can be served cheaply in bulk to satiate the male prison population. The diet therefore contains far too much starch and carbohydrate. For many of Connecticut's female inmates, this results in obesity and dietary diabetes. In prison, women complain about everything, but we can't seem to unite behind the common cause of advocating for a healthier diet.

At York, food wastage is off the charts. "As long as I oversee what's served, I don't care whether the inmates eat it or not," a dining hall supervisor remarked one day. "The pigs can have it, for all I care." Once upon a time, Connecticut's female inmates raised their own fruits and vegetables, their own beef cows and chickens and pigs. Today, their modern counterparts sit idle, gain weight, raise their blood pressure, and create havoc because of boredom and frustration. Each week, a local pig farmer picks up barrels of discarded food from the facility, paying the state so much per barrel for the slop.

VI. The Sisterhood of Misfits

Don't let the serene description of Danny and me watching birds at the feeder fool you. Last year, a woman hanged herself in Thompson Hall, where crows hover outside during the day, replaced by bats at night. Our red brick residence, bordered in front by pretty flower gardens, is home to unhappy, dejected women, many of whom have been abandoned by their families and friends. *I have no idea where I'll go if I'm granted parole. . . . I have no home left. My kids all moved to other states. . . . How will I get to work without a car? . . . How will I get health care?* These are common worries for women nearing the end of their sentences. The prospect of leaving prison can be frightening. The prospect of staying is worse.

Coming out of the chow hall one day, I notice an inmate sobbing. Two COs are chuckling nearby, holding their hands in the air as if grasping a noose. One of them asks the girl, "You gonna be the *next* hang-up?"

. On another day, a CO is standing near the basketball court, monitoring our double-file return from the chow hall to our housing unit. He seems to be pointing at me. "Did you want me for something?" I ask.

"Why do you say that?" he answers.

"I thought you were pointing at me."

"Naw, I was just doing a little target shooting."

One morning, I push the intercom button in my cell, and the CO on duty—a woman whose moods shift as abruptly as my mother's—tells me to state my emergency. "No emergency," I say. "I have to go to work."

If this were a normal day, the cell door would pop open, but this time the officer screams, "You're not going anywhere and don't ring this buzzer again! If they want you at work, they'll call for you!"

The volatility and abuse in my life before prison has prepared me for the volatility and abuse I find here. And because it's not in my best interest to challenge a CO, I take off my food prep uniform and lie on my bed. A little while later, the officer moves down our hallway, kicking our cell doors and screaming. "YOU ARE NOTHING BUT A BUNCH OF BITCHES!" Later still, the tier's main intercom clicks on. "I'm putting a request form under each of your doors!" she hollers. "So all of you can go right ahead and complain about my treatment because I DON'T CARE WHAT YOU THINK OF ME!"

Oh, god, four more hours until this crazy woman goes off shift. And when she returns in a day or so, she may be reasonable and sweet. No matter who shows up that day, I'll deal with her. We all will. We have no choice.

In this, the sisterhood of misfits, I live surrounded by chaos, raw language, expert manipulation, and ambiguous sexuality. Wives and mothers in the free world become lesbians in prison. Understanding and then breaking vicious cycles—changing yourself for the better—is hard work. Too hard for many women. Seventy-five percent of the inmates at York do not take advantage of school or counseling programs. Instead of changing self-destructive habits, they adapt them to their new environment. Separated from violent spouses, they opt to let their codependency rage on in the form of volatile relationships with other women. Commissary items such as dried ramen noodles, Honey Buns, and potato chips substitute for drugs, though an inmate can find drugs here if she wants them badly enough.

Still, it is possible for a woman at York to stay spiritually connected, and to rehabilitate herself if she wants to. Because the prison environment mirrors the abusive environment I was used to, I arrived knowing how to isolate myself to stay safe. Slowly and cautiously, I have established friendships with women I can trust, and I have stayed away from women who are addicted to drama, trouble, and illegal excitement. York offers limited opportunities in the areas of education, cultural programs, and counseling services. Through these, I have become increasingly self-aware. But I have also undergone some changes that I do not consider positive or rehabilitative. I am more suspicious now—untrusting, disillusioned, and bitter. I am sure some of this is the ever-lingering remnants of my post-traumatic stress disorder. Hypervigilance, flashbacks, dissociative amnesia, hypersensitivity to loud noises: these are among the symptoms that challenge and sometimes derail me. But step by small step, I move toward the light at the end of this ten-year tunnel.

Case in point: I have been learning how to practice visual meditation as a coping skill when I receive distressing news from home that I am powerless to do anything about, or when I'm assigned a difficult roommate. I begin with a breathing exercise that helps me focus and blocks out the noise around me. Then I bring to mind an image that makes me feel peaceful. I use a scene I witnessed in Germany once—acres and acres of sunflowers on both sides of a small two-lane road, in the countryside near Vilseck.

My latest roommate, Beth, is bipolar, and she has a history of violence. She is berating me because I left our cell door open with a shoe while

I ran to take a quick shower. "You *know* I got in trouble this morning for wearing my shorts on the tier!" Beth screams. "You *know* that CO hates me. So what do you do? You prop open our fucking door!" Her vulgarity aside, she has a point: it's a serious safety and security offense to prop open a cell door—an infraction for which an inmate can get a disciplinary ticket.

"I'm sorry, Beth," I say. "But you weren't even in the cell when I left my shoe in the door. And besides, I *asked* if I could leave the door ajar because I was going to be quick. I had permission."

"You think you're something else, but you're nothing but a fucking bitch! You think your shit don't smell, because staff likes you better than me. But you know something? You're just an inmate like me. In fact, you're worse than me, because you're a KILLER!"

Beth's attempt to unnerve me is successful. As she screams, her contempt becomes my mother's contempt, her face Mark's face. I am tangled again in that terrible night when I took his life.

So I lie on my bed and begin my meditation: *Breathe*, I instruct myself. *Evoke the calming image*. But something's wrong. I know the sunflowers in the field should be yellow with brown faces, but they're gray, absent of color. In my past life, I would tell myself at a moment like this that, gray sunflowers or not, I was strong. I was in control. I could handle this all by myself. But here in prison, I've become self-aware enough to recognize that I am verging on a crisis. I need to see a counselor—to call as loudly and insistently as it takes to get someone to help. Painful as it is, this is progress. This is rehabilitation.

VII. Waiting

Here at York, there's always gridlock—body traffic, not cars. "Clusterfucks" they're called, in prison jargon. "Hurry!" staff orders, and so we hurry up to wait. We wait in lines to go to school, to pass through the walk gate, to obtain our medications, to get our meals. Wherever we wait, we remain aware of our surroundings. A code can be called at any time, which means staff will come running or drive like bats out of hell to get to the emergency. When a code is called, we are directed to stand still and wait until given further directions.

Even though the compound has wide, white-painted crosswalks, staff vehicles cannot be relied upon to stop for pedestrian inmates. Once in a while, an officer will gun his engine as he approaches. His DOC van will barrel past, traveling too fast for these narrow roads. Hypervigilance keeps me aware of my surroundings, alert to who is standing too close to my personal boundaries. I don't like being touched by people I don't know very well, or touched unexpectedly. I like to know who is standing near me in case of confrontation or chaos. I have learned to enjoy being alone, or being in the loyal company of the puppy I am training.

In summertime, seagulls and hawks circle Thompson Hall. Praying mantises, butterflies, and hummingbirds grace our garden. Flying squirrels—those winged chipmunks—invade the bird feeder at night. Some of the girls have come across a snake in the garden, but, happily, I have not been one of them. It's been three years now that I've lived in Thompson Hall, and it still amazes me when birds perch on the razor wire. Why doesn't it cut their feet?

Behind our building is a lake inhabited by ducks and Canada geese. Osprey perch in the surrounding trees. Because the ocean is across the road from the prison entrance, I sometimes see a family of sandpipers scurry across the more secluded, sandy areas of our yard. These moments remind me of those happy afternoons when my mother took us hiking through the state parks, picking wildflowers and wading through brooks. Mom loved the ocean, too, though she never learned how to swim. I still see her there, at the water's edge, basking in the sun. She shrieks happily as the cold water breaks against her white legs, her white-laced spandex bathing suit. Mom has passed her love of nature on to me, and it has helped me survive this prison life.

It's early fall, and the side yard at Thompson Hall is a mass of moving black: wild turkeys milling about, scavenging for fallen seed. Danny, of course, is at the window, watching them. Because the puppies are our constant companions, unless they go off grounds with a volunteer for socialization, they are as imprisoned as we are, their interaction with nature as limited as ours.

Now it's late November, that time of year when the leaves are off the trees and darkness arrives by late afternoon. As I walk toward my current home, the lights from Gates Correctional Institute, the men's prison adjacent to ours, are reflected on the surface of the lake. From this vantage point, prison looks like any small town built near a body of water. For a moment, I pretend I am part of a peaceful community, walking down any quiet country road, leisurely and free.

Whoo, whoo, an owl calls. As a child, I was told it was bad luck to hear an owl in daylight. It meant death. But an owl's *whoo-whoo* at night is natural. I look up to the treetops but can't see his silhouette against the night sky. I'm in my fifties now; my eyesight is deteriorating as I age. Home is supposed to be where the heart is. My physical heart is housed here at York, but my emotional heart is walled up and waiting for the day when I return to my family.

I should have made peace with my mother before she died. I should have left Mark before I broke. I should not have squandered my life, racing to do everything I could for others at the cost of losing myself. After several years of imprisonment, my mind has slowed down enough to allow me the bittersweet gift of perspective.

Recalling the horror of those doomed victims leaping from the World Trade Center fills me with despair. Watching the birds and squirrels at the feeder gives me hope. Hope and despair: I do my best to acknowledge and balance both.

"Hi, Grandma!" Riley calls. My daughter Andrea, who lives with her family in Georgia, is in Connecticut for two weeks, and she's brought her children, Alesha and Riley, to York for a visit. Riley wraps his arms around me and squeezes. Alesha and Andrea give me hugs and kisses.

"Grandma, I want us to go to Madagascar when you come home," Riley informs me. "Because there are all kinds of animals there, and I'm going to be a zoologist."

"Grandma, after you leave here, can you take me to New York City?" Alesha asks. "I want to go shopping and see a play."

"Mom, we're going to build you a room over our garage when you get out," Andrea says. "That way, you can have your own space."

My mind races from that over-the-garage sanctuary to the imagined jungles of Madagascar to the bustling streets of Manhattan. When Andrea and her siblings were small, we would take the Brewster train into Grand Central Station to see the Fourth of July fireworks on the East River, the Macy's Thanksgiving Day parade, the ball drop on New Year's Eve at Times Square—all of us cheering another year finished, a new year just begun.

I am Barbara Parsons, who has been a health-care worker, a business manager, a homemaker, a gardener, and a killer—and who is consequently a state prison inmate. Good-bye to the trusting daughter, sister, wife, and mother I once was. I have one grandson and six granddaughters, and I live in fear that I will again learn that one of them has been harmed. I don't care who you are; I am sure you have a dark side. Look at me: who would have ever thought that I, an average neighbor from rural Connecticut, could be capable of murder?

Still, I am grateful that, at long last, I have acquired the inner strength I only used to pretend to have. I am grateful that my family's plans and dreams of the future include me. And I am grateful for the natural world that helps me endure the harsh, unnatural world of this maximum-security prison.

At my open window, with Danny beside me, I count the days.

Contributors

K*elly Donnelly*, a native of Boston's South Shore, was born in 1962. She has worked extensively as a bartender and a floral designer. Donnelly's hobbies include gardening and photography. Convicted of negligent assault in 2004, she is serving an eleven-year sentence. At York, Kelly Donnelly has worked as a recreational aide and a librarian's assistant. She has participated in the Prison Arts Program, the Poetry Project, the Avodah Dance Ensemble, Alternatives to Violence, and an art-appreciation course taught through Three Rivers Community College. Of her writing, Donnelly says, "I started keeping a journal many years ago to record my feelings. I use this as a form of therapy. Recently I've begun writing poetry and enjoy that very much."

Born in 1947, *Bonnie Jean Foreshaw* was raised in south Florida. She was convicted of first-degree homicide in 1986 and sentenced to a forty-five-year term at the Niantic Prison. At the time, this was the lengthiest sentence ever given an inmate at the women's facility. Foreshaw has been imprisoned longer than any other woman serving time at York CI.

Legal experts familiar with Bonnie Foreshaw's case maintain that her public defender failed to meet the minimum standard of competency provided by the Constitution and that, given the circumstances surrounding her case, she should have been charged with manslaughter, not first-degree homicide. Attorney Mary Werblin, who has done extensive pro bono legal work to get this case reexamined, contends that Bonnie Foreshaw's trial exposes the court's gender and class bias.

Bonnie Foreshaw has four children and four grandchildren. Prior to her arrest, she was a Bloomfield, Connecticut, resident who worked as a machinist and served as a union steward. She has also been an Avon cosmetics representative and a Jaycees president. At York, she has served for many years as a "big sister," surrogate mom, and mentor to younger inmates, particularly youthful offenders. Active in Literacy Volunteers, she has helped others attain their general equivalency diplomas and acquire computer skills. She was one of the first graduates of York CI's hospice program, and as a hospice volunteer has comforted terminally ill inmates in their last days and hours.

Bonnie Foreshaw's personal essay, "Faith, Power and Pants," was published in the anthology *Couldn't Keep It to Myself*. Excerpts from "Florida Memories," the essay published here, were featured in the Judy Dworin Performance Ensemble's production, *Time In*.

An articulate and respected leader of the writing workshop, Bonnie Foreshaw is one of its charter members. "I write to ease stress," she says, "and to purge myself of dreadful memories of the physical violence I've endured. I write what, for many years, I could not even verbalize and this helps me to heal and move on."

⁓

One of the writing group's most diligent participants, *Lynne Friend*, born in 1959, entered York CI in 1998. She is serving a twenty-five-year sentence for manslaughter. Before her incarceration, Friend was a restaurant manager who enjoyed tennis, reading, music, and movies. At York, she works for DataCon Data Entry Services, a prison employment program. Her pastimes include writing, reading, crossword puzzles, increasing her vocabulary, and participating in a book-discussion group. Excerpts from her essay "The Marionette," printed here, were incorporated into the script of the Judy Dworin Performance Ensemble's production of *Time In*. Popular with her fellow inmates, Lynne Friend says she prefers solitude to engagement with the daily dramas that life in prison brings.

"I write nonfiction as a way of exploring and making sense of the traumas that have charted the course of my life," Lynne Friend says. "I have written humorous stories, too, and these provide a welcome respite from the dark times I remember and write about out of necessity."

Convicted of larceny and conspiracy, *Lynda Gardner* was born in 1948. A mother and grandmother, she entered York Prison in 2005 and is serving a fifteen-year sentence, to be suspended after six years. She is in recovery from alcohol, drug, and gambling addictions. At York, Gardner is employed by DataCon Data Entry Services and enjoys sketching, reading, dancing, and "learning, learning, learning." She was a featured performer in York CI's production of the Judy Dworin Performance Ensemble's *Time In*, an exploration of female inmates' lives.

"I write to begin the process of forgiving myself and others," Lynda Gardner comments. After years of "drugging myself to a numb state" to escape the pain of her childhood, Gardner says she tries to honor the miracle of having survived by sharing her story of recovery.

In February of 1996, fourteen-year-old *Robin Ledbetter*, an alternative-to-detention program runaway whose drug-addicted parents had been unable to raise her, conspired with a fifteen-year-old male acquaintance to rob a Hartford cab driver. When the driver resisted, he was stabbed and later died of his wounds. Ledbetter contends that her co-conspirator stabbed the victim, a claim which state of Connecticut prosecutors refute. The year before Ledbetter's arrest, Connecticut's General Assembly had passed a law allowing juveniles who faced serious felony charges to be tried as adults. A jury convicted Robin Ledbetter of robbery, conspiracy to commit robbery, and felony murder. During her sentencing hearing, her judge spoke of the community's need to rescue "this great wash of children who are being lost to us" because of parents ill-equipped to raise them. He then sentenced the fourteen-year-old to a prison term of fifty years. Robin Ledbetter, born in 1981, became one of the first juveniles incarcerated at the maximum-security York Prison.

In an October 16, 2005, article titled "Sentence Wasting Another Life," *Hartford Courant* columnist Helen Ubiñas wrote of Ledbetter's trial and sentencing: "The juvenile justice pendulum that is continually swinging from merciful to merciless was on the punishment end of the arc. She took part in a killing at a time when Americans were sick of children with guns getting away with murder, when politicians and pundits throughout the country told Americans to brace themselves for a generation of 'super-predators.' When states embraced criminal justice policies for children without stopping to consider whether they would work." Of the judge's comments and his subsequent sentencing of the defendant, Ubiñas commented, "Do you get that logic? I don't. Save the child from her parents' fatal flaws by throwing the child away?"

In May 2005, the Juvenile Law Center of Philadelphia filed an amicus petition in the case of *Robin Ledbetter vs. Commissioner of Correction*, arguing that, at the time she confessed to her involvement in a felony murder, Ledbetter did not understand that she could be prosecuted as an adult defender. The petition presented research that confirmed that children are developmentally different from adults in their cognitive capacity, and that adolescence is a period of major neurobiological development, including the ability for abstract thought, cognitive abilities, and decision-making skills. Because of these factors, the petition further argues that juveniles require greater protections than adults to ensure that a confession is voluntary. The justices hearing Ledbetter's appeal affirmed the decisions of the trial court, concluding that justice had been served.

Twenty-six-year-old Robin Ledbetter, whose hobbies include drawing and crocheting, says she writes for rehabilitation and release. "But I struggle against giving up on myself when I focus on the length of my sentence." Having entered York Correctional Institution in 1996, she is not scheduled to be released until 2046. She has made two attempts to end her life. Ledbetter asked Helen Ubiñas, "How do you restart a life at 64 when you never started it in the first place?"

⟿

Christina MacNaughton has studied theater at home and abroad and was a featured performer in York CI's production of the Judy Dworin Performance Ensemble's *Time In*, an exploration of women prisoners' lives in song, word, and movement. In recovery from drug addiction, MacNaughton is serving an eight-year sentence and was recently released to a halfway house. At York, she was active in Alternatives to Violence, the Prison Pup Partnership, and Project RAP. She also served as a teacher's aide and a hospice volunteer. "I write because I've always wanted to live a million different lives and experience a million different things," Christina MacNaughton has said. "Writing has been a best friend, a lover, and even an enemy—my constant companion."

⟿

Born in 1975 and incarcerated in 1993, Brendalis Medina is one of the charter members of the writing workshop. Her essay "Hell and How I Got Here" was published in *Couldn't Keep It to Myself* and has been read and studied by middle school and high school students around the country. Medina is serving a twenty-five-year sentence without parole for a gang-related killing at which she was present. Ordered with three of her fellow gang members to accomplish a "beat-down" of a fourth woman, Medina contends that she was taken by surprise when one of her "sisters" stabbed and killed the victim during the fight. Each of the four teens was charged and later convicted of first-degree homicide. Medina maintains that she participated in the violence but is innocent of felony murder.

At York, Brenda Medina obtained her high school general equivalency diploma and had earned thirty-six credits toward an associate's degree before the state of Connecticut discontinued college-level courses for inmates. She has served as a janitor and a food-service worker. A bilingual tutor registered with Literacy Volunteers of America, Medina has also taught incarcerated Latinas to read, speak, and write English. In addition, Medina has served as reporter, photographer, and editor for the *York Voice*, an inmate newspaper. In 2002, Brenda Medina designed, organized, and implemented York's Latina Appreciation Week.

"I started writing to keep myself sane in this crazy place, but now it has become much more than that," Brenda Medina says. "Through my writing, I have come to a much better understanding of who I used to be, who I am, and who I want to be."

Prior to her incarceration, *Barbara Parsons*, a native of Kent, Connecticut, was a certified nursing assistant and the originator and owner of a business called At Your Service. Convicted of "manslaughter due to emotional duress" following the shooting of her abusive husband, she received a twenty-five-year prison sentence, to be suspended after ten years. She was incarcerated at York Correctional Institution from 1996 to 2005.

In 2003, the state of Connecticut sued Barbara Parsons and seven other York inmates for the per diem cost of their incarceration in response to the publication of their personal essays in *Couldn't Keep It to Myself: Testimonies from Our Imprisoned Sisters* (ReganBooks, 2003). In 2004, Parsons won the PEN/Newman's Own First Amendment Award, an international honor given to writers whose freedom of speech is under attack. Following her 2005 release from prison on parole, Parsons returned to her hometown where a group of local residents, the Friends of Barbara Parsons, eased her transition back to the community. Today Parsons, a nature lover, works at a seasonal gardening center and as a home health-care provider. She continues to train special-needs

dogs for the disabled. Shy by nature, she has become a sought-after guest speaker, addressing the subjects of domestic violence and prison reform. Parsons also cofacilitates a community writing group for the Susan B. Anthony Project for abused women. Her outreach work helps Parsons fulfill a promise she made to her fellow inmates shortly before her release: that she would speak on their behalf and not forget them.

"Writing helps me empty the file cabinet in my memory labeled 'trauma' so that I can live with some inner peace," Barbara Parsons has said. "I entered the writing class a broken woman with bleak thoughts about my future, but I eventually found my voice and reclaimed my life. I hope that by speaking and writing about my experiences, I can help other women find their voices, too. I am eternally grateful to Mr. Lamb and my peers at York because I honestly feel the class saved my life."

In May 2006, on the one-year anniversary of Barbara Parsons' release from York Prison, she returned to the Niantic facility. Parked on the side of the road, she gazed in at the compound, sending good thoughts to the women inside. Then she crossed that road, entered Rocky Neck State Park, and stared out at the ocean. Parsons said she wanted to see at last what, for ten years, she had only been able to smell and imagine.

─◦◉◦─

A native of Puerto Rico, *Carmen Ramos* relocated to Waterbury, Connecticut, and was a stay-at-home mom who enjoyed cleaning, watching television, attending church, and playing games with her children. Since coming to York, she has earned her high school equivalency diploma and has served as a maintenance worker, a teacher's aide, and a librarian's assistant. Her activities in prison include reading, listening to the radio, and playing Scrabble. A talented and exuberant dancer, Ramos has performed in the Judy Dworin Performance Ensemble's *Time In* and as a part of founding director JoAnne Tucker's Avodah Dance Ensemble. Born in 1967 and incarcerated since 1993, Ramos is serving a thirty-year sentence for first-degree murder.

"When I first came to the United States, the only language I knew was Spanish," Carmen Ramos observes. "It wasn't easy to live in a country and not have any clue about what people were saying. At York, I was offered the opportunity to go to school, and I took the offer because I wanted to learn English. Year after year, my English has improved, so much so that I wrote this story just to prove to myself and others that I could do it. In life, everything is a struggle, but we need to have faith in ourselves. I admit that I hate to write, but when I do, my pain and sorrow move from me to the paper. After that, I feel some relief. I try to remember to strive for success, not for perfection."

"I dedicate 'The Rainbow Ring' to my two boys, Junior and Gordo," Carmen Ramos says. "Mom loves ya!"

—◈—

"I write because I need to!" says *Deborah Ranger*, one of the writing workshop's most articulate members. "In writing, I find discovery, freedom, and peace." A New Britain resident, Ranger was convicted of second-degree larceny in 2001 and is serving a fourteen-year sentence. Prior to her incarceration, she was employed as an office manager and, in her spare time, enjoyed country line-dancing and scrapbooking. She was born in 1965.

At York, Debbie Ranger has served as a librarian's assistant and has participated in poetry and dance projects. In June 2006, she was a featured performer in the Judy Dworin Peformance Ensemble's multimedia presentation *Time In*. The following November, *Time In* was performed for the public at Hartford's Charter Oak Cultural Center, with professional dancers and singers standing in for the inmate performers. Debbie Ranger's daughters, Suzy, SamiJo, and Tabitha, sat jubilantly and tearfully in the audience, watching and listening to their mother's words brought to life.

—◈—

Jennifer Rich, a Torrington native, was born in 1983. She entered York CI in 2004 and is serving a seven-year sentence for conspiracy to commit armed robbery. Her hobbies have included camping, hiking, and scuba diving. Rich, a recovering heroin addict, says that prison has been rehabilitative only in that it provides an environment of enforced sobriety. True rehabilitation, she says, must be self-initiated and self-sustaining. Rich says she writes about her life because she finds it therapeutic.

—⊚—

Savannah is a pseudonym for a writer who wishes to remain anonymous. An animal lover, she trained dogs to become service providers for the disabled through York's Prison Pup Partnership. Having served an eight-year sentence, she was released in 2006. Savannah has worked extensively with the deaf and hearing-impaired community, providing interpreting services in American Sign Language. She writes to allow herself "the free expression of my innermost feelings" and notes that "society must realize that if women are denied proper therapy and resources while they are in prison, they face transitions back into society which can be as traumatic as the circumstances that led them to commit their crimes."

—⊚—

Upon her release in 2004, *Roberta Schwartz* spent her first year on parole working as a paralegal in Connecticut. In May 2005, she married "Alex," the lover who waited for her, and returned to Austin, Texas, where she is currently employed as property manager for Goodwill Industries of Central Texas. Schwartz says, "I love the mission of Goodwill, and although I can no longer practice law, I'm pleased to be able to use my background and education. This is a job I would have wanted even if I had never stolen money and gone to prison."

While at York, Roberta Schwartz served as a teacher's aide, trained dogs for the Prison Pup Partnership, and followed the defeats and victories of her beloved New York Yankees. Of her participation in the writing program, she says, "I have written and wanted to be a writer since I read *Harriet the Spy* in elementary school. From high school on, I was never without a notebook in my lap, recording my thoughts and impressions everywhere but at work. The interesting thing to me is that when I started to use cocaine during my courtship and first marriage, I stopped writing. The rule always had been: you can't lie to your notebook. I brought a black-and-white composition book with me when I went to rehab and have been writing ever since. When I got to York and found out there was a writing group with Wally, I felt that, even in prison, God was directing me to record my story and learn about myself."

Reflecting on her incarceration, Roberta Schwartz says, "I figured out in the first six weeks of prison that I had a choice—to be miserable or to try to be productive and useful. I chose the latter, and because of that, I was happier while I was incarcerated than I had been during the bad years when I was stealing and doing drugs. At York, I experienced a world that I never knew existed and learned many valuable things. I still don't fully understand how I will use all the lessons I learned in prison, but I know I will."

-—◦—-

Born in 1960, *Kimberly Walker* of Stratford, Connecticut, is serving a seven-year sentence for first-degree larceny. Prior to her incarceration, she was a payroll accounting manager whose favorite activities included cardio kickboxing and spending time with her children and grandchildren. At York, she has served as a recreational aide, taken instruction in yoga, graduated from the cosmetology program, and studied religion.

"I write to relieve stress, to heal the hurts of the past, to remember precious family memories, and to make my time here go by faster," Walker says. "When I came to York in 2003, I was frightened of what lay ahead. But I have been building a solid foundation with God and have kept myself busy with positive groups and activities. I am blessed to have supportive friends and family and when my prison journey has been completed, I hope to serve the Lord by helping other prisoners on their way to better lives."

-—◦—-

Chasity C. West's hobbies are writing and reading. Prior to her incarceration in 1998, she was employed as a licensed practical nurse at the Cheshire Correctional Institution. Born in 1974, she is serving a life sentence without parole for capital felony murder. West is appealing her conviction.

"I write to escape this reality," Chasity West says. "Writing offers me a kind of rehabilitation that prison doesn't provide: the healing of a broken heart and soul, the restoration of a crushed spirit. Writing makes me human again and allows for a kind of resurrection of self."

Lisa White, a nurse's aide from Bridgeport, Connecticut, and a recovering drug addict, was convicted of first-degree robbery in 2003. Born in 1968, she was released from York CI to a halfway house in the autumn of 2006. White enjoys listening to music, reading "good poetry that comes from the soul," and helping others. "When I write about the things I've seen and experienced, it cleans my mind and frees me from the painful past," White says. "I am grateful for the love of my family, particularly my daughters Simone and Iman, who help me to stay strong."

Charissa Willette, of Wolcott, Connecticut, was born in 1979. She entered York in 2000 and is serving a seventeen-year sentence for first-degree manslaughter following the death of the abusive boyfriend, five years her senior, with whom she became involved at the age of fourteen. Willette has served as a librarian's assistant and a teacher's aide at York's prison school. She says her writing helps her to better understand her thoughts, her feelings, and her past mistakes.

Kathleen Wyatt of Meriden, Connecticut, was born in 1959 and entered York Prison in 2002. She is serving a nine-year sentence for second-degree manslaughter, the result of an automobile-related fatality. Prior to her incarceration, Wyatt's hobbies included cooking, gardening, and music. A gifted artist, at York she has participated in the culinary arts and prison art programs. Of her participation in the writing group, of which she is one of the most eloquent spokeswomen, she says, "I was broken upon entering prison, but I believe one day I will be whole again. I write to find peace within my soul."

Facilitators' Biographical Statements

Following a tumultuous adolescence, *Susan Budlong Cole* says, she entered into a marriage for which—in retrospect—she was singularly unprepared. "Over time we managed to grow up together," Cole states, "and with two adolescents of my own—one going off to college that same fall—I became a college freshman at thirty-seven." Five years later, Cole graduated from Wesleyan University and began a twenty-five-year commitment to the treatment and prevention of alcoholism and other addictions. "That I stumbled into such a rewarding career still fills me with wonder and gratitude for the extraordinary role models I met along the way," Cole notes. "Blessed by a wonderful family and a fulfilling career, I retired in 2004. Two years later my thanks go out to Wally Lamb and former cofacilitator Dale Griffith who recognized I had something to contribute to the inmate writers' program. In fact it may be that everything I'd done prior to my association with Wally and the writers has prepared me for one of the most satisfying roles of my life. My thanks as well to the incarcerated women of our group who have taught me more than I can possibly hope to teach them."

Careen Jennings says, "I was born in a small midwestern city, the oldest of six, and taught to be a good Catholic girl during the smug, self-righteous, and superconservative 1950s. As was typical for my generation, I married young and was a mom before I was twenty-one. A bit less typical, I continued in college, scheduling classes around a babysitter's schedule and graduating just a year after my class. To my great delight, feminism and the civil rights movement changed the world before I was thirty, but with three children and the demands of a high school teaching career, I could only rejoice from the sidelines. After thirty-seven years in the classroom, I am retired, happily single, and working to reinvent myself. I have two surviving children, both grown, and one grandson."

Of her experience at York, Careen Jennings comments, "The women I work with, with sentences that stretch far beyond their rehabilitation, labor with pen and an occasional precious hour on the computer to make sense of their lives. I am just a helper, a bringer of verbal tools so that they can assert their humanity, their dignity, through their words. Their words, born of tears, can be free."

Wally Lamb's novels, *She's Come Undone* and *I Know This Much Is True*, were *New York Times* Notable Books of the Year and featured titles of Oprah's Book Club. Lamb is also the editor of *Couldn't Keep It To Myself: Testimonies from Our Imprisoned Sisters* (ReganBooks, 2003).

Honors for Wally Lamb include the New England Book Award for fiction, the Barnes and Noble Writers for Writers Award, a National Endowment for the Arts fellowship, and Distinguished Alumni awards from Vermont College and the University of Connecticut. *I Know This Much Is True* won the Friends of the Library USA Readers' Choice Award for best novel of 1998, the result of a national poll, and the Kenneth Johnson Memorial Book Award, which honored the novel's contribution to the antistigmatizing of mental illness.

Lamb is nearing completion of his third novel, *The Hour I First Believed*. He says, "What my fictional characters, my inmate students, and I have in common is that we are all imperfect people trying hard to become better people." Wally and Christine Lamb are the parents of three sons: Jared, Justin, and Teddy.

Continuation of Copyright Page

About the author

About the book

Read on

Insights,
Interviews
& More . . .

Wally Lamb
Braided Cords

Christine Lamb

SAY "CONNECTICUT" and you're likely to conjure in people's minds images of leafy bedroom towns whose tony residents commute to Manhattan, unwind at the country club, and send their kids to prep school. I come from the "other" Connecticut: east-of-the-Connecticut-River Connecticut. We're more feisty than fashionable, more liverwurst than pâté. Boston exerts a greater pull on us than New York, and so we drop our r's, root for the Red Sox, and use the word "wicked" as an adverb, as in *Manny Ramirez is a wicked good hittuh*. Norwich, the eastern Connecticut mill town where I was born and raised, is the prototype for Three Rivers, the fictional town where I have set two of my novels. Dominick and Thomas Birdsey in *I Know This Much Is True* and Caelum Quirk, the protagonist of *The Hour I First Believed*, were classmates as kids—baby boomers raised by their working-class families and by TV: *Howdy Doody*, *Shindig!*, *All in the Family*, the news. Each evening after supper (working-class Connecticut eats early), avuncular Walter Cronkite delivered the daily rise and fall: the worrisome advances of

Communists and cosmonauts, the Elvis and Beatles crazes, the assassination in Dallas, blood spilled in the South for a righteous cause and in Vietnam for a dubious one. The Birdsey brothers and Caelum Quirk were shaped by turbulent times, the tube, and an eastern Connecticut sensibility. So was I.

Located at the juncture of the Yantic, Thames (rhymes with "James"), and Shetucket rivers, Norwich was once the hunting and fishing grounds of two warring Native American tribes, the Mohegans and the Mashantucket Pequots. In the seventeenth century, the Mohegans cast their lot with the white settlers from Europe and thrived. The Mashantuckets did not and faced near-extinction. Thanks in part to those three intersecting rivers, Norwich became a boomtown during the nineteenth century. Its engine was textile manufacturing. Cotton was shipped up from the South, converted to cloth, then shipped to ports in Boston and New York. Norwich's wealthy mill bosses moved their families into splendid Victorian homes on fashionable Broadway and Washington Street. Factory laborers—the majority of them French-Canadian migrants and European immigrants who had crossed the Atlantic in steerage—settled their families into company-owned row houses and ramshackle riverbank tenements. Bucolic Norwich, the self-declared "Rose of New England," became a popular destination for the Manhattan millionaires who ferried across Long Island Sound and up the Thames for a weekend of rest and relaxation.

There were no pictures of my paternal grandfather, but I have his pocket watch. A railroad conductor from nearby Noank, he died in his early thirties, a victim of the influenza epidemic of 1918. His young widow was left with an infant son (my father) and no means of subsistence. Grandma took in laundry to survive, then got work as a housekeeper to a British gentleman and his two sons. She married the elder son, a factory worker who moonlighted as a banjo player in a radio orchestra. Like the Birdsey twins, my maternal grandparents were southern Italian immigrants whose families ▶

> " Grandma took in laundry to survive, then got work as a housekeeper to a British gentleman and his two sons. She married the elder son, a factory worker who moonlighted as a banjo player in a radio orchestra. "

had matched them for marriage. Grandpa was a cobbler, Nonna a homemaker who gave birth to eleven children. My mother, number eight, came into the world, like her siblings, on the kitchen table under the supervision of Auntie, Nonna's sister-in-law and midwife. "We never knew Mama was pregnant until Auntie showed up for the delivery," my mother once told me.

Ma was timid, devout, funny, and unfailingly kind. Like many raised in the Sicilian tradition, she wanted her children to remain in the fold when they came of age, kept safe from a world that could be hard-hearted and dangerous. "This is good, but don't get too smart," she once advised me, staring worriedly at a row of A's on my grammar school report card. "It's not good to be too smart." She herself was bright and had wanted to go to college to become a teacher. Nothing doing, her Old World father told her. Daughters didn't need higher education; they needed to help their mothers with the housework until they had a husband and a house of their own. Grandpa invited himself along on my parents' first date, sitting up front with his future son-in-law while his daughter rode in back. When Daddy entered the shoe shop to ask for my mother's hand, Grandpa gave him his blessing and a twenty dollar bill to be spent on groceries—a ringing endorsement, given the importance of food to southern Italians. At the time, Daddy worked as a dyer at the woolen mill. Shortly after the wedding, the factory boss offered him a foreman's position. My father wanted to accept, but it would have meant relocating to the state of Maine. Nothing doing, my mother told him. She couldn't live that far away from her family. So Daddy quit the mill and took a job shoveling coal at Norwich's Department of Public Utilities at half his factory pay. But if there was sacrifice on his part, there was reward as well. Having prioritized *famiglia* above career advancement, my father, a self-described "swamp Yankee" with only a skeleton crew of blood relatives, was brought into the fold of his wife's large and loving Italian clan. Through the years, Daddy rose through the ranks at the utilities company and retired as a superintendent. He never really liked being the boss, but he sure liked to make people laugh. He was a great storyteller—a raconteur with a million poems, ditties, limericks, and jokes in his repertoire, a good number of them inappropriate. ("Hey, did you ever hear about the nun who refused to wear underpants? She went to confession, and for her penance, the priest gave her three Our Fathers, three Hail Marys, and five cartwheels.") Daddy loved to sing, too. "Rock-a-Bye Your Baby with a Dixie Melody" and "When the Saints Go Marching In" were his two favorites. "Daddy! Stop!" I would plead as a child, clapping my hands to my ears and running from the room whenever his crooning began. Now I wish I could hear him sing again.

We lived on McKinley Avenue, a five-minute walk from downtown—or, as Norwichites called it back then, "downcity." The Four Horsewomen of the Apocalypse galloped thunderously through my formative years, and by this I mean not Conquest, Slaughter, Famine, and Death but Vita, Gail, Sandy,

4

and April, my bossy older sisters and the bossy girl cousins who lived just down the street. Vito Signorino, the only other boy on McKinley Avenue, threw rocks at me. That left me, by default, in the relatively safe clutches of Vita, Gail, Sandy, and April—and here I refer to physical, not psychological, safety. My sisters and cousins favored imaginative play over sports or board games. More often than not, I was the outside observer of their strange and exotic recreations, but occasionally I'd be recruited for one of the girls' games of pretend—cast usually in the role of victim. In "Hospital," they were nurses who got to "vaccinate" me with straight pins from my mother's sewing box. For "Death Drums," they fashioned sarongs from old dining room curtains and, as Amazons, locked me in the existential darkness of Nonna's canning closet. Beating on the skin of our Uncle Joe's conga drum, they chanted, with mounting hysteria, "Death drums! Death drums!"—a memory which gives me the shakes fifty years later. Inching toward puberty and inspired by a bolt of pink net fabric that had somehow found its way into our house, the Four Horsewomen invented a naughty game called "Kingy Boy." I was the titular Kingy Boy in this one—a seven-year-old sultan required only to sit cross-legged on the floor with a towel wrapped around my head turban-style while my sisters and cousins, harem girls wrapped in yards of pink net, danced and undulated around me, chanting, "Kingy Boy! O Kingy Boy!"

When the game was over, I was warned not to tell Ma about it. Instead, on my very first trip to the confessional in preparation for First Communion, I spilled the beans to Father Ziegler. "Bless me, Father, for I have sinned. It has been zero weeks since my last confession. These are my sins. I told three fibs, I called my sister a stupid snot, and I played Kingy Boy."

Father's shadow shifted behind the screen. "Well, all right, then. For your penance, I want you to say three Our Fathers and three Hail Marys. Now let me hear you make a good act of—you played *what*?" When I explained the gist of the game, Father told me Kingy Boy was probably not a sin, but he tacked on another couple of Hail Marys anyway.

In the middle years of the twentieth century, eastern Connecticut's textile companies began their migration to the South. By then, however, the Cold War had come along to rescue the local economy. The navy's submarine base and Electric Boat, just down the road in Groton, now employed thousands. Yet if the defense industry put food on the table, it made Norwich nervous. The sub base would be a likely target, everyone said, if that crazy Khrushchev decided to drop the bomb. The frequent wail of the civil defense siren through the windows of Broad Street Grammar School triggered in my classmates and me the desired Pavlovian response: hands atop our heads, we would crouch beneath our desks in the duck-and-cover position we had practiced, as if Formica and metal would protect us from atomic oblivion. Some Norwich residents installed underground bomb shelters in their backyards. We did not. "What would be the point?" I overheard my uncle say to my father during a game of pinochle. "If they drop the big one, we'll all just turn to ash." On Ash Wednesday, Father Ziegler reinforced that message. "From dust you ▶

Wally Lamb *(continued)*

came, to dust you shall return," he mumbled, pressing a thumbprint of ashes onto my forehead. An insomniac since childhood, I frequently find myself awake at night, worrying about the safety of my wife, my kids, my country, and my fictional characters. I'm fairly certain that the seeds of this nocturnal apprehension were planted during the "innocent" 1950s, when children were schooled in spelling, arithmetic, and fatalism. Fatalism was certainly what I felt that September day in 2001 when I sat slack-jawed before the TV and watched the Twin Towers fall. Different enemies, different weaponry, but "it" had finally happened. "You can't worship both God *and* money," Thomas Birdsey, who suffers from paranoid schizophrenia, warns in *I Know This Much Is True*. "America's going to vomit up its own blood."

Two institutions made Norwich unique: the Slater Museum, just off the town green, and, at its southern border, the sprawling Norwich State Hospital, the largest facility for the mentally ill in Connecticut. Both exerted a powerful influence on me as a child and, decades later, exerted an equally powerful influence on the writing of *I Know This Much Is True*.

Located on the campus of the Norwich Free Academy, Slater Museum houses an Egyptian mummy's hand, a replica of Michelangelo's *Pietà*, the ship's log of a whaling captain, and a suit of samurai armor—artifacts from no fewer than thirty-five centuries. The museum's jewel in the crown—its cast gallery of classical Greek and Roman sculpture—is alive with story. Niobe weeps for her children, whom the gods have slain. A serpent strangles writhing Laocoön, who, like Thomas Birdsey, bore the burdensome gift of prophecy. On the museum gallery's back-wall frieze, the three-dimensional battle between the Olympians and the Giants depicts, in the tortured eyes of the vanquished, the waste and suffering of war. Those anguished eyes haunted me as a child visiting the museum and they became, over the years, the eyes of battered women, abused children, and the victims of bigotry, oppression, and mental illness—in short, my characters' eyes. "The world is a very old place, so you'll never be able to tell a completely original story," one of my writing teachers, Gladys Swan, advised me shortly after I began writing fiction. "The best you can do is to put your own spin on the ancient tales—those stories have lasted because people *need* them to be told and retold. If you want to write fiction, study myth." Toward that end, my longstanding acquaintance with the Slater Museum had given me a leg up.

Norwich State Hospital came into existence in the early years of the twentieth century as the draconian treatment of the mentally ill gave way to more humane and progressive practices. Patients would get better if they were kept busy with work and recreation, the experts had come to believe, and so the hospital campus boasted a tannery, a working farm, a greenhouse, a theater, a baseball diamond, and an underground tunnel system through which patients were led to a central dining hall for meals and socialization. "Down below" was how the locals referred to Norwich Hospital, though it sat at the top of Laurel Hill. As a kid sitting in the backseat of my parents' station wagon, I would sometimes ride past the place, staring out the window with equal measures of curiosity and dread. *Crazy people live there! Look, there's one walking the grounds now!* In the early 1960s, lithium was developed at Norwich Hospital, given first to monkeys and then to men and women. By the late sixties, medication had replaced recreation as the treatment of choice; a drugged psychiatric patient was more docile—less of a headache for the hard-pressed staff. In the 1980s, Connecticut concluded that its mammoth state hospital was non-cost-effective. Short- and long-term patients were disgorged and the facility closed down, building by building, over a ten-year span.

There's an old Sicilian saying, *I più gran dolori sono muti*—very great griefs are silent. My mother never told me that her father had spent the last years of his life locked away in Norwich Hospital's forensic building. Illness had addled his brain and made him violent, and he had turned his ferocity against Nonna, his wife of fifty years. I found out about Grandpa's hospitalization from my cousin April when I was sixteen. Thirty years later, shortly after I had begun writing *I Know This Much Is True*, I had an eerie dream. I was my childhood self, walking across a frozen pond when I saw, at my feet beneath the ice, Nonna's face. She was alive, staring up at me, a plea in her eyes. But a plea for what? . . .

The next day, on impulse, I left my writing desk, drove down to the abandoned state hospital, and walked its ghostly grounds. Standing before the barred, broken windows of the forensic building that had housed a grandfather I had never known, I began to cry. Then I went home and created, in the vacuum, the character of Domenico Tempesta, Dominick Birdsey's grandfather and namesake. Once I had old Domenico's voice, his story spun out rapidly, and his unhappy, ego-driven life came to function as a cautionary tale for Dominick, who knows his troubled forebear only from the grandiose but revealing life story Domenico spoke into a Dictaphone machine in the months before he died. Fiction writing as wish fulfillment? Maybe. From—and about—my actual grandfather, there had been only silence.

Upon graduation from high school in 1968, I left Norwich and enrolled at the University of Connecticut twenty miles up the road. The four years I spent there were turbulent and seductive—an era in which world politics and cultural sea changes invited baby boomers like me to fight for social justice and "party hardy." The sexual revolution had arrived and marijuana smoke perfumed the dorm. The Vietnam War and the civil rights battle intensified, and the soundtrack of those years segued from *This is the dawning of the Age of Aquarius* to *By the time we got to Woodstock, we were half a million strong* to *Tin soldiers and Nixon coming. We're finally on our own.* Prepare ourselves for the "real world"? Shit, man, we were going to fix what was wrong with it. "I'm on strike!" I told my father over the phone after the invasion of Cambodia and the killings at Kent State. "The hell you are!" he shouted into the receiver. "You get to class!" But Richard Nixon and Walter Lamb Sr. were more or less interchangeable that spring, so I hung up the phone, stuck my fist in the air, and joined the protest.

At the end of that wild four-year ride at UConn, I did *not* launch myself ▶

into the chaotic world at large. My mother's son, I took a U-turn, returning to Norwich to teach English at the high school from which I'd graduated. My first classes were the ones no other teacher wanted, comprised of students who had been retained so many times, a few of them were my age, twenty-one. "The sweathogs," they were fond of calling themselves. My plan was to win them over by releasing them from the prison that school had been for them until my arrival. I would open their minds by making their education *relevant*. The sweathogs and I honeymooned for about a week, until the day when I approached Seth Jinks, a surly senior, and asked him to take his head off his desk and pay attention. Seth worked nights and slept at school during the day. He raised his head as I had asked, opened his bloodshot eyes, and said, "Why don't you go fuck yourself?" The class and I held our collective breath. I had no idea how to respond. Mercifully, Seth unfolded his long legs, stood, and ambled voluntarily out the door and up to the principal's office, thereby saving my teaching career. I remained at that school for the next twenty-five years.

I became a good teacher and was a good and dutiful son. I visited my parents often, attended family picnics, served as a pallbearer at my aunts' and uncles' funerals. Along the way, I fell in love with and married a pretty local girl of Italian, Portuguese, and Polish blood—a good friend from high school. Christine is, today, my bride of thirty years. We have three sons. When I count my blessings, Chris and the guys are at the top my list.

I was thirty when I wrote my first short story, and I have been writing fiction now for more than twenty-five years. In 1992, the phone rang and the caller at the other end of the line claimed she was Oprah Winfrey. Yeah, right, I remember thinking, and I'm Geraldo Rivera. But it really *was* Oprah, calling to thank me for having written my just-published first novel, *She's Come Undone*. "I couldn't stop reading it," she said. "You owe me two nights' sleep." Oprah called me again in 1997 to say that she had started a new feature on her show to promote the pleasures and challenges of reading. *She's Come Undone* became the third title of the phenomenally popular Oprah's Book Club. The following year, *I Know This Much Is True* became an Oprah's Book Club selection, too. "It's not just a book," she told her vast TV audience. "It's a life experience." These endorsements of my work have been both a boon and a blessing, and Oprah's philosophy—"Take what you need and pass on the rest to others"—has guided me as well. As I have received, I have tried to give back as generously as I can. That resolution led me to my volunteer work at York Correctional Institution, Connecticut's maximum-security women's prison. To date, my writing students there have published two collections of autobiographical essays, *Couldn't Keep It to Myself* (2003) and *I'll Fly Away* (2007).

After the Berlin Wall fell and the Cold War sputtered to an end, Electric Boat laid off thousands. Norwich became blighted, the once-elegant Victorian homes on Broadway and Washington Street falling into disrepair and decay. But in the twentieth century's last decade, those two warring Native American tribes, the Mashantuckets and the Mohegans, rose phoenixlike from the ashes to stanch the exodus and save the local economy. The mammoth Foxwoods and Mohegan Sun casinos have become two of the country's largest and most lucrative gaming operations, and the thousands of workers needed to run these gambling and entertainment meccas—many of them immigrants from Asia, Mexico, Haiti, Russia, and eastern Europe—have revitalized and brought cultural diversity to the dormant and dying Rose of New England, just as Grandpa and Nonna's generation had done a hundred years earlier.

The Four Horsewomen of the Apocalypse metamorphosed into conventional women: teachers, wives, mothers, grandmothers. At our last family reunion, I overheard them discussing varicose veins and osteoporosis. My mother's hearing was the first to go. Later, a series of strokes claimed her speech and her mobility and left her with dementia. But Ma's eyes still lit up whenever her children and grandchildren visited and she never lost her ability to laugh. My father, who by then had developed Parkinson's disease, took over the care of his wife and the McKinley Avenue home they had moved into in 1950, the year I was born. But a fall and a broken hip ended Daddy's ability to hold down the fort and so the fort was sold. During their last years together, my parents were roommates at a Catholic nursing home, where my mother, in her wheelchair, attended daily mass and my father held court and told his salty jokes, even to the nuns. "Ever hear about the nun who refused to wear underpants?" I once heard him ask Sister Gertrude. After she'd left the room, I lectured him on the inappropriateness of telling dirty jokes to the Brides of Christ. He waved away my fuddy-duddiness. "Sister Gert and I have an understanding," he said. They had a standing bet, too, whenever the Yankees played the Red Sox. The loser was obliged to buy the winner a Baby Ruth. Ma died peacefully in 2000. In 2005, my father's Alzheimer's-afflicted roommate walked down to the nurses' station and told the staff that Mrs. Lamb was in the room with Mr. Lamb, helping him get ready. Daddy died the next day.

In his wondrous memoir *Growing Up*, Russell Baker writes, "We all come from the past, and children ought to know what it was that went into their making, to know that life is a braided cord of humanity stretching up from time long gone, and that it cannot be defined by the span of a single journey from diaper to shroud." I am, when I write fiction, people other than myself. And many times each week, I am not just the fifty-six-year-old novelist I turned out to be, but also all the other selves I have been—the novice teacher, the student protester in tie-dye and love beads, the new father witnessing a delivery room miracle, Kingy Boy. I am also, as Baker suggests, all who have come before me. I was born before my father, as my sons were born before I was. The product of a specific time and place, each of us is much more than that. That's a lesson I relearn daily when I face the blank page, the glowing screen of the computer monitor. Though my lessons are far from over, writing and life have taught me this much at least. I know this much is true. ❧

A Change of Priorities
Author Turns Advocate

The following article, written by Donna Doherty, appeared in slightly different form in the New Haven Register *in 2007.*

LIKE THE TITLE of his first bestselling novel, author Wally Lamb has watched his share of women "come undone" over the years. But he's doing what he can to try and put them back together again.

For nearly a decade, the writing course that Lamb voluntarily teaches at York Correctional Institution, a maximum security women's facility in Niantic, Connecticut, has been giving incarcerated women a voice. The latest fruit of these labors is *I'll Fly Away*, a second collection of their short stories, essays, and poems, which have served as a kind of writing therapy for some of them and as an actual springboard to a writing career for a few.

Lamb is well aware that some of the women he teaches have not only turned their own lives upside down, but have also changed forever the lives of their victims. He makes no excuses for what they've done, but his only concern is what has brought them to his class. Lamb never even asks them why they are there. He says of several women with whom he's worked for four or five years, "I have no idea why they're in prison," and goes on to explain, "my job is not to judge; the state already has." More often than not, their history will come out in their writing—several are lifers, and one is awaiting sentencing for a crime that could bring the death penalty.

The class is a popular one, usually with a waiting list. The maximum number of women allowed is eighteen, and there are basic rules for entry.

"They have to be discipline-free for a year and have at least a year left on their sentence; so there is continuity. They have to submit the reasons why they want to be in the program," he says by phone from his home in Storrs. "I read over their little essays and decide. I'm

> " My job is not to judge; the state already has. "

not looking so much for aptitude as I am for the ring of truth as to the reasons they want to be in the program."

That ring of truth can be like a punch to the gut. The writing is raw, often profane, sad, angry, even wistful, and it is frequently about abuse, rape, drugs—the unpretty side of life. Some of the writers, such as Robin Ledbetter, are notorious charges within Department of Correction annals. Robin, aged twenty-six, was charged as an adult offender at age fourteen and sentenced to fifty years at York, which she called "big-girl jail." Lamb recalls her two suicide attempts and the question she asked a reporter, "How do you restart a life at sixty-four when you never started it in the first place?"

Battling Despair

Lamb believes that society often leaves the incarcerated without many tools to turn their lives around. He hopes his program does its small share to give them some feeling of redemption and rehabilitation. That's what brought him to York in the first place: women were committing suicide, losing the battle with the despair Lamb says inmates fight "on a daily basis" in prison. There seemed to be no outlet for them to release that despair, share it with others and learn that there could be something positive somewhere in their experience.

"Certainly, there's institutional failure," he says. "I think now there is more effort, more programs to rehabilitate, but there is still a long way to go. If you're going to basically put people in cages and not address how they can fix themselves or where things went wrong, you're going to have people back in the system. Under [the Connecticut Governor John] Rowland's administration in 1999, a lot of the more humane aspects of prison were discontinued, but now there is more humanity than there used to be."

Everyone's a Critic

Humanity and civility are demanded in Lamb's classes. While students critique each other's work, it must be constructive criticism—first ▶

❝ If you're going to basically put people in cages and not address how they can fix themselves or where things went wrong, you're going to have people back in the system. ❞

A Change of Priorities *(continued)*

the positives, then suggestions for improvement. The class, whose members range in age from the early twenties to fifty-nine, meets every week, with Lamb teaching every other week, sharing responsibilities with two other facilitators.

Even Lamb's work gets a look. Students previewed pieces of his third novel, offering their opinions on the work, which deals with a school nurse who witnesses the Columbine tragedy and is damaged by it to the point of ruin. He strongly believes it would not be what it is had he not been teaching this class.

"I probably couldn't have gone to that subject matter if I hadn't been exposed to this program," he says, "so there's a really wonderful give and take."

He teaches them rudimentary skills of fiction writing: recreating dialogue, setting a scene, exposition, and the necessity of rewriting. "Occasionally if they are really struggling with something personal, I suggest that rather than using 'I,' they give the character a different name."

It is not lost on Lamb that his two best-selling novels, *She's Come Undone* and *I Know This Much Is True*, also dealt with rampant dysfunction. York has inadvertently been a research lab. "As I've been trying to help those women with their education," Lamb says, "they've given me an education. One of the things they've educated me about is the reason women land in prison in America. And that has been a bleed-through to my own fiction."

Lamb cites domestic abuse, drug problems, poverty, depression, even guilt about not living up to expectations as some of the reasons women commit crimes. Contributor Roberta Schwartz was a lawyer who, unhinged by depression after her father's death and a bad marriage, started to embezzle, eventually spiraling into drug addiction. She calls her story "Lost and Found."

Barbara Parsons, who won a PEN/Newman's Own First Amendment Award for her essay in

> 66 One of the things they've educated me about is the reason women land in prison in America. And that has been a bleed-through to my own fiction. 99

the first volume, wrote the final piece in
I'll Fly Away, reflecting on York on the one-year
anniversary of her release in a piece rich with
the sights she could only observe from inside
a prison. Christina MacNaughton is another
award-winner; her essay "Just Another Death"
won the 2007 PEN Prison Writing Award for
nonfiction.

This volume had a much easier birth
than the first, *Couldn't Keep It to Myself.* In
2003, Attorney General Richard Blumenthal
sued both the writers for the cost of their
incarceration—one inmate would have owed
close to one million dollars—and Lamb because
the book was revenue-producing, even though
revenues were going to charity. As a result, the
computers were confiscated and the program
suspended. Eventually, with the help of the
press and an investigation by *60 Minutes,* the
case was settled and the class was restored.
Lamb calls the experience "demoralizing."
From his perspective, "it was hardest for the
women still inside. The women on the book
tour were getting positive feedback when we
did the readings. . . . But it was scary, because
none of them had dealt with that particular side
of the law." Lamb's battle was rewarded last year
with a Communitarian Award from New
Haven's Fellowship Place, a haven for people
with social and mental problems.

As Lamb found out, working with
"criminals" is an emotional hot button,
especially for their victims. While this time
it was smooth sailing, the lawsuit left its scars.
Lamb talks about the legal problems in the
introduction, where he also recounts his
experiences with the program, which has
actually pushed his own writing career down
on his priority list. After much anticipation,
his long-awaited third novel, *The Hour I First
Believed,* was published in the fall of 2008.

With the program reaching the decade mark,
Lamb reflects on his experience running the
program and publishing the stories it has
yielded: ▶

A Change of Priorities *(continued)*

"What has become important to me is educating the public," he says. "I think it's so easy to put people behind bars and put razor wire at the top of a fence. It's easy to forget. I think the silence makes the worst prisons.

"When I publish, it's to allow people on the outside to listen to voices on the inside and maybe discard some of these stereotypes about the way prisoners are treated and what happens when they are released." ∾

> ❝ What has become important to me is educating the public. ❞

Reprinted by permission of the New Haven Register.

Author's Picks
Twenty-one Books That Called Me to a Writing Life

TWENTY-ONE BOOKS that called me to a writing life, roughly in the order that I discovered them:

Mrs. Piggle-Wiggle by Betty MacDonald

Homer Price by Robert McCloskey

The Black Stallion by Walter Farley

The Adventures of Tom Sawyer by Mark Twain

To Kill a Mockingbird by Harper Lee

The Catcher in the Rye by J. D. Salinger

The Adventures of Huckleberry Finn
by Mark Twain

The Great Gatsby by F. Scott Fitzgerald

The Odyssey by Homer

Shakespeare's tragedies

My Antonia by Willa Cather

Of Human Bondage by W. Somerset Maugham

Walden by Henry David Thoreau

Great Expectations by Charles Dickens

The Complete Stories by Flannery O'Connor

Pigeon Feathers and Other Stories
by John Updike

What We Talk About When We Talk About Love
by Raymond Carver

Growing Up by Russell Baker

The Hero with a Thousand Faces
by Joseph Campbell

The King and the Corpse by Heinrich Zimmer

Unto the Sons by Gay Talese

Have You Read?
More by Wally Lamb

THE HOUR I FIRST BELIEVED

Wally Lamb, author of two number one *New York Times* bestsellers and Oprah's Book Club picks, delivers his first novel in over a decade—an extraordinary work of prodigious scope and ambition that explores the consequences of violent events in human lives blown irrevocably off course.

Combining myth, psychology, faith, and multigenerational family history, Wally Lamb's *The Hour I First Believed* is a literary tour de force, at once a meditation on the human condition and a compassionate, unflinching evocation of character.

Moving to Littleton, Colorado, forty-seven-year-old Caelum Quirk and his young wife, Maureen, find work at Columbine High School. In April 1999, while Caelum is away due to a family emergency, Maureen cowers in a cabinet in Columbine's library, hiding from two students on a murderous rampage. Though she miraculously survives, Maureen cannot recover from the trauma. Seeking solace, the couple returns to Connecticut, to illusory safety on the Quirk family's farm.

As Maureen fights to regain her sanity, Caelum discovers a cache of forgotten memorabilia spanning five generations of his family, from the Civil War to his own troubled childhood. As he painstakingly reconstructs the lives of his ancestors—and uncovers their unimaginable secrets—Caelum must confront his family's painful past and fashion a future from the ashes of his own tragedy. His personal quest for meaning and faith becomes a mythic journey that is both contemporary and quintessentially American.

"A modern-day Dostoyevsky." —*New York Times*

Around the world, millions of readers have been captivated by Wally Lamb's incredible talent in representing the lost and the lonely. In this number one *New York Times* bestseller, Lamb weaves the story of Dominick Birdsey, whose entire life has been shaped by anger and fear, with that of his paranoid schizophrenic twin brother, who he deeply loves and resents. The two brothers share a family history that includes an adoptive father, Ray, and a long-suffering mother, Concettina, a timid woman with a harelip and a huge desire to protect her troubled son, Thomas, as the demons of his schizophrenia become increasingly apparent.

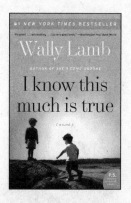

But as Thomas commits an act which sends him to strict confinement for the mentally ill, Dominick's life spins even further out of control. He attempts to come to terms with his desire to rescue his brother and his fears about his own psychological health and inability to love. Dominick's journey is illuminated, and further complicated, by a fable-like account of his grandfather Domenico Onofrio Tempesta's life.

As Dominick continues to face the pain of loss, he must rebuild himself in the shadow of his twin and come to grips with his anger in order to forgive. *I Know This Much Is True* is a masterfully told story of alienation and connection, power and abuse, and devastation and renewal. Readers everywhere will continue to be moved by this joyous, heart-wrenching, mystical, exquisitely written, and profoundly human masterpiece.

"An amazingly ambitious book. . . . An epic in every sense. . . . A first-person narrative that sweeps you up on the first page and is never less than enthralling." —*Rocky Mountain News*

"[It] never grapples with anything less than life's biggest questions."
—*New York Times Book Review*

Read on

COULDN'T KEEP IT TO MYSELF

In a stunning work of insight and hope, *New York Times* bestselling author Wally Lamb once again reveals his unmatched talent for finding humanity in the lost and lonely, and celebrates the transforming power of the written word.

For several years, Lamb has taught writing to a group of women prisoners at York Correctional Institution in Connecticut. In this unforgettable collection, the women of York describe in their own words how they were imprisoned by abuse, rejection, and their own self-destructive impulses long before they entered the criminal justice system. Yet these are powerful stories of hope and healing, told by writers who have left victimhood behind.

In his moving introduction, Lamb describes the incredible journey of expression and self-awareness the women took through their writing and shares how they challenged him as a teacher and as a fellow author. *Couldn't Keep It to Myself* is a true testament to the process of finding oneself and working toward a better day.

"Hope permeates the book."—*Los Angeles Times*

"The twelve riveting, touching autobiographical accounts look past the bars to lay bare lives that would normally have gone unheard."
—*Entertainment Weekly*

Don't miss the next book by your favorite author. Sign up now for AuthorTracker by visiting www.AuthorTracker.com.